I0349843

Emotional intelligence: Does it really matter?

A guide to coping with stressful experiences

Phillip W. Bowen

Cognitive Science and Psychology

VERNON PRESS

Copyright © 2020 Vernon Press, an imprint of Vernon Art and Science Inc, on behalf of the author.

All rights reserved. No part of this publication may be reproduced, stored in a retrieval system, or transmitted in any form or by any means, electronic, mechanical, photocopying, recording, or otherwise, without the prior permission of Vernon Art and Science Inc.

www.vernonpress.com

In the Americas:
Vernon Press
1000 N West Street,
Suite 1200, Wilmington,
Delaware 19801
United States

In the rest of the world:
Vernon Press
C/Sancti Espiritu 17,
Malaga, 29006
Spain

Cognitive Science and Psychology

Library of Congress Control Number: 2019937914

ISBN: 978-1-62273-901-1

Also available:

978-1-62273-679-9 [Hardback]; 978-1-62273-812-0 [PDF, E-Book]

Product and company names mentioned in this work are the trademarks of their respective owners. While every care has been taken in preparing this work, neither the authors nor Vernon Art and Science Inc. may be held responsible for any loss or damage caused or alleged to be caused directly or indirectly by the information contained in it.

Every effort has been made to trace all copyright holders, but if any have been inadvertently overlooked the publisher will be pleased to include any necessary credits in any subsequent reprint or edition.

For Sonia

Table of contents

	List of tables	xi
	List of diagrams	xiii
	Acknowledgement	xv
	Introduction	xvii
	Background	xxi
Chapter 1	Emotional intelligence	1
	A little background to emotional intelligence	2
	The main models of emotional intelligence	3
	Ability model paradigm (Salovey and Mayer, 1990)	4
	Mixed model paradigm (Goleman, 1995, 1998a, 1998b)	6
	Mixed model paradigm (Bar-On, 1997)	8
	Trait model paradigm (Petrides and Furnham, 2001)	11
	Oxymoron	14
	Lack of consensus	15
	Critique	16
	Limitations	17
	Summing up	18
Chapter 2	Stress	19
	Perspectives of stress	19
	Work related illnesses	20
	Eustress and distress	23
	Cortisol, oxytocin, serotonin and noradrenaline	25
	The modern workplace	27
	Positive emotions and links between stress, coping and emotional intelligence	29
	Emotional dissonance	29

	Demands of the job and well-being on the academic	30
	Impact of stress on the academic	34
	Chronic stress and possible outcomes	37
	The traditional organisation and rational thinking	38
	Burnout	38
	Stress and work/ life balance	42
	Summing up	43
Chapter 3	Understanding and processing emotions	47
	Different emotions	48
	Understanding your own emotions and those in others	51
	Teaching and emotional intelligence	53
	Learned optimism and learned helplessness	56
	Bullying and harassment	61
	Therapy	62
	Toleration of negative emotions	63
	Emotion-focused therapy	64
	Emotion-processing therapy	64
	Cognitive Behavioural therapy	65
	Summing up	66
Chapter 4	Coping	69
	Coping strategies	69
	Methodological study of how academic cope	72
	Academic sample	72
	Planning	80
	Active coping	82
	Acceptance	83
	Positive reframing	84
	Emotional support	84
	Instrumental support	86
	Self-distraction	89

	Humour	89
	Venting	89
	Self-blame	91
	Religion	91
	Behavioural disengagement	92
	Denial	93
	Substance use	93
	Comparison between studies	96
	Summing up	97
Chapter 5	Personality and individual differences	99
	Background	99
	Personality and coping	102
	Personality and stress	104
	Personality (The "big five") and job performance	106
	Personality (The "big five") and trait emotional intelligence	106
	Personality (The "big one") and trait emotional intelligence	107
	Summing up	107
Chapter 6	Intelligence and groups	109
	Intelligence	109
	General intelligence	111
	Groups and groupthink	116
	A nudge in the right direction	118
	Social networking	119
	Social intelligence and loneliness	122
	Group/ team/ intelligence	122
	Group emotional intelligence	123
	Management business perspective	124
	Group stress and group psychological strain	127
	Financial cost	129
	Group coping	130

	The beehive	131
	Summing up	132
Chapter 7	Emotional intelligence and well-being	135
	Physical/ psychological well-being	137
	Infection, illness, introversion and negative thinking	143
	The widening gap in inequality	143
	Passiveness and "*I can take it*" syndrome	146
	Emotions and memory	147
	Emotions and creativity	148
	Self-help	149
	Telomeres	150
	The dark triad	152
	Emotions and cognitive thinking and control	155
	Exercise mind and body	155
	Summing up	157
Chapter 8	Training and development	161
	Motivating and inspiring	162
	Mindfulness	165
	Walking/ talking and smiling	168
	Reframing the mindset	169
	Developing self-awareness	170
	The white room	172
	Summing up	174
Chapter 9	Emotional intelligence: Does it really matter?	177
	Memory	179
	Life's a journey	181
	The working environment	181
	Right or wrong?	184
	Breaking point	186
	IQ and multiple intelligences	187

Conforming	188
Pessimism, optimism and hormones	188
Dissent in the ranks	190
"I can take it"	190
It could have been worse	191
Emotional intelligence: does it really matter?	191
Bibliography	*195*
Index	*249*

List of tables

Table 1.1. Main theorists/ models. 4
Table 1.2. Emotional intelligence model (Ability model, Salovey and Mayer). 5
Table 1.3. Emotional intelligence (Mixed model, Goleman). 7
Table 1.4. Mixed emotional intelligence (Bar-On,1997). 9
Table 1.5. Trait emotional intelligence (Petrides, 2009). 11
Table 1.6. Main models and theorists. 16
Table 1.7. Performance and self-report measures of E.I (Matthews et al., 2004). 17
Table 2.1. Perspectives of stress. 20
Table 2.2. Teacher retention rates UK (2017). 32
Table 2.3. Higher education staff statistics: UK, 2017/18 (HESA, 2015, 2019). 34
Table 2.4. Students achieving first or higher degrees. 35
Table 3.1. Theories of emotion. 49
Table 3.2. Emotional style. 51
Table 3.3. Characteristics of highly effective teachers. 53
Table 3.4. Criteria for major depressive disorder. 57
Table 3.5. The DSM-5 criteria for major depressive disorder (MDD). 57
Table 3.6. Permanent (Pessimistic) verses Temporary (Optimistic). 60
Table 4.1. Types of stress. 70
Table 4.2. Coping mechanisms (Carver et al., 1989). 71
Table 4.3. Coping strategies. 74
Table 4.4. Coping (Carver et al., 1989) (Summary of items). Totals. 75
Table 4.5. Coping strategies (Summary of do this a lot and a medium amount). 75
Table 4.6. Emotional and instrumental support (Responses). 76
Table 4.7. Emotional and instrumental support (Summary of paired items). 77
Table 4.8. Information of those interviewed. 78
Table 4.9. Summary of those interviewed. 79
Table 4.10. Examples of how those interviewed cope. 94
Table 4.11. Examples of coping strategies used by those interviewed. 95
Table 4.12. Coping with interpersonal relationships (interviews). 96
Table 5.1. Cattell's sixteen dimensions of personality. 100
Table 5.2. Tupes and Christal's five dimensions. 100
Table 5.3. The *big five*. 101

Table 5.4. Personality and coping. 103
Table 5.5. Examples of research undertaken on personality type. 103
Table 6.1. Thurstone's seven (7) primary mental abilities. 112
Table 6.2. Guilford's independent abilities. 113
Table 6.3. Hierarchy of intelligence (Vernon, 1950). 114
Table 6.4. Carroll's three (3) stratum hierarchy. 114
Table 6.5. Cattell, Horn and Carroll theory. 115
Table 6.6. The number of global social network users. 120
Table 7.1. Five (5) domains of well-being. 137
Table 7.2. Types of physical activity. 138
Table 7.3. Examples of physical inactivity. 139

List of diagrams

Diagram 6.1. Group psychological strain. 129
Diagram 7.1. Illness/wellness continuum. 137
Diagram 8.1. The *"I can take it"* continuum. 162

Acknowledgement

I am continuing to learn and gain new experiences every day and this book has gone so far in achieving my aspirations and lifetime goals. To say I have spent hours reading through content associated with this book would be an understatement. Reading has gone well beyond those discussed in the content. Therefore, I would like to thank all those sources who have helped contribute to the content of this book. There are too many to name under this section, but quite a few are shown in the bibliography. I would like to take the opportunity to Daniel Goleman who initiated and maintained my interest in emotional intelligence. Thanks also go to John D. Mayer, Peter Salovey and David Caruso together with Konstantinos V. Petrides who developed my interest further, much further. I would also like to thank authors Malcolm Gladwell, Michael Marmot and Nicholas Taleb who demonstrate a master class in thought-provoking writing that is engaging, clear to read, and unproblematic to follow.

A very big thank you to my wife, Sonia, who has been super supportive throughout the process. I am also very fortunate to have been assisted by a great support team at Vernon Press including Carolina Sanchez, Argiris Legatos, James McGovern, Javier Rodriguez and colleagues, who recognises the passion and commitment I have in this area. A massive thank you to the reviewer of the draft text who kindly provided excellent pointers and thoughts that I have included into the final text.

I have to include a special mention for colleagues and friends who have been there to give me moral and academic support: Joe and Deborah Clarke, Professor Richard Rose, Professor Andy Pilkington, Professor Simon Burton-shaw-Gunn and Professor Gail Kinman. I cannot thank each of you enough. A further thanks to all the students and colleagues I have met throughout the years, all of which have added to my skills and knowledge.

As the years have passed, I have recognised that the more I have read and absorbed the less smart I realise I am. Einstein commented that the more he learned, the more he realised how much he didn't know. If the quote is from Einstein, I think it is safe and acceptable to acknowledge this myself. However, I keep learning and continue to seek further information and knowledge.

Thank you all for your love, kindness and joy you have all given me over the years.

Phil

Introduction

The content of this book is directed at those who are interested in the topics of emotional intelligence, stress, coping and education. It crosses the boundaries between psychology, sociology, anthropology, philosophy, health and education. The desire is to integrate the findings into a lucid explanation connecting many of the dots that may be lacking or located in different sources. The book engages the reader with understanding about the term and role emotional intelligence has to play in the workplace and in the social environment. We are influenced by the world around us and yet we think that we are able to make decisions independently that are rational and common sense. The book integrates discussion around wider concepts that may influence decision making, demonstrating how complex we are as human beings and how challenging it is to make the right and wrong decisions.

The purpose of the book is to ask if emotional intelligence really does matter. To answer this question, the background is discussed in the next section, delving back to the times of classical Greece to explain how the dualistic view, of separating rationalistic thought and emotions has become entrenched through the last two and a half millennia. We seem to continue to separate rationalistic thinking from emotions and yet they are integral to what makes us human. It was not until the late nineteenth (19th) and twenty-first (21st) centuries that theorists and researchers appear to take the term "*emotions*" as an area worth looking into in greater depth. It is now apparent that much of what and how we think are influenced by emotions. There is a growing acceptance that there may be multiple intelligences of which emotional intelligence is just one. The background concludes by identifying that, whereas studies into emotional intelligence have been carried at school level, little research has been carried out in higher education, including universities, which suggests that it is an area in which research can be undertaken.

The content of the book continues with Chapter One (1) that begins by asking the question of whether or not emotional intelligence exists. The main theoretical models associated with emotional intelligence are identified and a critique is provided around the findings suggesting that there is a lack of consensus in clearly defining the term and how and what it measures. The chapter clearly identifies and critiques the three (3) main models: 1) the ability model (Salovey and Mayer, 1990; Mayer and Salovey, 1997), 2) the mixed Model (Goleman, 1995,1998; Bar-On, 1997, 2000) and, 3) the trait model (Petrides, 2009, 2011; Petrides and Furnham, 2001).

Chapter two (2) discusses the term stress and how it impacts on mental health. Eustress, distress and chronic stress are reflected upon and discussion provided around the physical impact stress has on human biology and how the modern workplace can lead to burnout. Chemicals can be released into the body that can affect psychological and physical well-being. Examples are identified and discussed. The human body has been developed to reflect the hunter-gather mentality that our ancestors faced each day. We are not made for the modern workplace and yet we have to cope with pressure and stress that the workplace brings. The influence that the modern workplace has on us is discussed and is followed by a reflection of how positive emotions link with stress, coping and emotional intelligence. The demands of the workplace and modern living can lead to emotions being experienced such as anger and fear. These may not fit with the demands and expectations of the organisation where emotional display is felt to be unprofessional or unwanted. This can give rise to emotional dissonance that is discussed in this chapter. The demands of the job and the impact stress has on the academic are reflected upon, followed by a discussion about the impact chronic stress can have on work/life balance.

Chapter three (3) probes more deeply into the different emotions we experience and how emotional intelligence can be used in the teaching environment. Discussion is given over to teaching and emotional intelligence followed by a section on the terms learned optimism and learned helplessness with suggestions as to ways in which to cope with challenging experiences. Bullying and harassment is also discussed as it seems to occur in almost every working environment and suggestions are made as to how to cope with such experiences. The final part of this chapter is made over to different therapies that are available from professional sources.

Chapter four (4) uses the coping strategies provided by Carver (1997) in his journal article "*You want to measure coping but your protocol's too long: consider the brief COPE.*" The chapter delves into the different coping strategies that can be used providing anecdotes and case study examples from university academics. Consideration is given to individual difference that can influence which coping strategy is used. The tolerance levels can vary where one person may regard an experience as mild pressure while another person may feel high levels of stress. The findings suggest that people may use more than one coping strategy and that it is context dependent.

Personality relates to how people cope with challenging experiences and to emotional intelligence. Chapter five (5) reflects upon personality and individual differences, factors that may influence how and why people respond to experiences in different ways. The chapter makes use of Costa and McCrae's (1992) theoretical model of the "*big 5*" personality types and considers the relationship personality has with coping and stress. The *big one* personality type is also discussed. This chapter also reflects upon the relationship personality has with job performance and emotional intelligence.

Chapter six (6) delves into the term "*intelligence*" (IQ) and how theory has developed over the twentieth (20th) century to include groups and teams. Groupthink is identified, and discussion expanded to reflect upon the influence of social networking and why social interaction is so important. This chapter also considers how the term "*group*" is associated with intelligence, stress and coping. The chapter concludes making use of the "*beehive*" model comparing how similar we are as human beings to bees.

Chapter seven (7) focuses on the role emotional intelligence has on well-being. The traditional view of emotions in western society is to separate them from rational thinking. We are encouraged to engage with work to such an extent that it can become overpowering and overbearing that can impact upon personal well-being. The macho approach encourages the mentality of *"I can take it"*. This chapter discusses the effect the modern working environment has on physical and psychological well-being and how it can give rise to a serious illness that can have a cost upon family and organisation. A section is made over to the effect the modern working environment has on creativity. The chapter delves into the "*dark triad*" (narcissism, Machiavellian and psychopathic dispositions) where people use emotions to manipulate others while having self-centred, grandiose opinions of themselves. The chapter concludes by suggesting ways in which to cope with challenging experiences.

Chapter eight (8) draws upon the findings from earlier chapters and provides suggestions and helpful tips to cope with challenging experiences. The chapter begins by focusing on the terms motivating and inspiring behaviour followed by a discussion around the term mindfulness. Reframing the mindset and developing self-awareness is important, focusing on positive and constructive thoughts. Suggestions are made to engage in physical exercise and to talk with friends and family. The chapter concludes by providing a short exercise entitled "*The white room*", that can help bring back focus to the "*now*".

Chapter nine (9) includes sections on memory, the working environment, conforming and reference back to the stoic view that things may be less serious than they actually are. The final part of this chapter reflects upon the title of the book "*emotional intelligence: does it really matter*", pulling together final thoughts and conclusions.

Background

To appreciate the meaning and terms of emotion and emotional intelligence, it is helpful to reflect on how these concepts have developed over time. It is also helpful to establish the background to how and why focus is given to a rationalistic approach within western thinking where emotions and rationalism have been separated for millennia.

The historical view, from the times of Greeks, is that intelligence and thinking are superior while feelings and emotions are considered inferior. Wisdom and reasoning should be in control and emotional impulses suppressed (Sparrow and Knight, 2006). Solomon (2010) refers to the metaphor of the master and the slave where wisdom (that is associated with of reason) is in control and dangerous impulses (associated with emotions) are suppressed or channelled so that they are in harmony with reasoned thinking. Damasio (1994) explains that this high reason view of decision making assumes that logic will obtain the best solution for any problem. This view has been embedded into western culture and thinking from the time of Socrates and Plato.

It appears that everything that we know about Socrates (470BC-399BC) relies on sources such as Plato (428BC-347BC), Xenophon (431BC-354BC), Aristophanes (446BC-386BC), and subsequent interpretation. It is not even known as to what he did for a living. However, it does look as though Socrates acknowledges that emotions are integrated into understanding oneself and interpersonal relationships (Bowery, 2007; Schultz, 2013). According to Plato's "*Philebus*", Socrates refers to three (3) types of pleasure and pain that are described as passions (in Greek- "*pathos*") (Fortenbaugh, 2014; Meinwald, 2008). Each of the passions are considered to be very different from each other. The first (1st) is associated with the body. Socrates provides an example of finding pleasure and relief from scratching a painful itch. The second (2nd) is associated with both body and soul. Socrates explains that a person who is hungry, and expecting to be fed, may feel the pain of an empty stomach but finds pleasure from the thought that they are about to be fed. The third (3rd) is associated with soul, that is thought to be independent of the body. For example, feelings of fear, love, envy, and anger that are later described as emotions (Fortenbaugh, 2014). Emotions continue to lurk in the background that can lead to poor decision making and cloud judgement (Brickhouse and Smith, 2015; Solomon, 2010). It provides a foundation for those that follow, separating emotions from rational thinking.

Plato, a pupil of Socrates, regards the soul as being a separate entity to the body (Crivellato and Ribatti, 2007). He suggests that the soul is made up of three (3) basic energies that *"animate"* the human being (Plato, 380BC) (Kraut 2010). These are reason, emotion and appetite. Reason is given the highest value. Emotion and appetite are regarded as lower *"passions"*. Plato explains that the soul is ordered and is governed by reason, therefore keeping the lower passions (emotions and appetite) under control. Plato views emotions as being wild and uncontrollable. They are non-rational and serve no psychological purpose. Emotions challenge reality and reason and are considered to be a hindrance, clouding judgment rather than facilitating it (Dalgleish and Bramham, 1999). He therefore places reason above emotions where reason is immortal and independent of the body while emotions are perishable, similar to internal organs of the body (Schirmer, 2015).

Aristotle (384BC- 322BC) is a student of Plato. In *"Rhetoric"*, Aristotle explains that emotions are part of the process for those seeking to gain a greater understanding of oration and persuasion (Aristotle,1992). Emotions are associated with reason that are reflected in how events are experienced. Aristotle (350BC) considers emotions central to identifying who we are as human beings. If they are central, then minimising/ removing emotions could change or hide the identity of the person. Whereas he appears to one of the first people to identify emotions, he is selective, referring to emotions to help illustrate discussion. It may be that he delved into further depth about emotions in other treatises that are now lost to history. Aristotle refers to emotions such as: calmness, anger, friendship/enmity, fear/ confidence, shame, kindness, pity, indignation and envy. However, he does not use the word *"emotions"*, preferring the term *"pathos"*, the idea being, to appeal to the audience's emotions gaining sympathy, empathy, awaken emotions with the purposes of inducing a desired judgement. *"Ethos"* refers to the credibility, and character, of the speaker and includes factors such as the way the speaker dresses, their position in society and, vocabulary that is used (for example a barrister, university professor, doctor). *"Logos"* refers to the use of reasoning by presenting arguments that appear logical to the audience. Together pathos, ethos and logos are referred to as modes of persuasion, rhetoric appeals, or ethical strategies. Aristotle (1992) places emotions into three (3) categories:

1. Emotions that are directed at oneself (for example: confidence)

2. Emotions directed at other people (for example: friendship) and

3. Emotions directed at external events (for example: fear)

Zeno of Citium (334BC-262BC) is the founder of stoic school of philosophy who believes that it is not what the person says but how they behave (Irvine, 2009). He was born in Citium, now known as Cyprus. He arrives in Athens having been shipwrecked and becomes a student of Crates of Thebes (365BC-285BC) a cynic philosopher. While in Athens, he later establishes his own stoicism school at the Stoa Polikile in the Agora (Irvine, 2015). He comments about his new life that *"I made a prosperous voyage when I suffered a shipwreck"* (Diogenes Laertius, 2018) eminently describing his stoicism. Stoicism reminds us of how short our lives are and how unpredictable the world is clearly identifying the importance of overcoming destructive emotions and how they can affect us. The focus is on our own behaviour, recognising that we can only control ourselves and not external events or experiences (Holiday, nd). Stoics regard virtue as the only good and external things such as wealth, pleasure and health are neither good nor bad. Virtue is considered sufficient to bring happiness. Being stoic is being resilient to destructive emotions while remaining calm. Zeno of Citium identifies four (4) main emotions: pleasure, grief, fear and desire. He distinguishes destructive emotions as being sinful, irrational and unnatural to the soul that Chrysippus (280-206BC) finds *"disobedient to reason"* (Dufour, 2004). Chrysippus elaborates by suggesting that emotions are associated with two approaches to judgement. The first is if an experience is good or bad and the second what decisions are made about the experience. Zeno of Citium defines an emotion as being a *"horme pleonazousa"* (an excessive impulse) and divides people into two groups: those who are wise and those who are foolish. A wise man performs every action well. The fool fails everything (Lyons, 1999). Thus, emotions can be associated with being foolish and are, therefore, regarded as being negative and unnecessary. This view is reinforced by Cicero (106BC to 43BC) who feels that emotional disturbances are a sickness of character. For example: a likeness of women is similar to a fondness of wine (Gross, 2006). This stoic viewpoint is reinforced by Seneca (4BC to 65AD) who considers that emotions such as grief, fear and anger are irrational, emphasising that virtue is sufficient for happiness (Irvine, 2009; Vogt, 2006). The virtues that the stoics recognise are: wisdom, justice, temperance and courage. Happiness is found by accepting the present moment and not allowing yourself to be influenced by the fear of pain or the desire for pleasure.

Galen (129AD to 198AD) continues to regard passion as a disease of the soul that interferes with daily conduct of life (Magai and McFadden, 1995). He compares those who are intemperate with wild beasts who allow themselves to be influenced by the irrational power of the soul. Emotions such as anger and jealousy, therefore, need to be controlled and tamed. However, Irvine (2015) explains that stoicism isn't someone who simply holds a stiff upper lip and stands there while taking whatever is thrown at them. Being stoic is building on strategies that recognise between things that can be controlled and those that cannot. He adds that energy is much better spent on things that matter and things that we have control over rather than spending time worrying about things outside our control.

Hippocrates (460BC- 370BC) is accredited to applying the four (4) humours (blood, yellow bile, black bile and phlegm) to medicine that are thought to have their origins in ancient Egypt (Van Sertima, 1992). Galen extends the application of the four (4) humours to temperament that is developed further in medieval times where the: 1) dominance of blood suggests the person to be sanguine, warm-hearted, active and social; 2) dominance of yellow bile suggests a person to be choleric, short-tempered and irritable; 3) dominance of black bile suggests that the person is likely to be melancholic, wise and quiet, and; 4) dominance of phlegm suggests that the person is likely to be phlegmatic (calm and relaxed) (Watson and Evans, 1991).

The Greeks consider that emotions are contained within the body and not the brain. However, with modern understanding and appreciation as to how the body and mind works, it is apparent that both the mind and the body contributes to feelings and emotions. Notwithstanding the two millennia between the times of Aristotle and Galen and that of present day, phrases associated with irrational emotions are still used that resonate from the past. For example: *"breaking your heart"* and *"pouring your heart out"* (Schirmer, 2015).

The teachings from the earlier philosophers are passed down into the Roman era and subsequently medieval times and incorporated into Christian teachings. Little further study is undertaken on the human body as it is regarded as a sin to hinder or impede the transfer of the soul into the next world which has continued into recent and modern times. Views and thoughts are therefore often expressed based upon earlier teachings and personal interpretations. This is exemplified by Thomas Aquinas (1225 to 1274). He considers that emotions affect pure thought and are perversion of reason, hostile to rationality. Throughout the middle age's emotions are linked to ethics and sin and, are integrated into Christian psychology that have become the *"seven deadly sins"*: lust, greed, sloth/ laziness, gluttony, envy, anger/ wrath and pride (Solomon, 2010). However, virtues such as hope, love and faith are not regarded as emotions and are equated with reason. This does appear to be a contradiction. For example, a person who may have strong faith may influence others to carry out atrocities on others. Another person may love another. However, that love may be inappropriate.

In the seventeenth (17th) century Rene Descartes (1596 to 1650) puts forward the dualist *"Cartesian"* viewpoint in which the mind is higher than the body. In his *"treatise on the passion of the soul"*, Descartes suggests that emotions are neither separate nor a simple function of the body or soul (Descartes, 2017). For example, categorising emotions may be ambiguous when associated with passivity, rational thinking, objectivity, personal identity, and thought dependency. He explains that passions are associated with the soul, the seat of consciousness, while emotions are perceptions of the soul (De Sousa,1990). Descartes adds that emotions are contaminates of thought that need to be eradicated and passion is undesirable as it interferes with clear thinking (Hergenhahn, 2009). This long help dualist viewpoint may go a long way to explain why western philosophy has such strong underpinning influences that reinforce the rationalisation of emotions within social values and stereotyping of genders (Fineman, 2003).

Making a rational decision suggests that we are thinking sensibly and logically. Rationality implies that we have access to all relevant information to make decisions and that we have the capacity to reason. The reality is that we may likely bias our decision making and it is almost impossible to gain full detailed knowledge and understanding of an experience. We are not computers. Simon (1997) explains this as *"bounded rationality"* acknowledging that our knowledge of the world around us is likely to be incomplete and that decisions are made based upon the information that is available. Taleb (2012) comments that making errors can be the most rational thing to do as they may lead to discoveries (for example, chemotherapy and penicillin). However, in his book *"the skin game"*, Taleb (2019) acknowledges that there are risks that cannot be taken. The skin game concedes that sacrifices have to be made so as to protect those higher in the organisation or help the collective survive. What is important is that you pay attention to what people do and *not* what they say. However, our *"pseudo rationalistic"* decision-making focuses on beliefs rather than the consequences and, in western culture, rationality continues to be valued more highly that feelings and emotions and is regarded as someone of higher, greater intelligence and strength of character (Kingelbach and Phillips, 2014). This may also go some way to explain why there appears to be little investigation into the emotions before the late nineteenth (19th) century.

Towards the latter part of the nineteenth (19th) century interest in the term emotions began to raise interest again. One of the first to this is James (1884, 1902) who suggests that emotions consist of different patterns that are associated with organ sensations. He argues that it is the sensations from muscles and the skin are the main causes for emotions. He adds that each person has the capacity to adapt their own personality to demands they face and to enact the social self to take care of things they value. Wundt (1904) considers that emotions are made up of feeling experiences that are associated with dimensions of quality, activity, and excitement. Ekman (1973) and Izard (1977) suggest that there are a small number of basic emotions that include happiness/ joy, sadness, anger, fear, and disgust. Plutchik (1980) adds: surprise, anticipation and trust to this list. However, others add substantially to this list to include terms such as *"engaged, grateful, exhilarated and, calm"*. To complicate the picture further, these terms are in English, limiting the number of terms that can be used. Words are used in other languages and cultures to explain a particular emotion, emotions that cannot be clearly defined in the English Language.

In 1937, Papez (1995) looks into cases of brain damage and identifies those who experience blunted or exaggerated emotions. He suggests that the damaged areas of the brain must work together in, what is later described as, the limbic system. Discussion ensues as to what happens within the limbic system and what emotions activate different parts of the brain. This continues to the present day. However, there is also on-going debate as to the boundary of the limbic system and what parts of the brain it interacts with. For example, Carter (2010) points out that there doesn't appear to be such a thing as an emotion facility. Recent thought is that emotions interact with different parts of the brain depending upon the context and experience (Davidson and Begley, 2012). However, findings do suggest that when an emotion is experienced it stimulates the amygdala that sends signals, directly or indirectly, to the frontal cortex. The indirect signal passes through the hypothalamus that sends hormonal messages to the rest of the body creating physical changes such as increased heart rate and blood pressure. Feedback is then sent through the somatosensory cortex to the frontal cortex that is then interpreted as an emotion. If neural pathways are blocked, emotions cannot be experienced (Carter, 2010).

Whereas emotions appear to be associated with feelings, hormones, and *"fight or flight"* response, there is argument as to an agreed definition of the term *"emotion"* (Scherer, 2005). Cultural influences and background of individuals may also influence how an emotion is experienced. People are now living and working in a globalised environment where there are interactions between those from different cultures and backgrounds. Communities and organisations may have their own cultures. However, those who live and work in it bring their own culture and background to the environment that in turn may influence the wider culture. How one person responds may differ to how another responds. To state that a person is angry may be interpreted by one person as an emotion where a person shouts and swears, throws things about, uses intimidating body language, and becomes red in the face. Another person may simply internalise the feeling of anger and show little outward signs of the emotion being experienced. Therefore, using terms to describe an emotion only goes so far as to explain what is experienced.

Consideration has to be given to the individuality of each person as he/ she may have similar experiences but feel different types of emotions. Those who are able to detect and control their own emotions and to handle social interactions may be more inclined to be successful and perform well in their job and can be considered as more emotionally intelligent. However, a person with low emotional intelligence may compensate by using other strengths (Mayer, 2012). For example, they may be excellent verbal communicators while lacking in empathy. They could be highly successful without being emotionally intelligent (Brody, 2004, Mayer, 2012). They may be skilled in technical detail and understanding but lack self-awareness of the emotion being felt. Furthermore, emotions felt may be mixed. The person may feel pleasure at the same time as feeling pain or fear. To add to the complexity, there could be a multiple of emotional intelligences that underlie emotion (Zeidner, Matthews and Roberts, 2001).

The challenge that we face is that the workplace is traditionally considered as being a logical, non-emotional, and rational place to work where emotions are considered as being irrational and the antithesis of rational thinking (Ashforth and Humphrey, 1995; Ashkanasay, Zerbe and Hartel, 2002). However, the work environment is saturated with emotions, which includes the teaching profession where emotional intelligence and emotions are integral to interpersonal interactions (Mortiboys, 2012). To regard emotions as the antithesis of rationality is too simplistic. As pointed out by Cian, Krishna and Schwarz (2015) rationality and emotion are fundamental elements that make us human. Manufacturing and heavy industry has declined in recent decades in many of the countries in the western world, including the UK. People are more likely to be employed within the service sector where they are required to be more emotionally engaged with the customer, leading to greater interest in emotions, emotional intelligence and psychology in the workplace (Briner, 1999). What is apparent is that nothing seems to happen in isolation that does not involve our emotions (Kringelbach and Phillips, 2014). Emotions are fundamental to understanding the world around us and how we relate to it. The nature of work is changing and appears to gather pace, where we are now moving quickly into the age of artificial intelligence. There is increased global competition and as such greater demands and expectations are placed upon workers to be more productive. Those working in the teaching environment are not exempt. They often feel tired and stressed with a high percentage of those in academic positions leaving the profession or regret entering the profession in the first place (Kinman, 2001). Work-related stress can have a negative impact upon a person and on those around them. Stress is complex, and people respond differently depending on that being experienced (Aldwin and Park, 2004). Each person may respond in different ways to a particular experience. Therefore, defining a particular experience as stressful is situation dependent upon the capacity of the person to cope.

Stress is associated with well-being, with a link being identified between emotions and physical/ mental health and that mismanaging negative emotions can lead to illness that include: hostility, heart disease and hypertension (Dembroski, MacDougall, Williams, Haney, et al, 1985; Friedman, 1990; Gross, 1998; Hammen, 2005, Jorgensen, Jonson, Kolodziej and Schreer, 1996; Julkunen, Salonen, Kaplan, Chesney, et al, 1994; Schwabe and Wolfe, 2010; Suls, Wan and Costa, 1995; Wang, 2005). Furthermore, minor illnesses can also be exacerbated by inhibition of emotions that can lead to more serious illnesses such as cancer and heart disease (Fawzey, Fawzey, Hyun, Elashoff, et al, 1993; Pennebaker, Kiecolt-Glaser and Glaser, 1988; Pennebaker, 1990; Spiegel, Bloom, Kraemer and Gottheil, 1989).

Studies have been undertaken on emotional intelligence associated with burnout, bullying and discrimination and is influential in helping teachers cope with stressful experiences (Kinman, Jones and Kinman, 2006; Lewis, 2004; O'Boyle, 2001; Nelson, Low and Nelson, 2006; Simpson and Cohen, 2004). In their study of five hundred and thirty-three (533) university academics titled "*The relationship between emotional intelligence and well-being in academic employees*", Bowen, Pilkington and Rose (2016) find that there is an invert relationship between perceived stress and managing emotions. The greater the perceived stress the academic experiences, the less they manage emotion. This suggests that there is a relationship between emotional intelligence, stress and coping.

Woods (2010) points out that research in emotional intelligence has been carried out at school level, but little research has been undertaken with academics in higher education. Research around emotions within the organisational context also appears to be limited in higher education (Briner, 1999, 2005; Kumar and Rooprai, 2009). There, therefore, appears to be an area in which research can be carried out.

Reflections are provided throughout the book with the purpose of prompting a little thought.

Chapter 1

Emotional intelligence

A challenge that social scientists have experienced over the 20th century is to clearly identify the existence of different types of intelligence, including emotional intelligence. There has been a difference of opinion as to whether intelligence is fixed or can be learned. There is also debate as to what intelligence actually is and how it can be defined. A further challenge that researchers have had is that, until very recently, it has not been possible to look inside a person's brain to see how it works. Religious convention limited access to cadavers as any interference to the body could impede the soul from gaining access to the afterlife. More recently, brain scanning has been undertaken, identifying parts of the brain that may react to stimuli. However, this is undertaken in the laboratory and may not equate to "*real life*" experiences. As technology develops, it may provide further insight into how the brain works. It raises the question as to whether or not there are multiple intelligences. There does appear to be an agreement by researchers that emotional intelligence does exist (for example: Goleman, 1995; Bar-On, 1997; Salovey and Mayer, 1990; Petrides and Furnham, 2001), however, there are different theories and models associated with measuring emotional intelligence. Furthermore, there is no agreed standardised test. It may be that multiple intelligences, including emotional intelligence, are simply part of the personality and cannot be separated from the characteristics that we inherit from our parents and that which we learn as we develop.

General intelligence (cognitive intelligence) (IQ) has been identified and discussed over the twentieth (20th) century, and there are instruments that have been devised to help measure how intelligent we are. However, IQ does not appear to capture how gifted a person may be in areas such as: music, emotions, sport, and interpersonal/intrapersonal relationships. Intelligence can, therefore, be thought of in different ways. Emotions may also play a part and influence the decision-making process. A person may be good at managing, regulating and identifying emotions in others using intuitive "*intelligence*" to his/her advantage. He/she may rely on emotional decision making and not just making use of rationalistic thinking. In other words, they use emotional intelligence.

In his book "*Frames of mind: The theory of multiple intelligences*", Gardner (1983) puts forward the idea of multiple intelligences that include: spatial, musical, verbal, language, sport, and interpersonal/ intrapersonal relationships. For this reason, intelligence can be thought of in different perspectives (Gardner,1983, 1999). People experience the world in different ways, undergoing different emotional and social reactions and feelings. A person who may be talented at sport may not have high IQ scores. A person with a high IQ may not be so talented at personal interaction and picking up social cues. Multiple intelligences, identified by Gardner, may not exist. Furthermore, like multiple intelligences, emotional intelligence could be a popular fad and an invention of theory that is too complex to gain a consensual definition and agreed means of measurement. The aims and objectives of this book are not to seek to prove or disprove the existence of emotional intelligence. However, there does appear to be more to a person than general intelligence and that may include abstract and intuitive reasoning associated with multiple intelligences. Whereas there does not appear to be a consensus as to the definition and measurement of the terms: *"intelligence"* and *"emotional intelligence"*, studies have been undertaken throughout the world using different tools and measurement techniques suggesting that different types of intelligence can be defined and measured that include emotional intelligence. It is on this premise that this book accepts the existence of emotional intelligence. However, further research is needed to help define and measure the concept of emotional intelligence.

This chapter begins with a little background information about emotional intelligence and continues with identifying three (3) main theories: ability model, mixed model and trait model. It is apparent that where there is an agreement by the authors associated with these theories that emotional intelligence does exist, there does not appear to be a consensus as to how it can be measured, nor an agreed definition. The chapter provides a critique of the different models identified and concludes by identifying limitations associated with the approaches used to measure emotional intelligence.

A little background to emotional intelligence

The workplace is traditionally considered as being logical, rational and non-emotional with the idea that emotions are irrelevant and get in the way of effective performance (Briner, 1999). The workplace is also regarded as a rational environment in which emotions are considered to be the antithesis of rational thinking. Whereas rational thinking maintains a strong hold on social and work behaviour, it is becoming more acceptable to recognise that emotions have a strong influence on how people interact and behave. With an increase in those working in the service industry, staff are required to be more emotionally engaged with customers and this leads to greater interest being given to emotional intelligence, emotions, and psychology in the workplace. Work is saturated with emotions that include joy, frustration and fear, and to regard emotions as being antitheses of rationality is too simplistic. Since the 1990's, theorists have shown growing interest in the role of emotional intelligence in the workplace. It appears that it is no longer a question as to whether or not emotions have a role in the workplace. The focus appears to be more on how emotions can be managed, how staff in organisations cope with emotions, and how this may impact on other factors within the working environment.

The term emotional intelligence first appears in a German publication in 1966: "*Praxis der Kinderpsychologie und Kinderpsychiatrie*" (Leuner,1996). Wayne Payne (1986) appears to be the first person to use "*emotional intelligence*" in an English unpublished dissertation. Emotional intelligence is brought to mainstream academia in 1990 by Salovey and Mayer. However, it becomes a popular construct following the publication of Daniel Goleman's (1995) book titled "*Emotional Intelligence: Why It Can Matter More than IQ*".

Emotional intelligence is associated with social interactions, individual adaptability and psychological well-being. However, there does not appear to be an agreed definition and means of measuring emotional intelligence. Matthews, Zeidner and Roberts (2004) suggest that emotional intelligence is a competence that helps us identify, express and understand emotions. It also helps regulate positive and negative emotions both within yourself and with other people. Emotional intelligence is considered to be the ability to understand your own emotions (self-awareness), and understand emotions in others, allowing a person to decode attitudes and intentions and to respond accordingly (Keltner and Haidt, 2001). Emotional intelligence is, therefore, an important construct in enabling a person to express, understand and perceive feelings and to be able to control emotions. This is the overarching explanation of emotional intelligence that is used in this book and that which is generally accepted within academic literature. However, further agreement by researchers is still illusive. It is therefore helpful to investigate and discuss the main theories associated with emotional intelligence in further depth.

The main models of emotional intelligence

Since the 1990s, researchers identify different models (for example: ability, mixed, trait) and assert the existence of emotional intelligence. The table below provides a summary of the main theorists/ models associated with emotional intelligence which are then discussed in further detail.

Table 1.1. Main theorists/ models.

No	Theorist	Model	Concepts/ framework
1	Salovey and Mayer (1990) Mayer and Salovey (1997)	Ability	Cognition and emotion
2	Goleman (1995 and 1998a, 1998b)	Mixed	Social and emotional competencies (Cognitive and personality traits) Everything that is not IQ
3	Bar-On (1997)	Mixed	Social and emotional intelligence (Non-cognitive and competency and skill)
4	Petrides, 2009a, 2009b, 2011; Petrides and Furnham (2001, 2003)	Trait	Emotional traits Associated with personality

As an analogy, emotional intelligence can be regarded as a bowl of fruit. Each model identified can be regarded as a particular type of fruit, for example: apple, orange, banana. They are all fruit but look, feel and taste different. To add to the analogy and complexity of describing emotional intelligence, the mixed model could be seen as a combination of several fruit giving rise to challenges in defining exactly what it is.

Ability model paradigm (Salovey and Mayer, 1990)

The first model is put forward by Salovey and Mayer (1990), who define emotional intelligence as an ability to monitor your own emotions and feelings and to discriminate how to use the information to guide thinking and actions. It is the ability to understand and manage emotions that relate emotion with cognition. The ability model focuses on the actual emotions and how they interact with thought. It is considered to be an ability that is associated with intelligence- hence the ability model of emotional intelligence. Within this model, emotional intelligence enables a person to monitor his/her own emotions and the emotions in those around them. It also enables the person to distinguish between emotions so that he/she can take the right action or make the right decision when required. Emotional intelligence is therefore an *actual* intelligence. It is a mental skill, an ability, as opposed to a trait or characteristic.

(Salovey, Brackett and Mayer, 2004). There are four (4) categories within their ability model. These are: 1) perceiving (to identify the person's own emotions); 2) facilitating (emotional facilitation to think); 3) understanding (to understand and analyse emotions and emotional knowledge; 4) managing emotions (to reflect and regulate emotions in oneself and others. The table below summarises the categories and year of publication.

Table 1.2. Emotional intelligence model (Ability model, Salovey and Mayer).

No	Categories	Year
1	Perceiving emotions	1990
2	Emotions used to facilitate thinking	1990
3	Understanding emotions	1990
4	Managing emotions	1997

Mayer, Salovey, Caruso and Sitarenios (2003) argue that it is the only published performance measure of emotional intelligence abilities that can assess *actual* emotional skills rather than desired or perceived skills. The approach to this model is that each of the dimensions exists within particular circumstances or contexts and that each person differs in their abilities and how they react and relate to different circumstance. The four (4) categories of emotional intelligence are related to other mental abilities (for example: verbal intelligence) which, when tested, are shown to be reliable. The ability model acknowledges that emotional intelligence is associated with cognitive intelligence as well as higher levels of thinking. It is about thinking, learning and adapting to the environment. By definition, the ability model can therefore be regarded as an intelligence (Mayer, Caruso and Salovey, 1999).

The ability model relies on external assessment, making use of maximum performance. This approach relies on consistency and that the base levels for assessment are the same for each person. However, each person has different backgrounds, experience and understanding of how they see the world and his/ her base level and responses/ reactions may vary to others who undertake exactly the same test. Furthermore, another weakness with this model is that it relies on true and accurate interpretation of data and that it is possible to directly correlate one set of answers to another. "*Operationalisation*" of ability emotional intelligence is, therefore, subjective and is based upon emotional experience that cannot be objectively assessed (Barchard and Russell, 2006; Matthews, Zeidner and Roberts, 2007; Robinson and Clore, 2002). An interesting analogy of the ability model is that of a person who may be verbally dexterous, has the ability to communicate, but may not be emotionally intelligent. For example, Michael has good short-term memory for verbal dexterity and is an excellent conversationalist, however, he is not aware of how emotionally engaged he becomes, that in turn upsets those he is in conversation with. Furthermore, Michael is not able to pick up very easily on emotions that others display and to manage the emotions experienced, therefore suggesting low emotional intelligence. In comparison, Patricia is extremely good at recognising her own emotions and those in others and is adept at managing these emotions effectively. However, when she undertakes an IQ test, she is shown to be slightly lower in cognitive skills than normal.

Zeidner, Matthews and Roberts (2012) suggest that emotional intelligence is associated with personality traits, whereas the ability model is associated with cognitive intelligence. The test associated with the ability model is widely used but it doesn't appear to measure intelligence, nor does it measure dimensions of psychological interest. This conflicts with the view that the ability model is associated with intelligence.

The ability model is clearly identified as an ability (one type of fruit), however, the mixture of cognition, skill and emotion suggests that it is a made up of more than one type of fruit. The Oxford Dictionaries (2016) refer to intelligence as an "*ability*" that helps us acquire and apply skills and knowledge; whereas emotion is defined as a strong "*feeling*" that is derived from the circumstances in which we are in as well as our "*mood*" and relationships with others. They appear to be separate constructs. If the ability model is associated with cognitive "*intelligence*", it cannot also be associated with "*emotions*" and emotional intelligence.

Mixed model paradigm (Goleman, 1995, 1998a, 1998b)

The next model discussed is referred to as "*mixed*". Emotional intelligence comes to mainstream reading in 1995 when Daniel Goleman publishes his book "*Emotional Intelligence: Why It Can Matter More than IQ*". He defines emotional intelligence as the capacity to recognise how we feel and how others feel that, in turn, motivates how we manage the emotions. This appears to be a wide overarching definition that could be used to define any of the models discussed in this book. However, when delving into the mixed model, Goleman relates emotional intelligence with traits that include motivation, persistence, sociability and self-awareness. Therefore, the model includes mental abilities related to intelligence, emotion and, personality dispositions and traits. Hence the name given to the model as "*mixed*". The mixed model relies on self-assessment and that the person is being truthful and honest when answering. The challenge with self-assessment is that it relies on the person being able to respond honestly and accurately. Each person may have different perspectives as to how they answer the questions. There is no base level from which every person can relate to. For example, the results may be influenced by feelings of bias. The person responding may be experiencing a good, happy day and respond differently to that which they would on another day when they are not feeling so happy.

The mixed model includes five (5) dimensions 1) self-awareness; 2) self-regulation; 3) motivation; 4) empathy and 5) social skills. Goleman (2000) subsequently amends the model to four (4) dimensions of 1) self-awareness, 2) self-management, 3) social awareness and 4) social skills. The table below outlines each of the dimensions.

Table 1.3. Emotional intelligence (Mixed model, Goleman).

Goleman (1998a,1998b) Dimensions	Goleman (2000) Dimensions		Competency
1. Self-awareness	1. Self-awareness	Recognition	Personal competencies
2. Self-regulation	2. Self-management	Regulation	
3. Motivation	3. Social awareness	Recognition	Interpersonal competencies
4. Empathy	4. Social skills	Regulation	
5. Social skills			

Personal competencies identified in the mixed model are made up of the dimensions of self-awareness and self-management. Self-awareness is a deep understanding of a person's own emotions, identifying strengths, weaknesses, motives and values. Self-awareness includes passion for direction and purpose and is central to achieving emotional literacy. Self-awareness includes passion for direction and is central to achieving emotional intelligence (Coco,2011; Orbach,1994). This self-awareness leads to self-realisation, whereby the person can sense his/her own levels of self-confidence in any given situation. It is also the person's ability to recognise how his/her own emotions impact upon others.

Self-management differs from self-awareness as it relates to the control of the person's own emotions and to managing their behaviour. In other words, the person responds to their own perception and understanding of themselves in a particular situation. Goleman places self-awareness and self-management with personal competencies, while social awareness and social skills are placed with interpersonal competencies. Whereas he removes "*motivation*" from the hierarchy, it is subsumed into the other competencies in the hierarchy (Goleman, 2000). Goleman also divides the hierarchy into recognition and regulation. Self and social awareness are associated with recognition, where a person can identify the emotional state of others. Self-regulation and social skills are associated with regulation; being able to manage emotional states in oneself and in others and to maintain good personal relationships. Social awareness is the ability to understand others; to empathise with other people's emotions and also to empathise at the organisational level, recognising the needs of the organisation's customers. Social awareness also includes how the needs and interests of others (including the organisation) can be met. Social skill is the ability to inspire and guide others with the intention of encouraging people to reach their full potential.

Goleman's model is developed into a self-report, 360-degree emotional competency model, combining earlier research undertaken by Boyatzis (1982, 2006). The instrument measures how a person deals with, or expresses, emotions both in life and the work environment and consists of: 1) self-motivation (Initiative, planning, achievement orientation, self-confidence); 2) self-awareness/ regulation (taking a risky stand, self-control, adaptability, conscientiousness, values learning); 3) people management (oral presentations, networking, leadership, coaching, empathy, influence, facilities learning, distinguishes the firm's reputation and resources); 4) social awareness, and; 5) social skills. The mixed model includes: mental abilities, skills, intelligence, emotion, personality dispositions, and traits. In the analogy used in this book, it is neither one fruit nor another, it is several mixed together. It is a wide use of a term that appears to lack focus. However, it is widely used and referred to in modern literature.

Mixed model paradigm (Bar-On, 1997)

Bar-On (1997, 2000, 2005) puts forward his own model associated with the "*mixed*" approach to emotional intelligence. He initially describes it as being an emotional social intelligence model, which he later develops into the Emotional quotient inventory (EQi) that includes factors associated with personality and emotional and social competencies. Bar-On (1997) defines emotional intelligence as a selection of non-cognitive capabilities, skills and competencies that influence how we cope with environmental pressures and demands.

Bar-On identifies emotional intelligent scales which measure dimensions and competencies. The model is divided into two: 1) theory (conceptualisation of emotional social-intelligence) and 2) psychometric (the measure of emotional intelligence- based on theory). The scales Bar-On uses are: intrapersonal, interpersonal, stress management, adaptability and general mood. The intrapersonal scale contains the dimensions of: self-regard, emotional self-awareness, assertiveness, independence, and self-actualisation. Self-regard is the ability of the person to perceive and understand themselves and to accept themselves for who he/ she is. Emotional self-awareness is the ability of a person to be aware of their own emotions. Assertiveness is the ability of a person to be able to express their emotions clearly and effectively. Independence is the ability to be self-reliant and not having to depend on other people to provide emotional support. Self-actualisation is the ability a person has to achieve their own goals and to achieve their potential and is summarised in the table below. The table below provides a summary of Bar-On's mixed model of emotional intelligence.

Table 1.4. Mixed emotional intelligence (Bar-On, 1997).

Scales	Dimensions	Explanations
1. Intrapersonal	Self-regard	The ability to perceive and understand oneself
	Emotional self-awareness	To be aware of one's own emotions
	Assertiveness	The ability to express emotions
	Independence	The ability to be self-reliant and not having to depend on others emotional support
	Self-actualisation	The ability to achieve goals and potential
2. Interpersonal	Empathy	To be aware of others feelings
	Social responsibility	The ability to relate with others in a cohesive manner
	Interpersonal relationships	The ability to relate to others creating a mutually satisfying relationship
3. Stress management	Stress tolerance	The ability to manage emotions constructively and effectively
	Impulse control	The ability to control one's own impulses
4. Adaptability	Reality testing	The ability to validate one's own thinking in relation to external environment
	Flexibility	The ability to adapt to new situations
	Problem solving	The ability to resolve challenges
5. General mood Scales	Optimism	The ability to look on the brighter side of life
	Happiness	How content one feels

The interpersonal scale incorporates the dimensions of: empathy, social responsibility, and interpersonal relationships. Empathy is being aware of other people's feelings and understanding how others feel. Social responsibility is the ability of a person to identify and relate with others in their own social group and to cooperate with others in a cohesive manner. Interpersonal relations can be described as the ability of a person to relate with others creating a mutually satisfying relationship. The scale of stress management includes the dimensions of stress tolerance and impulse control. The competencies associated with stress tolerance relate to the person's ability to manage emotions both constructively and effectively. Adaptability is associated with change management and includes the dimensions of reality testing, flexibility and problem-solving. Reality testing is the ability to objectively validate one's own feelings while thinking of and relating to the external environment. Flexibility is the ability of a person to adapt their own feelings to new situations. Problem-solving is the ability to effectively resolve challenges of intrapersonal and interpersonal nature.

General mood is associated with self-motivation. The dimensions associated with this are optimism and happiness. Optimism is the ability to look on the brighter side of life. Seligman (2006) refers to the term "*learned optimism*"; the power of feelings in helping a person overcome adversity to help them achieve their goal and happiness how content the person feels with themselves and others. Seligman (2006) also refers to pessimistic thinking where a person interprets setbacks as being permanent (long lasting), pervasive (affects everything), and personal (he/she is responsible for the set back). A person may score highly on being optimistic, therefore raising their emotional intelligence scores. However, optimism may not be appropriate on every occasion. If the cost of failure is high, then the use of optimism may not be the right strategy. Seligman (2006) adds that it is possible to accept pessimistic thoughts, and this could be a more intelligent strategy to adopt depending on circumstances being faced.

Both Goleman and Boyatzis associate the mixed model with social and emotional competencies that include cognitive and personality traits. This differs from Bar-On as he includes non–cognitive competencies. It appears that the mixed models put forward by Bar-On (1997) and Goleman (1995, 1998a, 1998b) are spread across different levels. The mixed models treat mental abilities and a variety of other characteristics such as motivation, states of consciousness and social activity as a single entity. The mixed model also appears to be based upon "*unstated assumptions*" and is linked to biological factors. However, there does not appear to be research to support this. For example: Bar-On refers to Darwin's (1872) theory of evolution and that, emotional intelligence is associated with the adaption to environmental stress. Greater clarity is needed. However, the term "*mixed model*" encompasses so many scales and dimensions, clarity may be illusive. Furthermore, tests associated with the mixed model appear to overlap with personality traits such as emotional stability and extroversion introducing factors that may not necessarily be associated with emotional intelligence. This then questions the validity of the mixed model.

The definition of the mixed model is broad and includes emotional characteristics, personality traits, human abilities and motivation. The model mixes attributes associated with emotion, intelligence and emotional intelligence together with the emotional intelligence concept and when put together, can create considerable confusion. The mixed model appears to include emotional characteristics, personality traits, human abilities and motivation. The package of factors such as persistence, good social skills and perceptiveness can be acquired or learned when they may actually consist of different and possibly opposing qualities. Although the theory associated with the mixed model appears to be popular, there seems to be little information about its psychometric properties within scientific journals. The mixed model appears to include everything except intelligence quotient (IQ) and also lacks academic rigour.

Trait model paradigm (Petrides and Furnham, 2001)

The third (3rd) model discussed in this chapter is put forward by Petrides and Furnham (2001) who differentiate between trait emotional intelligence and ability emotional intelligence. They seek to provide greater clarity and explanation as to the term emotional intelligence. Trait emotional intelligence can be described as: a constellation of emotional self-perceptions which are located at the lower levels associated with personality hierarchies and includes factors from personality (for example: assertiveness, empathy).

Trait emotional intelligence incorporates self-perceived abilities via a personality framework that identifies items that include behavioural dispositions and self-perceived abilities, that can be measured through a self-report. The full Trait Emotional Intelligence Questionnaire (TEIQue-) is a self-report inventory that includes one hundred and fifty three (153) items, measuring: adaptability, assertiveness, emotion appraisal (self and others), emotion expression, emotion management (others), emotion perception, emotion regulation, impulsiveness, relationship skills, self-esteem, self-motivation, social competence, stress management, trait empathy, trait happiness, trait optimism. The table below provides a summary of explanations associated with each of the trait facets.

Table 1.5. Trait emotional intelligence (Petrides, 2009).

Trait facet (dimensions)	Explanations
1. Adaptability	How flexible and willing one is to adapt to new situations.
2. Assertiveness	How far one stands up for their own rights.
3. Emotion appraisal	How well one can assess emotions in oneself and others.
4. Emotion expression	How well one can communicate their feelings to others.
5. Emotion management	How well one can influence how others feel.
6. Emotion perception	How clear a person can identify their feelings and those in others.

7. Emotion regulation	How well one is at controlling their own emotions.
8. Impulsiveness	How well one is at controlling their own urges.
9. Relationship skills	How well one is at maintaining personal relationships.
10. Self-esteem	How self-confident one is.
11. Self-motivation	How well one is at facing challenges.
12. Social competence	How well one is at social interactions/ skills.
13. Stress management	How well one is at coping with pressure and regulating stress.
14. Trait empathy	How well one is at relating to another person's point of view.
15. Trait happiness	How happy or content one is with their own lives.
16. Trait optimism	How well one is at looking at the "bright side of life".

The first trait facet (dimension) is adaptability, assessing a person on how flexible and willing he/ she is to adapt to new conditions. Assertiveness is how far a person will stand up for their own rights. Emotion expression is how capable the person is to communicate their feelings to others. Emotion management in others is how capable a person is in influencing how other people feel. Emotion perception relates to how clear the person is about their own feelings and those of others. Emotion regulation is how capable the person is in controlling their own emotions. This can be exemplified, that when faced with fear or anger, self-regulation enables the person to make decisions when he/ she is in a crisis. It is recognising how a person feels when faced with these emotions. Impulsiveness is how likely it is for the person to give in to their own urges. Relationship skill is how capable a person is in maintaining a personal relationship with others. Self-esteem is how successful or self-confident the person is. Self-motivation is how a person faces challenges and adversity. Social competence is how well the person's social skills are. Stress management is how capable the person is to withstand pressure and regulate stress. Trait empathy is how well a person can relate to another person's perspective. Trait happiness is the measure of how happy or satisfied he/ she is with their own lives and trait optimism is looking on the *"bright side of life"*.

Trait emotional intelligence is independent of cognitive ability and overlaps Costa and McCrae's (1992) *big 5* personality types; these being neuroticism, extroversion, openness, agreeableness, and conscientiousness (Freudenthaler, Neubauer, Gabler and Scherl, 2008; Petrides and Furnham, 2001; Petrides, Vernon, Schemer, Lighart, et al., 2010); Russo, Mancini, Trombini, Baldaro, et al, 2012; Vernon, Villani, Schermer, Kirilovic, et al, 2009).

Research carried out by Petrides and Furnham (2003) explores whether people with high trait emotional intelligence are more sensitive to emotion-laden stimuli when compared to those who are low in trait emotional intelligence. The study is associated with fifteen (15) students who have high trait emotional intelligence scores and fifteen (15) who have low trait emotional intelligence scores. The students are then asked to complete an inventory on their mood states on three different occasions. The first is a baseline, prior to the test. The second is after the students have seen a disturbing World War II documentary. The third occasion is following the students watching humorous home videos. The students are then called in on two separate occasions to undertake the tests. The findings show that those from the low trait emotional intelligent group are less sensitive to mood changes within the experiment when compared to those students with high emotional intelligence. In other words, those with higher emotional intelligence are more inclined to experience statistically significant mood changes (for example depression, anger, tension) during the tests when compared to those with lower emotional intelligence. The experiment shows that the effects are significant after the *big 5* controls have been included, demonstrating the validity of using the Trait emotional intelligence questionnaire (TEIQue).

The TEIQue is able to predict outcomes much better than other questionnaires (Freudenthaler, Neubauer, Gabler, and Scherl, 2008; Gardner and Qualter, 2009). The TEIQue covers each factor in the trait emotional intelligence sampling domain, whereas other questionnaires may exclude factors associated with trait emotional intelligence (Cooper and Petrides, 2009). Another advantage Cooper and Petrides (2009) identify is that other measures, that are self-report, appear to have problems associated with their reliability, whereas the TEIQue demonstrates excellent psychometric properties. Petrides and Furnham (2001) add that trait emotional intelligence is also concerned with behaviours and subjective judgements. For example, trait emotional intelligence can predict goal orientation and mood recovery (Martinez-Pons, 1997; Salovey, Mayer, Goldman, Turvey et al., 1995). Trait emotional intelligence is also linked with depression and anxiety (Dawda and Hart, 2000; Russo, Mancini, Trombini, Baldaro, et al., 2012). There appears to be a well-established link between persistent pain and depression and a negative predictor associated with psychopathology (Gardner and Qualter, 2009; Harma, Katiala-Heino, Rimpela and Rantanen, 2002; Williams, Daley, Burnside and Hammond-Rowley, 2010). Trait emotional intelligence also reveals links associated with addiction, gambling, ecstasy, behavioural genetics, neuroscience and, psychopathology (Ali, Amorim and Chamorro-Preuzicl, 2009; Craig, Fisk, Montgomery, Murphy, et al, 2010; Mikolajczak, Bodarwe, Laloyaux, Hansenne, et al, 2010; Parker, Taylor, Eastabrook,

Schell, et al, 2008; Vernon, Villani, Schermer and Petrides, 2008; Uva, de Timary, Cortesi, Mikolajczak, et al, 2010).

Petrides and Furnham (2001) argue that emotion-related traits together with perception have been demonstrated to affect psychological and behavioural variables (For example: Beyer, 1998; Beyer and Bowden, 1997; Katz and Campbell, 1994; King and Emmons, 1990, 1991; Taylor and Armor, 1996; Taylor and Brown, 1988). It can also have strong predictive qualities associated with the socio-emotional criteria. For example, facial expressions, leadership, overall social competence and peer evaluations of kindness (Mavroveli, Petrides, Sangareau and Furnham, 2009; Mavroveli and Sanchez-Ruiz, 2011). Mavroveli, Petrides, Rieffe and Bakker (2007) add that those with high trait emotional intelligence may be at an advantage due to greater emotional self-regulation and are therefore more likely able to moderate their emotions when faced with such challenges. Emotion regulation is how capable the person is in controlling their own emotions. Bharwaney (2007) exemplifies this, that when faced with fear or anger, self-regulation enables the person to make decisions when he/ she is in a crisis. It is recognising how a person feels when faced with these emotions. A further argument in support of the trait emotional intelligence model is that research carried out on those who have experienced brain damage suggests that emotional intelligence is neurologically based and is unrelated to standard intelligence measures (Damasio, 1994, 1996; Robbins and Judge, 2013).

Emotional intelligence is, therefore, an important construct in enabling a person to express, understand and perceive feelings and to be able to control emotions (Redman and Wilkinson, 2002). Trait emotional intelligence is referred to as a group of self-perceptions that are located at the lower levels of personality hierarchy (for example: assertiveness, empathy) (Petrides, Pita and Kokkinaki, 2007). This book therefore refers to trait emotional intelligence (TEIQue) that is associated with personality traits (Petrides, 2009, 2011).

Oxymoron

As described by Damasio (1994,1996) it appears that emotional intelligence is neurologically based and is unrelated to standard intelligence measures. Therefore, trait emotional intelligence cannot be an *intelligence* as well as being associated with *personality traits*. They are mutually exclusive of each other. If *emotional intelligence* is associated with *personality traits*, as proposed by Petrides and Furnham (2001, 2003), it gives rise to a conflict in terminology. It cannot be both and thus leaves an oxymoron (a contradiction in terms). As argued by Mayer and Ciarrochi (2006), Petrides and Furnham's (2001) definition of trait requires a *non-standard definition* of the term trait as the definition of trait includes abilities such as intelligence as identified by

Eysenck (1947, 1958, 1973, 1991). To avoid confusion, Petrides and Furnham replace "*trait emotional intelligence*" with "*emotional self-efficacy*" and the term "*traits*" is replaced with "*dispositions*", thus distinguishing them from abilities. This may be considered as semantic, but it is helpful in clarifying the terminology and it resolves the confusion.

Lack of consensus

It is apparent from the different definitions, models and explanations discussed, there appears to be no consensus as to the definition nor means of measurement of emotional intelligence. A consensual structure of emotion is needed in psychology (Russell and Barrett, 1999). Emotion is a broad class of events, too broad to be considered as a single scientific category and emotion has to be considered individually, broken into more coherent units.

The field of emotional intelligence continues to lack a universally accepted definition and has led to inconsistent and, at times, contradictory findings (Davies, Stankov and Roberts, 1998; Epstein, 1998; Matthews et al., 2004; Mavroveli et al., 2007). Furthermore, correlation between trait emotional intelligence and ability emotional intelligence is low, there, therefore, needs to be a distinction between the approaches (Brannick, Wahi, Arce, Johnson, et al., 2009). Trait emotional intelligence is associated with personality, and ability emotional intelligence is associated with cognitive ability (Petrides, 2011). It is on this premise that it is acknowledged that emotional intelligence does exist.

Emotional intelligence can also reflect on feelings of well-being, how we see ourselves and how others may see us. For example, subjective well-being refers to how people see themselves and how they evaluate their own lives. They may smoke, take little exercise and drink too much. However, they are feeling happy and content with their lifestyle and feelings of well-being. They experience things from a hedonistic viewpoint where they have an internalised viewpoint of the world while maximising pleasure and minimising pain, satisfying needs and desires (Diener, 2009; Fredrickson, 2001; Henderson and Knight, 2012; Kahneman, 2011). They enjoy the cigarette, the bottle of wine while relaxing in front of the TV. If the person experiences feelings of high subjective well-being, they experience happiness. Whereas feelings of sadness and anger are associated with low subjective well-being. Using emotional intelligence can assess and evaluate how you are feeling delving into the emotional state and taking thoughtful action, thus improving feelings of intrapersonal subjective well-being.

Those who look in at this person, as an observer and, from a eudaimonic perspective, may consider that their lifestyle is unhealthy. The eudaimonic approach is where well-being is evaluated from a more objective approach. Assessment is from outside looking at the person; reflecting on a person's life being virtuous while asking *why* someone is happy rather than *if* he/ she is happy (Henderson and Knight, 2012). Asking why someone is happy or sad engages in more deep-seated thought and reflection from which analysis and assessment can develop into thoughtful action. Emotional intelligence can help place emotions in context reflecting upon interpersonal relationships, connecting to the emotional state and acting in a sensible and considered way.

For all the differences between each of the theories, there is an agreement between the theorists and models that emotional intelligence does exist and that it can influence the intra and interpersonal relationships, as well as feelings of well-being.

Critique

It is clear that there is a lack of consensus as to the definition and the means of measuring emotional intelligence. To add to the confusion, Perez, Petrides and Furnham (2005) points out that correlation between different models of emotional intelligence is weak and most of the studies are carried out in, what appears to be, a "*theoretical vacuum*". The mixed and trait model relies on self-report while ability emotional intelligence relates to ability and is measured through maximum performance tests (Mayer, Salovey and Caruso, 2000). The table below provides a summary of the models and ways of measurement.

Table 1.6. Main models and theorists.

No	Model	Theorist	Way of measurement
1	Ability	Salovey and Mayer (1990) Mayer and Salovey (1997)	Maximum performance
2	Mixed	Goleman (1995, 1998a,1998b); Bar-On (1997)	Self-report
3	Trait	Petrides and Furnham (2001)	Self-report

Self-report relies on the person being able to accurately assess and evaluate their own emotions. Challenges may be experienced where self-report data and paper-pencil tests are imprecise and can carry different meanings (Mayer and Ciarrochi, 2006). However, a self-report is shown to outperform the performance-based instruments associated with emotional intelligence by a large margin (for example: Martins, Ramalho and Morin, 2010; O'Boyle, Humphrey, Pollack, Hawver, et al., 2011). Matthews et al. (2004) summarises them in the table below:

Table 1.7. Performance and self-report measures of E.I (Matthews et al., 2004).

No	Performance based emotional intelligence	Self-reported emotional intelligence
1	Maximal performance	Typical performance
2	External appraisal of performance	Internal appraisal or performance
3	Response bias minimal (or non-existent)	Response bias may be great
4	Administration time long; testing complicated	Administration time short; testing easy
5	Ability like	Personality like

There is a clear distinction between maximum performance and self-report measures of emotional intelligence. Each has its own identifiable limitations. Researchers have found that there is a difference in the constructs of performance and self-report as they use different approaches to measurement and give different results (for example: Freudenthaler and Neubauer, 2007; Martins et al., 2010; Petrides and Furnham, 2001). Cooper and Petrides (2009) add to the critique that whereas other measures that are self-report appear to have problems associated with their reliability, the TEIQue demonstrates excellent psychometric properties.

Limitations

A challenge of measuring emotional intelligence is that each person has their own way of thinking and understanding of the world around them and this can change one moment to the next. Trying to measure and compare individual responses, as to how he/ she feels, may be unrealistic. A further challenge is that the person undertaking the research can only interpret and create understanding from the information heard and/ or seen. The person undertaking the test may have beliefs and values that influence their decisions. Furthermore, the person that is undertaking the study may also have beliefs and values that influence the interpretation of the findings. The difficulty is that it is not possible to detach the person from their beliefs and values when undertaking research.

Another limitation is that a person may not wish to tell the truth. They may lie. Furthermore, the person undertaking the test may not be able to remember details accurately and misinterpret their own experience. Their view may also conflict with another person's understanding of the same experience. There are unlikely to be objective observations as a person is seldom likely to give a full account about what they experienced. However, the findings can help with informing and contributing to theory.

Summing up

This chapter provides a little background to how emotional intelligence came into mainstream academia in 1990 by Salovey and Mayer, and into widespread use in 1995 following Daniel Goleman's book titled "*Emotional Intelligence: Why It Can Matter More than IQ*". There appear to be three (3) main theories associated with emotional intelligence: the ability model, the mixed model and, the trait model. There are different definitions and means of measurement with little or no consensus. It would therefore be helpful to have a single explanation and definition; however, emotion is a broad class of events that may be too broad to be considered as a single scientific category. The chapter also reflects on a contradiction of terms, an oxymoron, explaining that trait emotional intelligence cannot be an *intelligence* as well as being associated with *personality traits*. They are mutually exclusive. Petrides and Furnham therefore replace "*trait emotional intelligence*" with "*emotional self-efficacy*" and the term "*traits*" is replaced with "*dispositions*", thus distinguishing them from abilities. The chapter then explains that there is a lack of consensus as to what emotional intelligence actually is and how it can be measured. The chapter concludes by looking into a few limitations associated with studying emotional intelligence. For example, each person has their own way of thinking and understanding of the world around them and this can change one moment to the next. Undertaking a study where a participant completes a questionnaire relies on them being honest and to remember how they felt at the time. Undertaking observations of others relies on true interpretation by the observer. Trying to measure and compare individual responses as to how he/ she feels may be unrealistic. For all the differences between each of the theories, there is an agreement between the theorists and models that emotional intelligence does exist and that it can influence intra and interpersonal relationships, as well as feelings of well-being.

Chapter 2

Stress

Stress is a complex area of study as people respond differently depending on the nature of the experience and how they feel. What one person may experience as being stressful another may see it as nothing more than a small irritation. The term stress seems to be embedded into everyday life. Getting up in the morning and having to catch a train or bus may rise the stress level. Working with loud people or with those who have irritating habits can cause stress. The demands of the job may be overwhelming and support from management may not be forthcoming. It seems that these experiences have always been with us. However, it is only in recent decades that the term stress has become part of the English lexicon.

The Health and Safety Executive (UK 2018b) associate work-related stress with six areas: demands, control, support, relationships, role and change. Each of the aforementioned are associated with three main perspectives of stress: 1) Stimulus 2) Response, and 3) Interactional, and are discussed in this chapter. This chapter also provides interesting data around findings on stress and what drives us as human beings to feel the urge to *"fight or flight"*. The chapter continues by reflecting on demands placed upon academics and the impact this may have that can lead to chronic stress and burnout. This chapter discusses the importance of positive emotions and how they can help improve feelings of distress. The nine to five job appears to be disappearing quite fast and replaced by a more flexible approach to work where staff members can work away from the traditional workplace desk. There is greater pressure on work/life balance where work extends into the evenings, weekends and into holiday time. This chapter concludes by reflecting upon the need to have a sensible and reasonable work/ life balance, where people can break away from work-related matters, enabling them to focus on personal interests, interests that can help reduce stress levels. It is, therefore, worth looking into the *"perspectives of stress"* and reflect upon the terms.

Perspectives of stress

Masuda and Holmes (1967) refer to stimuli where *"things"* cause stress. Each person has a tolerance to a stressful experience and if the stress is too great it may affect his/ her well-being, possibly making them psychology and physically ill (Masuda and Holmes, 1967; Holmes and Rahe, 1967; Bartlett, 1998). The second refers to the *"response"* given when the person experiences the stress. Selye (1956) explains that rather than "*things*" causing stress it is the internal reaction/ response to the stress. The third perspective is described by Lazarus (1966) as the imbalance between the "*interaction*" of ability and demands of coping with a stressful experience. It is where the demands of coping with the stressful experience become too great, overpowering the ability to cope. The table below provides a summary of each of the perspectives.

Table 2.1. Perspectives of stress.

No	Perspective	Explanation
1	Stimulus (Masuda and Holmes, 1967)	"Things" cause stress
2	Response (General adaption syndrome) (Systematic) (Selye,1956, 1976)	"Response" to stressful experiences
3	Interactional (Psychological stress) (Lazarus, 1966, 1982,1990,1991,1993)	Transactional. "Interaction". Imbalance of ability and demands to cope

Work related illnesses

Stress appears to be endemic within society. It has become a significant health and safety factor within the workplace. In the 1990's work-related environment, stress is reported as being second to musculoskeletal disorders (Jones and Hodgson, 1998). In 2017/18 The Health and Safety Executive (HSE) (2018a) report that in the UK, 1.4 million workers experience work-related ill health, of which stress and depression accounts for 44% of work-related ill health ahead of musculoskeletal disorders at 35%. This has remained at a similar percentage for more than ten (10) years. The Chartered Institute of Personnel and Development also find that in their Health and Well-being survey (2019) that mental ill health is reported as the main reason for long term absence (59%), followed by stress and musculoskeletal injuries, both at 54%. The occupations that have the highest rates are healthcare workers, teaching professionals, business, media and public services professionals. The Mental Health Foundation (2018a) find that in the past year 74% of people have experienced stress that has been so overwhelming that they feel they are unable to cope and that, one in six people have experienced a mental health problem in the last week. 51% of adults who feel stressed also report feeling depressed. The National Health Service (England) (NHS) (2018) reports that one (1) in four (4) adults experience a mental illness that include: anxiety, depression, phobias, obsessive-compulsive disorder, panic attacks and, post-traumatic stress disorder. More alarmingly of those who feel stressed, 16% self-harm and 32% have suicidal thoughts. The HSE (2018a) also add that systematic reviews and longitudinal studies show that work-related stress is associated with depression, anxiety, and heart disease, and may also be related to some musculoskeletal disorders.

The main factors that cause work-related stress, depression or anxiety include workload, tight deadlines, long working hours and too much responsibility and lack of management support. This is supported by findings from the HSE (2018a) that report between 2009/10 and 2011/12 causes of work-related stress, depression and anxiety are associated with too much responsibility, lack of managerial support and tight deadlines. The CIPD (2019) find in their Health and Well-being at work survey that the main cause of stress-related absence is associated with workload, accounting for 62%. Management style accounts for 43%, followed by relationships at work (30%). A noteworthy observation that the CIPD (2019) make is that 24% of participants feel that financial well-being is a significant factor that leads to feelings of stress. In a study undertaken by Sparks, Cooper, Fried and Shirom (1997) they find that working long hours can impact upon health and well-being and yet academics appear to work beyond the normal number of hours during term time. Participants report an average working week of fifty-five (55) hours during the term time (Court, 1996). This was in the 1990s and workload pressures do not appear to have eased at all. The World Economic Forum (2019) finds that, in Europe, the UK has longest working hours with the average working week for full-time employees at 42.3 hours with Denmark being lowest at 37.8 hours per week. Worldwide it appears that Turkey has the longest working week with full-time employees working an average of 49.4 hours. Peter Fleming (2018) reports in the Guardian newspaper that technology was thought to help liberate us from the daily work. However, it appears to make things worse. For example, in 2002, less than 10% of office workers checked emails outside of office hours. That has now increased to 50%. Fleming (2018) points out that the nine to five job appears to be a relic of a bygone era. We may spend more time checking emails and working outside the traditional nine (9) to five (5) job; however, hours worked do not seem to equate to output/ productivity. Furthermore, our sedentary lifestyle seems to add to the challenges of coping with the stressful working environment. Because people work longer hours doesn't necessarily equate with productivity. The Organisation for Economic Co-operation and Development (2019) find that the level of Gross Domestic Product (GDP) per capita, for 2017, is highest for Ireland (85.9) followed closely by Norway and Luxembourg (80.7 and 79.5 respectively). The USA lies in sixth place with a ratio of 64.1 (estimate), behind Denmark (64.9) and Belgium (64.8) and just ahead of The Netherlands (62.6), Sweden (61.7) and Germany (60.5). The UK lies in sixteenth place with a ratio of 52.5. The ratio for Turkey is estimated to be 38.1 while Chile and Mexico lie at the foot of the table with a ratio of 21.9 (estimate) and 18.8 (estimate) respectively. It is, therefore, not surprising that stress levels remain high in the UK. Staff members work longer hours and are less productive than their counterparts in other countries. Demands, expectations and pressure are placed upon staff members to perform. However, it is not a simple numerical comparison that needs to be made. It is important to consider the nature of work and how interesting and motivating it is to the member of staff. Work needs to be intrinsically motivating and meaningful, and the hierarchy less authoritarian. Work should not become a chore where creativity is sucked out staff members (Fleming, 2018). Inspiring and trusting members of staff is intrinsic to productivity. Staff members may work fewer hours and productivity may increase. Staff members will feel wanted and seek to come to work and engage in work activities. They may also feel less stressed, anxious and depressed. It is creating an environment that is conducive to well-being.

The consequences of mental health problems are not just felt by the person experiencing it. It impacts upon the organisation as well. Stress-related illness can affect a person physically and psychologically and may impact/ affect those around them including family, friends and colleagues. Furthermore, if a person does not feel well, they are less likely to perform at their maximum potential. This can lead to lower productivity and output and cost the organisation both in financial and competitive terms. The HSE (2018a) find that work-related stress, depression and anxiety has increased in recent years with a prevalence of one thousand eight hundred (1,800) cases per one hundred thousand (100,000) workers in 2017/18. The HSE (2018a) also report that in 2017/18, more than half a million people experienced work-related stress, depression or anxiety. As a result, 15.4 million working days were lost due to work-related stress, depression or anxiety. This equates to just under twenty-six (26) days per person. Not only is there a cost to the health of the individual, there is also a financial cost to the organisation and to the Country. The CIPD (2019) find that approximately 40% of those who respond to their survey say that that organisation's approach to health and well-being is reactive, rather than proactive. Addressing issues associated with stress and well-being is important. Notwithstanding the evidence that work-related stress is having it appears that much more work is needed.

Delving further into the discussion, stress is a major cause for work-related illness within the education sector (Cartwright and Cooper, 1997; Clarkson and Hodgkinson, 2007). This was reported in the 1990s and 2000s. However, similar findings are found more recently. For example, the HSE (2018a) find that within professional occupations health workers, public service workers and those in teaching show higher levels of stress. It is apparent that stress continues to be a problem that is linked to health outcomes including cancer, asthma, arthritis, diabetes and heart disease (Johnson, Perry and Rosensky, 2002). The challenge with working in academia is that it appears that work is never-ending and that the demands on academics may involve competing demands that may lead to internal conflict, pressure and stress (Fisher, 1994; Wortman, Biernat and Lang, 1991). Furthermore, the nature of the work undertaken by academics can lead to blurring of boundaries both professionally and personal (Austin and Pilat, 2000). The nature of the job can therefore lead to increased work/ home life conflict and stress. This can impact upon well-being.

Eustress and distress

Stress can be seen from two points of view- eustress (that is regarded as "*good*") and distress (that is regarded as "*bad*"). If directed correctly the response to stress can be beneficial, putting the person's body and brain in an optimal position to perform a task or face a situation (Crum, Salovey and Anchor, 2013). Selye (1956, 1976) describes this as eustress where positive feelings are experienced that arise from challenging or conflicting situations that may yield benefits (Alpert and Haber, 1960). For example: it can lead to initiative taking, enabling a person to meet the demands of their job (Fay and Sonnentag, 2002). It can lead to improved memory and increase the speed by which a person processes information (Cahill, Gorski, and Le, 2003; Hancock and Weaver, 2005). It can also help enhance immunity and improve feelings of well-being (Dienstbier, 1989).

Whereas eustress can be beneficial, distress can have a debilitating effect on physical and psychological well-being. It is the amount, frequency, duration and/ or intensity of the external stressor that is likely to influence how a person reacts and, whether they experience the stress as enhancing (eustress) or debilitating (distress) (Holmes and Rahe, 1967). In his book *"Antifragile"* (Taleb, 2012) discusses the role of hormesis where small doses of harmful substances can be beneficial to the body. Too little may have insignificant effect. Too much and it can be harmful. It is finding that equilibrium. A reasonable level of stress is therefore good, whereas too much can damage the body and the mind. A further point that needs to be acknowledged is that one person may be able to cope with a substantial amount of stress, whereas another person may not. Not all stress is debilitating and is dependent upon how a person perceives and reacts to the environment they are in.

The mindset of the person may have an influence on how a person experiences a stressful experience, whether it is the experience of "*stress-is enhancing*" mindset or "*stress is debilitating*" mindset (Crum et al., 2013). A mindset is how a person perceives and reacts to the environment they are in. Adopting a particular mindset could, therefore, influence behavioural, psychological, and physiological outcomes. Notwithstanding the mindset and the resilience of a person to withstand particular stressful experiences, there is a critical point where the stress can become debilitating (Alpert and Haber, 1960). It is at this point that stress can become overwhelming and the person is unable to cope. It is an unpleasant psychological process that may happen as a response to environmental pressures and where a person's resources to cope are disabled (Hobfoll, 1989, 1998; Weinberg and Cooper, 2007). Distress occurs when resources are threatened or are low. It could include anything that a person values (including possessions or relationships. It could also relate to knowledge or money). Factors that appear to be agreed by researchers is that distress is associated with threats, harm or challenges and has become a significant health and safety factor within the workplace (For example: Kinman, 1996, 1998, 2001, 2008, 2010, 2014; Kinman and Jones, 2003, 2008; Kinman and Wray, 2013; HSE, 2018a, b; Lazarus, 2007; Lazarus and Folkman, 1984, 1986; Lazarus and Launier, 1978).

Stress may come from more than one source pushing and pulling a person in different directions. This is described as psychological strain, where stress can severely affect well-being (Journal of Occupational and Environmental Medicine, 2015). This is exemplified in a study of American and Chinese students undertaken by Zang, Liu and Sun (2017), who find that there is a relationship between psychological strain and suicide, anxiety, and depression. Academics who feel they experience greater stress than they can cope with are less likely to be involved in student interaction, decision making, and committee work and therefore are less productive (Klenke-Hamel and Mathieu, 1990; Wilke, Gmelch and Lovrich, 1984). This can lead to people leaving the teaching profession (Lambert and McCarthy, 2007). Kelly, Charlton, and Jenkins (1995) goes as far as to suggest that academics are 50% more at suicide risk when compared to the average worker.

Stress does appear to be linked with high job demands and low control over what people do in the workplace. This impacts upon well-being. For example, in a meta study of thousands (1000's) of people, undertaken by Steptoe and Kivimaki (2013), those who experience high demand and low control have an increased likely hood of experiencing heart disease. This finding is supported in a study of ten thousand (10,000) people who work in the civil service in the UK (Bosma, Peter, Siegrist and Marmot, 1998). In another study undertaken by Sundquist and Johansson, (2000), the findings suggest that those who experience high demand and low control are also more likely to experience mental illness points out that most people can cope with being busy. This is supported in a recent study by Li, Atasoy, Fang, Angerer et al. (2019) who find that those trapped in a pressurised situation, and have little or no control, can experience effect on well-being. The tipping point is where demands become too much and there is a feeling of lack of control (Marmot, 2015). It depends on factors such as context, personal traits and the ability to cope with challenging and stressful experiences. However, as pointed out by Li, Atasoy, Fang, Angerer et al. (2019), those who experience high blood pressure, problems with sleeping, and job stress are risk factors on their own. There is an increasing risk of early death from cardiovascular disease when added together. It is, therefore, important to have a sensible diet, exercise, have a good sleep and engage in relaxation strategies to help reduce the likelihood of heart disease, maintaining positive psychological and physical well-being.

Cortisol, oxytocin, serotonin and noradrenaline

It is not just psychological factors that affect the way people respond to a stressful experience. There are also biological factors that come into play that includes different chemicals and hormones in the body. For example, distress is associated with the release of cortisol which helps us to *fight or flight*. Cortisol is a hormone that is often referred to as the *"stress hormone"*. Cortisol helps to control sugar levels, reduce inflammation, regulates the metabolic rate and influences memory retention. Cortisol also affects blood pressure and the levels of salt and water within the body. It is therefore a very important hormone that can impede or help with well-being. Cortisol is associated with stress and there is a point where stress can be overpowering at which point cortisol levels are increased and the body becomes overwhelmed and the reaction is the feeling of being distressed. The production of cortisol reduces protein that is stored in the body and the immune system can then break down (Kanoy, Book and Stein, 2013).

When stressed, the liver continues to produce glucose as fuel. However, glucose levels may not reach other parts of the body. The body's response is to disengage in the growth and repair of the body tissues. If this is over a short time, it may have little effect. However, if this goes on over a prolonged period, the outcome can have a dramatic impact upon the body and well-being. For example, when effort, energy and time has been given to work outputs, it is disheartening when someone gives critical negative feedback, pointing out what is wrong. Impact on the receiver of negative feedback can result in feeling stressed simply by trying to understand why the person made such negative comments. The intent may be to *"say it like it is"*. As human beings, we tend to be self-critical and receiving negative feedback can affect confidence and motivation. If it is on one occasion, it may not have a long-lasting effect. However, if further critical comments are made, they can send the person into rumination, worrying and worrying about that said. If the matter is ruminated over time, it can affect psychological and physical well-being and result in feelings of distress. Stress can also affect interpersonal relationships both at work and at home. We can tell ourselves not to worry. However, as a human being, we dwell on negative experiences for longer, trying to understand what happens so that next time the stressors can be avoided or dealt with more effectively. However, distress can lead to depression and anxiety. Depression can lead to changes in eating and weight that may be linked with levels of glucose and cortisol that is released into the body, encouraging the person to eat higher calorie foods. The increased demands placed on the system demands greater use of protein, sugar and insulin that in turn demands the body to eat the "*wrong food*". Eating the wrong food can lead to an increase in weight (Anisman, 2015).

Whereas cortisol is associated with distress, eustress is associated with the production of oxytocin in the system. As it is released into the body, it provides an experience of pleasure such as receiving praise. Oxytocin is found to reduce activation of the amygdala and *fight or flight* response (Kirsch, Esslinger, Chen, Mier et al., 2005). Oxytocin regulates social interaction and is regarded as the "*love drug*" that is released during and after birth that also helps bond couples in adulthood (Helm, 2016; Kazim, 2011). Cortisol is likely to stay in the system much longer than oxytocin. (Oxytocin can be removed in about five (5) minutes compared to one (1) to two (2) hours (or even longer) for cortisol (Burnett, 2016). The benefits of oxytocin and the downside of too much cortisol may help partly explain the challenges people experience with negative thinking, anxiety and depression (Lubuschagne, Phan, Wood, Angstadt et al., 2010; Sabihi, 2017)

Serotonin is a chemical that the nerve cells in the body produces and is associated with well-being and happiness. It is located throughout the body and is used to regulate digestion, bone density, blood clotting, together with the way a person feels. Low serotonin levels are associated with stress, depression, getting annoyed easily and difficult to control impulses. Ways to improve levels of serotonin include exercise and sunlight. It is also helpful to focus on good thoughts and memories and try and reduce, or remove, negative memories and thoughts (Perreau-Linck, Beauregard, Gravel, Paquette et al., 2007, Young, 2007).

Noradrenalin (also known as norepinephrine) is sometimes referred to as a stress hormone, stimulating the release of cortisol into the body. Noradrenalin and cortisol are controlled by the amygdala activating the body and brain to respond to the world around us warning the body against the stressor (Labar, 2010). Noradrenalin is associated with aggression and sex drive. When this hormone is increased, it inhibits the production of insulin and releases glucose into the body (Ghosh and Collier, 2012). It can lead to increased heart rate, shortness of breath, increased heartbeat and blood pressure, and narrowing of blood vessels. In other words- *fight or flight* (Eysenck, 2004; Peterson, 2007). When high, there is an impulsivity to crimes incorporating violence and sex and is thought to be associated with post-traumatic stress disorder (PTSD) (Masters, 2004).

Feeling pumped up and excited can engage in feelings of eustress. It can improve performance. However, the above discussion shows how important it is to recognise feelings of distress and the damage that it can do to the body and mind. We live in a world in which we seem to have to face up to one type of stress, one after another, day after day. We need to find ways of coping in a more effective way, relieving the potential damage that distress may have. We need to find that balance where stressful experiences are placed in context and understood. However, that is very easy to say when we work in such a fast-moving lifestyle where stress seems to be inbuilt into our home and work lives.

The modern workplace

Stress has become a significant health and safety factor within the workplace. Demands and expectations upon the workforce appear to increase year on year. This may be the need to meet with the introduction of new software and/ or hardware. It may be facing a new line manager who has a confrontational approach. It may be increased demands that mean work has to be undertaken in the evenings and weekends or when on leave. For example, in the Health and Well-being at work survey for 2019, the CIPD (2019) find that 63% of people work when they are off sick or on holiday. Technology now allows us to work from almost any location. Whereas this can provide more efficient and effective ways of communicating information, the new technology requires adaption and engagement that lead to new working practices that place pressure on time that is already limited. The increased demands that are placed on us, add to the pressure and feelings of stress. For example, greater focus is given to addressing the concerns and complaints of the customer. In the case of the academic, this is likely to be the student. Understandably universities must compete for students and income, therefore it is important that the student's concerns and complaints are listened to. However, the increased demands that are experienced can remove the focus from other roles and responsibilities and impinge into time that may otherwise be given over to family, impacting work/life balance. For example, there may be less time to undertake research and read up on the latest information. There may be less time available to prepare and design programmes and modules. There may be less time in which to engage in hobbies and interests. There may be less time in which to spend with family and friends. The challenge of meeting with the competing demands may place greater stress on the body both physically and psychologically. Something has to give.

Stress doesn't just impact upon the person experiencing it. It can also affect others around them. For example, academics who feel they experience greater stress than they can cope may feel more withdrawn and are less likely to be involved in student interaction and decision making. They may be less productive. Furthermore, it can lead to absence from work and to people leaving the teaching profession. Members of staff may take short or long periods of absence from the workplace. Valued and experienced members of staff may feel psychologically and physically damaged as a consequence of work-related stress and this may be reflected within their homelife and future work prospects. It is important to reflect upon both human and financial costs both to the staff member and organisation.

It seems that we still have some way to go in health and well-being training being embedded into organisations policies, procedures, training and skills. The CIPD (2019) find that 40% of managers are trained to support those experiencing mental health issues and that 30% of managers feel confident to hold sensitive discussions with members of staff, pointing them in the right direction to those who can provide expert help. Whereas it is good that these managers have the requisite skills and knowledge it suggests that there remains a large percentage that lack the competencies in dealing with health and well-being issues. Organisations may have in place policies and procedures to support members of staff who feel stressed, anxious or depressed, however, there may be a more systematic failure where pressure and stress are considered to be inbuilt and deemed to be part of culture and cultural/ organisational change. A cynical observer may say that if people cannot face the pressure and stress, then maybe they shouldn't be working in that environment in the first place. A more considered view may suggest that organisations could engage with deeper reflection and build into their policies and procedures more detailed advice and guidance that helps support those who are feeling stressed. Whichever approach is considered higher education is in the process of developing borderless states (Becher and Trowler, 2001). The post-industrial environment is characterised by competitiveness, uncertainty, information overload, and turbulent change (Cameron and Tschirhart, 1992). It is therefore understandable that members of staff feel stressed, anxious and/or depressed. It is acknowledged that these findings are from earlier research in previous decades and temporal aspects may influence change. However, it does appear that academics continue to be faced with increased challenges that include: competition, finding new ways of working, gaining income, and learning new skills. It is no wonder that teaching is reported as one of the most stressful professions (Noriah, Iskandar and Ridzauddin, 2010; Nelson et al., 2006). It is likely that issues associated with health and well-being may become more prominent, having greater human and financial cost both to the individual and organisation. To help face these challenges, it would be helpful if such skills were included into all management training and development and that it becomes a central tenet of management roles and responsibilities.

Positive emotions and links between stress, coping and emotional intelligence

If a person develops their psychological resources making use of positive emotions, it can improve emotional well-being (Fredrickson, 2001). Furthermore, those who demonstrate higher levels of positive emotion are less likely to develop a cold (and those who express lower levels of positive emotions are more likely to have a stroke (Cohen, Cohen, West and Aiken, 2003; Ostir, Markides, Peek and Goodwin, 2001). This does suggest that there is a link between stress, coping and emotional intelligence. Relationships are key to managing stress, psychological well-being and health (Myers and Diener, 1995; Ryff and Singer, 2000). This is supported by Bowen, Pilkington and Rose (2016), who find that, in a study of five hundred and thirty-three (533) academics, there is an inverted relationship between perceived stress and managing emotions. The greater the perceived stress the person experiences, the less they are able to manage emotions. Those who have lower levels of emotional intelligence are likely to be more inclined to experience higher levels of stress and may find it more challenging to manage emotions. Those who have higher emotional intelligence may share stressful experiences with friends or families (depending on the context and receptivity) and are therefore more inclined to cope and to manage emotions more successfully (Salovey, Bedell, Detweiler and Mayer, 1999). They are also more inclined to have a healthier balance of feelings (Barrett and Gross, 2001).

Emotional dissonance

Employees are often required to emotionally engage with the customer and colleagues as part of the job requirements. This may be face to face which increases the demand to emotionally engage. The emotions that are required may not be those that the employee really feels. They may be having a *"bad day"* and yet they are required to show a smiling face and happy demeanour. Their overall personality may be inclined towards pessimistic emotions and they need to show optimism. The inner emotions felt may therefore contradict those being expressed demonstrating lack of authenticity and falseness giving rise to emotional dissonance. Emotional dissonance is the conflict experienced between emotions experienced and those expressed Abraham, 1998a, b,1999). It can result in job dissatisfaction, absenteeism, exhaustion, depression and reduced commitment to the organisation. In her book *"The Managed heart"*, Hochschild (1983) provides a metaphor of the employee who is the actor, who has to display emotions that are required as part of the job- emotional labour. She goes on to explain surface acting is where facial expressions, verbal (tone and content) and body language are used to support an emotion required as part of the job. This may contradict with the internal emotion being felt. Deep acting requires effort and engages with a true emotion being felt that comes from deep inside the employee, eliminating emotional dissonance that may otherwise be felt. The challenge with this is that deep acting can engage with true feelings and emotions that can in turn reflect upon the long-term mood and well-being of the employee. For example, if the employee has to counsel others or to provide pastoral care, the negative emotions that are experienced may have negative implications on physical and psychological well-being. Whereas social interpersonal actions can help overcome emotional dissonance, it is recommended that too strong and too weak emotions should be avoided in the teaching environment as emotional dissonance can have long term negative consequences including stress, burnout, job exhaustion losing contact with true feelings.

Demands of the job and well-being on the academic

Kinman and Wray (2013) find that academics experiencing stress has increased significantly since 1998. For example, a large percentage of participants' report that their job has become more stressful in the previous five (5) years of which approximately 75% report they work longer hours including weekends and evenings and 40% are considering leaving higher education (Kinman and Jones, 2003). Working long hours can impact upon health and well-being and yet academics appear to work beyond the normal number of hours during term time. McInnis (1999) finds that in a sample of two thousand six hundred and nine (2,609) Australian academics, 40% report experiencing added stress that includes working more than fifty hours a week. They are also required to undertake pastoral and academic support, fundraising and developing materials for new technology, adding to the stress being experienced. In a study across fifteen (15) Australian universities, Gillespie, Walsh, Winefield, Dua and Stough (2001) find that stress levels fluctuate throughout the year. However, stressors that are identified include: work overload, poor management/ leadership, lack of opportunity (reward, recognition, and promotion), not enough research funding, and lack of technical/ human resources. Other stressors experienced include: relationships with others, bureaucracy and time pressures, lack of promotion opportunities, lack of public recognition, and inadequate salary. To add to the challenges of the modern work environment the traditional view of the organisation being logical and non- emotional appears to continue. Simply put, emotions get in the way of effective performance (Briner, 1999). The assumption is that perfect decision making is associated with complete rational thinking. However, being completely rational may be a utopian view as emotions are integral to the way a person thinks and can influence how he/ she behaves (Briner, 1999). Stress does appear to be part of a larger set of issues incorporating emotions (Lazarus, 1999) and cannot be addressed as separate fields. Therefore, separating emotion from rationalist thinking may not be as realistic as traditionalists argue.

The Health and Safety Executive (HSE) (2013) report that the number of work-related stress cases has remained relatively flat over the decade (2002 to 2012). In 2011/12, there are just over one million work-related illnesses that are reported of which, 40% are related to stress, anxiety or depression. In their more recent report the HSE find that, in 2017/18, this figure has increased to 44%. The HSE (2013) also state that highest reported work-related stress over three years to 2012 (averaged) is in nursing, two thousand seven hundred and thirty (2,730) cases per one hundred thousand people. This is followed by teaching and education with two thousand three hundred and forty (2,340) cases per one hundred thousand people and; welfare and housing associates professionals, two thousand two hundred and ninety (2,290) cases per one hundred thousand people. Similar findings are found in the HSE (2018a) report for 2017/18 where nursing is reported to have two thousand seven hundred and sixty (2,760) per one hundred thousand people; teaching with three thousand and twenty (3,020) cases per one hundred thousand people and; welfare professionals with four thousand and eighty (4,080) cases per one hundred thousand people. It suggests that teaching and education is a high-stress environment in which to work and is becoming more so with approximately 22.5% increase between 2011/12 and 2017/18. Change appears to gather pace within the education sector. There is increased global competition that incorporates the private sector in offering students qualifications. Government legislation has changed in the UK where students are now responsible for funding their own degree. Government legislation also removes the cap on the number of students that universities can attract. Programmes and modules need to be developed that meet with the demands and expectations of the modern workplace and student. The findings of the HSE is, therefore, not surprising.

In the USA, The National Education Union (2018) find 15% of teachers report having a good work/ life balance and 81% of teachers have considered leaving in the last year because of workload. 40% of those who respond say that they spend more than twenty-one (21) hours a week working at home during weekends and evenings. The UK Government website, Gov.UK, (2018) report that in the academic year 2016-2017, 9.9% left the teaching profession. Retention rates for the first three years has dropped from 80% in 2011 to 73% in 2017.

Table 2.2. Teacher retention rates UK (2017).

Year	Percentage of teachers retained
End of year 1	87%
End of year 2	73%
End of year 3	67%

Source: Gov.UK.

The findings reinforce the challenges that those in the teaching profession are having to face. There seems to be a need to have a sea change in the way education is delivered. However, the direction that it presently sails appears to be increasing in pace, placing greater pressure and stress on those in the teaching profession.

As an individual working in the teaching profession, it is possible to develop skills in coping with stress and pressure. For example, becoming more aware of your own emotions and those expressed by others and managing them can be learned. It is possible to develop constructive ways of thinking when faced with challenging and stressful experiences. However, from a wider point of view, organisations could develop their policies further to support members of staff, constructing and building processes that create an environment in which staff members look forward to coming to work, enjoy the work, and are inspired to be actively creative.

Repeated studies show that those working in academic positions at universities are experiencing increased stress levels (For example: Blix, Cruise, Mitchell and Blix, 1994; Boyd and Wylie, 1994; Gillespie, Walsh, Winefield, Dua and Stough, 2001; Kinman, 2001, 2008, 2010, 2014; Kinman and Jones, 2003; McInnis, 1998). Research identifies that stressors that are being experienced by university academics include: heavy workloads, excessive administrative work; long working hours; inadequate opportunities for promotion; home/work life conflict; short term contracts and job insecurity; social environment; over commitment on work/life balance; and the feeling of remote management (Cross and Carroll, 1990; Daniels and Guppy, 1994a, b; Doyle, 1998; Doyle and Hind, 1998; Early, 1994; Ferrie, Shipley, Marmot, Stansfeld and Smith, 1998; Jackson and Hayday, 1997; Kinman, 1996, Bolton, 1998; Kinman and Jones, 2008; Repetti, 1993; Tytherleigh Webb, Cooper and Ricketts, 2005; Winefield, Gillespie, Stough, Dua, Hapuarachchi and Boyd, 2003). These factors are examples of stress being experienced in higher education that can affect the well-being of academics as they continue to experience greater time constraints, lower levels of influence and support, and greater work/ home demands.

In a sample of one hundred and seventy-eight (178) academic and general staff at fifteen (15) Australian universities job-related stress is found to be a large influencer, impacting upon work and personal life (Gillespie et al., 2001). To help cope with the stress, academics and staff members seek support from colleagues and management. Staff also find that personal coping strategies helped with stress. These include: work/life balance, stress management techniques, and lowering of their own standards. In another study of nine thousand (9,000) staff, across seventeen (17) Australian universities, psychological distress is identified as being higher in academic staff compared to general staff (Winefield et al., 2003). Academics who are working in the older universities in Australia appear to be better off when compared to staff at the newer universities. Stress being experienced could be due to the organisational change where control has moved further from the academic and towards the senior managers in the university. Academics are also encouraged to seek external funding which may not have been part of their job in the past and with decreased funding, and greater accountability, academics are more likely to experience increased stress levels. The majority of those who respond feel that there is work/ home life conflict. Similar findings are also identified by Sagaya, Vasumathi and Subashini (2015) in a study of academics in Tamil Nadu, India. One of the main points that comes out of their study is the misunderstanding and/ or conflictual relationships that most academics have with superiors. They also find that academics experience misunderstanding and/ or conflict with family members. In a study of twenty-four (24) academic chairpersons at a South African University, Cilliers and Pienaar (2014) report that staff members who experience stressful events are unable to cope and this is more likely to impact upon work performance. Staff report being tired, and cognitively, unable to cope too well. Staff feel they are overwhelmed by demands placed upon them and that their psychological well-being is being attacked. Furthermore, it appears that the university system does not provide support, leaving staff feeling isolated. This impacts upon difficulties with interpersonal relationships, psychological and physical functioning. Similar findings are identified by other researchers (for example: Benson, 2012; Chang and Tseng, 2009). A further comment that Cilliers and Pienaar (2014) make is that the academics demonstrate diligence and are highly intelligent. However, notwithstanding the feelings of being trapped and unhappy, the academics did not do anything about their situation and appear to accept that the circumstances they are in is natural. Acceptance is a factor associated with ways of coping which is discussed later in this book.

There appears to be a dichotomy where universities have to compete in the global market while staff members may have to cope with increased challenges associated with the work demands placed upon them, including: workload, information technology, student numbers and expectations, research and research bids. The way a person copes with the demands can impact upon their well-being and their interpersonal relationships with family members and colleagues. For example: a good relationship between staff and student has shown a positive impact upon student retention and performance (In other words, a caring relationship can have a positive impact upon achievement and aspirations (Gleaves and Walker, 2006; Rhodes and Nevill, 2004; Thomas, 2002).

Stress does appear to be an evitable part of daily life and academics are not immune to the same feelings and emotions as other occupational groups.

Impact of stress on the academic

The Higher Education Statistics Agency (HESA, 2015, 2019) find that the total number of academics employed (full/ part time) has increased from One hundred and fifty thousand, six hundred and fifty-five (150,655) in 2004/05 to two hundred and eleven thousand, nine hundred and eighty (211,980) in 2017/18; an increase of 29%. Non-academic support staff has increased from one hundred and eighty-five thousand, six hundred and fifty (185,650) to two hundred and seventeen thousand five hundred and eighty (217,580); an increase of 15%. The table below shows the number of staff employed over the period 2004/05 to 2017/18.

Table 2.3. Higher education staff statistics: UK, 2017/18 (HESA, 2015, 2019).

Academic year	Academic (full/ part time)	Non-academic	% difference between academics and non-academics (University and College Union report, 2012)	Total
2017/18+	211,980	217,580	2.57	429,560
2016/17+	206,870	212,835	2.80	419,710
2015/16+	201,770	208,750	3.43	410,515
2014/15+	198,335	205,500	3.49	403,835
2013/14+	194,235	201,545	3.63	395,780
2012/13*	185,585	196,935	5.76	382,515
2011/12*	181,385	196,860	7.86	378,250
2010/11*	181,185	200,605	9.68	381,790
2009/10*	181,595	205,835	11.78	387,430
2008/09*	179,040	203,720	12.11	382,760
2007/08*	174,945	197,510	11.42	372,455

2006/07*	169,995	194,165	12.45	364,160
2005/06*	164,875	190,535	13.47	355,415
2004/05*	150,655	185,650	18.85	346,305

Source: HESA (2015)
+ Source HESA (2019)
Note: data is regularly updated on previous years by HESA.

The above data suggests that in 2004/05 that the difference between academics and non-academic members of staff is 18.85%. By 2010/11 this reduces to 9.68% and by 2017/18 the difference is 2.57%. Whereas there has been an increase in the number of staff (both academic and non-academic) the percentage difference between each group has substantially reduced suggesting that academic staff are likely to have increased workloads and more likely to undertake responsibilities that, in the past, would have been covered by support staff.

In the UK, students achieving a first and higher degree have increased exponentially in the 20th century and into the 21st century. For example, in 1920, just over four thousand three hundred (4,300) achieved a first degree and seven hundred (700) achieved a higher degree. In 1950, approximately seventeen thousand three hundred (17,300) students achieved a first degree and two thousand four hundred (2,400) a higher degree at UK universities. In 2010 this increases to approximately three hundred and thirty-one thousand (331,000) and one hundred and eighty-two thousand, and six hundred (182,600) respectively (Bolton, 2012). In 2013/14, just fewer than five hundred and twenty thousand (520,000) students achieve a first degree and approximately two hundred and fifty-seven thousand (257,000) students gained a higher degree (HESA, 2015). By 2017/18 four hundred and ninety-two thousand (492,000) achieved a first degree and two hundred and eighty-four thousand and six hundred (284,600) gained a higher degree (HESA, 2019). The table below summaries reported data for students achieving a first degree and a higher degree.

Table 2.4. Students achieving first or higher degrees.

Year	First degree	Higher degree
1920	4,357	703
1930	9,129	1,323
1938	9,311	1,480
1950	17,337	2,410
1960	22,426	3,273

1970	51,189	12,901
1980	68,150	18,925
1990	77,163	31,324
2000	243,246	86,535
2010	330,720	182,610
2013/14+	519,685	257,935
2014/15+	483,410	261,620
2015/16+	480,575	262,150
2016/17+	491,170	266,125
2017/18+	492,385	284,620

Source: HESA (2015)
+ Source HESA (2019)
Note: data is regularly updated on previous years by HESA.

The ratio of students to academics is 10.2: 1 in 1938. It falls to 7.3: 1 in 1954 and, rises again to 7.8: 1 in 1961. This increases to 8.5: 1 in 1971. In 1974, the University Grants Committee amend the way statistics are reported to include, for example, those employed part-time. The statistics are amended again in the early 1980s when full-time equivalent student numbers are calculated (but not academic staff). By 1989, the ratio of students to academics is 11.8: 1 and this increases again to 14.6: 1 in 1993. The Higher Education Statistics Agency is then set up and reports the academic / student ratios that includes former polytechnics. By 2010 the ratio is 17: 1 and has remained around this figure since that time. These findings are interesting as they highlight the increased demands placed on universities by simply coping with increased numbers of students. This likely means that each academic has increased marking, supervision and interpersonal relationships with students. Whereas there has been an increase in the number of academics this does not appear to have kept pace with the number of students. It is acknowledged that there could be other factors that could explain the differences. For example, the use of computer hardware and software could help improve service delivery and student experience. However, it does appear that demands have increased on academics and this could partly explain the studies reporting increased levels of stress with demands such as workload, interpersonal relationships, excessive administrative work, long working hours and overcommitment on home/ work-life balance.

Each person may have experiences that give rise to emotions in different ways and extent. Experiences could include: insufficient time to undertake a good job, intense pressure, challenges to balance work and home life (Raiden and Raisanen, 2013). Shin and Jung (2013) also find similar findings, from nineteen (19) higher education systems, where stress experienced in the work environment could overflow into personal life. The main causes of stress, they identify, are associated with market orientated managerial reforms together with performance-based management.

Together with a rapid increase in student numbers, over the recent years, universities in the UK have also become financially self-reliant, no longer receiving finance from central Government. Students no longer have grants, but instead loans that are first introduced in 1998, capped at £1,000; increased to £3,000 in 2006; and increased again to £9,000 in 2012 (Ball, 2014). A further challenge academics have to cope with are complaints from students. Saul (2014) points out that twenty thousand (20,000) students have complained to their university demanding more for the £9,000 fee they pay. Not only do academics have to cope with increased numbers of students, students may also become more demanding, expecting academics to be more responsive to their demands, as they now pay their own fees. This could add to the stress that academics may experience. Universities are understandably seeking to be more competitive and streamlined, where they increase income and reduce costs. This could include increased use of online technological support such as online learning. The academic, therefore, needs to develop technological and software skills and knowledge that they may feel is outside their existing area of skills and knowledge. This could place increased personal demands on the academic leading to increased levels of stress, being able to cope, and home/ work life conflict. Academics appear to experience excessive administrative work and inadequate opportunities for promotion and this can have an impact on the health of academic staff.

Job insecurity, that includes including short term contracts, maybe also be a reason for work-related stress. The demands, pressure and stress placed on academics does not appear to have reduced. There appears to be a move from a collegiate culture of cooperation and shared values towards the business/ industrial approach that includes a bureaucratic and less participate style of management which could lead to deskilling and de-professionalisation (Tapper, 1998, Trow, 1993). This may add to feelings of increased stress, lower moral, and crisis of professional identity (Sarros, Gmelch, and Tanewski, 1998). The factor that appears to worry people most is job security and that stress experienced by university staff appears widespread.

Chronic stress and possible outcomes

It does appear that stress is unavoidable in a person's life, whether this is associated with their personal or work life (Kinman, 1998). It is therefore important to acknowledge and respond proactively to feelings of distress. If not addressed, distress can develop into chronic stress, that can result in people having difficulties with cognition (thinking- including memory, attention deficit and being absent minded) and behaviour (substance misuse, aggression and absenteeism). Studies undertaken suggest that there is a relationship between feeling stressed and health outcomes that include: cancer, asthma, arthritis, liver disease, diabetes and heart disease (for example: Chandola, Britton, Brunner, Hemmingway, et al, 2008; Chandola, Brunner and Marmot, 2006; Cohen, Janicki-Deverts and Miller, 2007; Johnson, Perry, and Rosensky, 2002). As well as having an impact on physical health, stress is also linked to absenteeism from the workplace, loss of productivity and death (Atkinson, 2004; Schneiderman, Ironson and Siegel, 2005). Stress can also lead to mental illness, cognitive impairment, depression and aggression (Bodenmann, Meuwly, Bradbury, Gmelch et al., 2010; Hammen, 2005; Schwabe and Wolf, 2010; Wang, 2005).

The traditional organisation and rational thinking

One of the challenges that people appear to face is the traditional view of organisations that are viewed as logical, non-emotional and rational where emotions are irrelevant and get in the way of effective performance (Briner, 1999). The assumption is that perfect decision making is associated with complete rational thinking. However, being completely rational may be a utopian view as emotions are integral to the way a person thinks and can influence how he/ she behaves. Carter (2010) adds that neural transmission is greater coming from the limbic system to the cortex when compared with the opposite direction. In other words, emotions may have greater influence over decision-making processes. This suggests that emotions may have a greater influence on behaviour than rational thinking. The human body has been developed over millennia and has learned to react with stressors leading to *fight or flight*. Feelings of stress are integrated into how the body reacts to stimuli. It is only in recent generations that we have adapted to work in offices and factories. It is therefore understandable that the body maintains the ancestral strings that pull on the emotions and feelings that can affect physical and psychological well-being. Therefore, stress does appear to be part of a larger set of issues incorporating emotions and separating emotion from rationalist thinking may not be as realistic as traditionalists argue.

Burnout

The stress that academics experience can lead to physical, emotional and mental exhaustion that can be better described as burnout. Freudenberger (1974) is the first person to define *"burnout"*, explaining it as a state of frustration or fatigue that is brought about by commitment to a particular cause, a way of life, or a relationship that did not provide the expected reward. Maslach and Jackson (1981) define burnout as having three (3) components. These are :1) emotional exhaustion (tiredness, worn out, low energy, a feeling of being overworked); 2) depersonalisation (objectifying others, negative and cynical attitudes towards others) and; 3) lack of personal fulfilment (no longer believing in oneself as being effective and, having negative feelings towards oneself). Whereas the term burnout is used in the lexicon of the English language, it isn't recognised as a psychological disorder as there is a lack of consistency between those who experience it. However, the person experiencing burnout is likely to encounter chronic stress levels that may lead to detachment and cynicism together with feelings of lack of accomplishment and ineffectiveness. They may be less warm and pleasant when interacting with others and less prepared. The person may also feel like giving up and lack motivation. This can result in them being less productive. Burnout/ exhaustion can have a significant impact upon performance and can lead to increased absence from work. At the same time, those experiencing burnout may also feel trapped within their profession and find it difficult to make decisions to move. It may explain findings from Cilliers and Pienaar (2014) that notwithstanding been highly intelligent and diligent academics do not do anything about their situation and simply accept what is delivered to them. Academics may dread going into work and feel physically drained and exhausted. There may be a resistance to change and to blame others for failure or lack of achievement. However, they do not take action to try and resolve the challenges being faced. This can add financial costs to the organisation and personal costs to the person who's work life/ balance may be affected. It is acknowledged that burnout can be caused by different reasons that may include poor diet/ lifestyle, personality type, interpersonal relationships and personal lifestyle choices. However, a person who is more inclined to be a perfectionist is also likely to be at greater risk of burnout (Taris, van Beek and Schaufeli, 2010). When stress develops, to the point of exhaustion and burnout, the body's immunity system is affected, and this can lead to a predisposition to catching colds and flu.

In a study undertaken by university teachers in south India, Reddy and Poornima (2012) find that 40% of the teaching posts are reported as being vacant. This could add to the pressure/ stress experienced by staff. The findings from this study suggest a significant positive relationship between professional burnout and occupation stress and recommend that there should be intervention from the organisational level. To help manage stress, recommendations are made that encourages emotional intelligence training, social support systems, cognitive behavioural management, and counselling services. A recurrent theme of studies undertaken on workplace stress amongst teachers is heavy workload and demands placed upon time, together with multiple role expectations. The research suggests that stress in the teaching environment has not declined. Indeed, the findings show that pressure of work and feelings of stress remain increasingly high. The days of the traditional view of university teaching where it is considered a low-stress job appear long gone.

The consequence of experiencing burnout is not just on the person but those around them. For example, they may seek to blame others and be less productive. The challenge is how to identify stress and predict burnout.

An analogy could be given of running a marathon. A person can train every day, day after day, week after week until they have the stamina, physical strength, and will to succeed. They may complete the marathon in a reasonable time but not able to meet with the time set by the front runners. If they try to keep pace with the front runners, they may fall out at an early stage and not complete the marathon. They may find that walking part of the marathon means that they can regain strength to allow them to complete in a time that reflects their own performance times. It may be helpful if organisations used a similar analogy when placing increased demands upon staff members. Some may perform and meet with the demands and expectations placed upon them. Others may not.

Organisations could be more flexible in their approach to demands and expectations and place a more considered workload/ demand on staff members. While monitoring factors (for example: staff levels, staff working beyond the normal hours, and absenteeism) organisations could look out for possible signs of stress and burnout and take action to resolve. It is sometimes difficult to recognise internal stress levels. The accumulation of stressful experiences may trigger overwhelming levels of stress that can no longer be coped with. It is, therefore, important to regularly assess and evaluate feelings and to take action to resolve the challenge before it becomes overwhelming. It is also helpful that colleagues look out for each other and to consider taking action to help if signs of stress are experienced.

In a study of one hundred (100) professors from different universities in Karachi, Pakistan, Iqbal and Abbasi (2013) find that there is a significant negative relationship between job burnout and emotional intelligence. The greater likelihood of burnout, the lower the level of emotional intelligence. This may not be a causal relationship as there may be other factors that are influencing the findings. However, Akbari and Khormaiee (2015) argue that a purpose of life, social relationships and a sense of independence are important to maintaining good mental health. They also identify that resilience is a predictor of a healthy psychological state which plays a partial mediating role between psychological well-being and emotional intelligence. The findings suggest that emotional intelligence does have a role to play where burnout and stress are concerned. Brackett (2013) states that emotions matter. Adults who have higher levels of emotional intelligence are more likely to manage stress and interact with others more effectively and to have greater empathy (Brackett, Mayer and Warner, 2004). They are less likely to be associated with alcohol and drugs and smoke less. Furthermore, they are likely to be less anxious and to experience depression. This concurs with the research undertaken by Tsaousis and Nikolaou (2005) who carry out two (2) studies of three hundred and sixty-five (365) people, and two hundred and twelve (212) people respectively. They find that there is a relationship between emotional intelligence and well-being (Emotional intelligence negatively correlated with smoking and drinking and positively correlated with exercising).

It may not be the right time to make rational decisions when feeling burned out. However, sometimes hard decisions need to be made. If the cause of burnout and exhaustion is associated with the work environment, discussion can be held with managers and those within the human resource department. It is also helpful to discuss with friends and loved one. However, there may be no other option than to extract yourself from that environment and find a job that is less likely to cause such feelings of stress.

Reflection: Burnout

On a scale of 1 to 5 where 1 not at all, 3 sometimes, and 5 very much so, ask yourself how you feel?
1. Do you feel physically exhausted much of the time?
2. Do you feel mentally exhausted much of the time?
3. Do you feel that you are ineffective?
4. Are you prone to get agitated easily?
5. Do you experience panic attacks?
6. Are you prone to quickly react to situations?
7. Are you concerned that you may make errors, and someone may pick up on them?
8. Do you find it difficult to wind down and relax at the end of a working day?
9. Do you find it difficult to breathe or do you experience rapid breathing?
10. Do you find it difficult to enthuse/ build yourself up to do something?

Responses:
1 to 15. You don't have very much to worry about
15 to 30. It is worth reviewing the causes for you to feel this way.
30 to 40. Warning signs suggest that action be taken to resolve the reason you feel this way.
40 to 50. Urgent action is recommended. Identify the causes. If they cannot be resolved, if possible remove yourself from the cause. This may mean change or move job.

Stress and work/ life balance

Stress can also have an impact upon work/life balance. In a study undertaken in 1995, Bradley and Eachus find that stress associated with work/ home life is higher with university staff than those in other occupations. In another study, Boyd and Wylie (1994) find that 80% of those surveyed, feel that their workload had increased. In a further study, Doyle (1998) finds that of thirty (30) female academics from one university in the UK, 33% feel that their family are adversely affected by the work demands placed upon them and that the heavy workload experienced have contributed to relationship breakdown. Whereas these studies are carried out in the 1990s, stress/ pressure experienced by academics appears to remain high. In a meta-analysis, Mitra (2015) finds that where employees experience change, there are few people to provide moral and mental support. The stress experienced could therefore lead to ill health and mental disability impacting on the way a person performs. The stress being experienced includes: excessive workload, low job security and an unhealthy work environment that can give rise to a negative impact on work/ life balance.

The Mental Health Foundation (UK, 2018a) find that 33% of employees feel unhappy or very unhappy about the amount of time that is devoted to work, with more than 40% neglecting other aspects of their life because of work commitments. 27% of participants feel depressed, 34% feel anxious and 58% feel irritable. The Mental Health Foundation (the UK, 2018b) also point out that the more time that is allocated to work commitments, the more participants are likely to worry and to feel unhappy.

The studies identified in this book are carried out over several decades and the findings do suggest that there is evidence to support the view that demands placed upon academics can impact on their work/ life balance and lead to negative impact on their well-being, and those close to them, and that higher emotional intelligence can help people cope with stressful experiences. It is therefore helpful to draw a line between work and personal life and to try and reduce stress levels by taking exercise, meditation, yoga and hobbies. Maybe taking up a musical instrument, going to the gym, socialising with friends and family.

Reflection: work/life balance
1. Keep a diary of the *times* each day that you start and finish work. Add up the hours you spend working each week. Consider giving yourself time limitations each week.
2. Keep a note of *what* you spend your time doing. For example: emails, meetings. Reflect upon what you can do to reduce the time on these items.
3. Note down the concerns/ worries you have. Identify how these concerns/ worries can be overcome. Remember that the more hours you work, the more tired and less productive you are likely to be.
4. Outside work, identify what you get the most please from. How much time do you allocate to this interest? Could you spend more time on this outside interest?
5. Review your diary and what you spend time doing on a regular and frequent basis.

Summing up

This chapter has discussed perspectives of stress that are described as "*things*" that cause stress, "*response*"/ internal reaction by the person experiencing stress and, "*imbalance*" the ability and demands of coping with a stressful experience. This chapter has identified key findings associated with mental health. Where 74% of people have been overwhelmed or unable to cope with stress and one (1) in six (6) people have experienced a mental health problem in the last week. Stress is associated with psychological illness that include: anxiety, depression, phobias, obsessive-compulsive disorder, panic attacks and, post-traumatic stress disorder. Of those who feel stressed 16% self-harm and 32% have suicidal thoughts. Organisations may have policies and procedures in place, however, experience of stress continues to be a challenge that individuals and organisations need to address.

Eustress can have benefits that increase adrenalin and attention to the matter at hand. It can also enhance memory and immune system. However, where stress is felt over more frequent occasions and to be more intense, it can become debilitating and impact upon the person's ability to perform and deliver on tasks. This can result in feelings of distress and eventually to chronic stress. It may become so overwhelming that it leads to severe mental and physical ailments that the person may experience over a long period, possibly a lifetime. This may lead to them taking time off from work increasing the pressure and stress on other members of staff. The feeling of stress can lead to long term absenteeism from work that can place increased pressure on other members of staff, who have to cover the responsibilities, and to increased financial costs to the organisation This may also impact upon student experience that is reflected in the student feedback impacting on the university ranking. The cost of addressing this may ultimately fall on the health services that are paid for by the taxpayer or through higher insurance payments. It reinforces the importance of addressing feelings of physical, emotional and mental exhaustion that can eventually lead to burnout.

It is only in recent generations that we have had to move from hunter-gatherer to agrarian lifestyles to work in factories and offices while living in compacted spaces. It is therefore understandable that the body maintains the ancestral *fight or flight* reaction to stressful experiences. It is understandable that managers and owners of organisations seek to decompartmentalise this idea of keeping emotions out of the workplace while maintaining a logical, non-emotional and rational approach. However, separating emotion from rationalist thinking may not be as realistic as traditionalists argue. Davidson and Begley (2012) explain that the emotions overlap with rational and cognitive thinking enabling us to navigate the world of work and relationships. Furthermore, trying to maintain the traditionalist approach may simply compound stress as those experiencing it may seek to suppress the emotion or display emotions that may not accord with what the body is telling them. They may use emotional labour that adds to the feeling of stress.

The chapter concludes by identifying statistical data from the Mental Health Foundation (UK) (2018a, b). A third of those surveyed say that they feel unhappy or very unhappy about the amount of time that is devoted to work and, over 40% neglect other aspects of their life because of work commitments. Over a quarter of participants feel depressed, over a third feel anxious, and over half feel irritable. The more time that is given to work commitments, the more participants are likely to worry and to feel unhappy. Demands placed upon academics can impact on their work/ life balance and lead to a negative impact on their well-being. Stress levels can increase to such a point that it is no longer tolerable. Whereas it is helpful to separate work and home life and to make recommendations to that end, there continues to a blurring of the line, where people are working from home and in a flexible manner that may not have been thought of just a few short years ago. It creates work/ life conflict that adds to feelings of being stressed. Issues associated with health and well-being continue to have a significant impact upon the individual and the organisation. There is both a human and financial cost. From an individual point of view, it may also be helpful to take up a musical instrument, go to the gym or, socialise with friends and family. Taking exercise, meditation, yoga and hobbies may also help redirect thoughts and reduce stress levels. However, when emotions are heightened, and pressure of work appears unrelenting, it is easy to forget outside interests. From an organisational point of view, it would be helpful if such skills, associated with health and well-being, were included into all management training and development and that it becomes a central tenet of management roles and responsibilities. It appears that we have a long way to go to resolve the challenges between organisational success/failure, management, customer demands, and staff well-being.

Chapter 3

Understanding and processing emotions

The term *"emotion"* is derived from the French word "émotion", meaning physical disturbance and, arrived in the English lexicon in the seventeenth century (Dixon, 2012). Until the nineteenth-century mental states were categorised as sentiments, affections, passions or appetites. It was not until the mid-nineteenth century writers began to publish books on the *"emotions"* (for example: Bain, 1859; Cooke, 1838, Ramsay, 1848). Basic emotions appear to be universal that are associated with two (2) modes of appraisal (the interpretation of an event or experience): 1) deliberate, reflective and conscious and, 2) automatic, unconscious and unreflective (Lazarus, 1991a, b). In their study of facial features and emotions with isolated tribes in New Guinea, Ekman and Friesen (1971) identify six (6) basic emotions that are universal: anger, disgust, happiness, fear, surprise and sadness (Ekman, Friesen, O'Sullivan, Chan et al. 1987). Plutchik (2002) identifies eight (8) basic emotions: anger, fear, surprise, anticipation, joy, sadness, trust and disgust. There is a continuing debate as to how many emotions there actually are and to confuse matters further, emotions can be mixed where anger, love and fear could form jealousy. There is no consensus as to what the term means and there is ambiguity around its place in science. After more than one hundred (100) years, there still does not appear to be one accepted consensual understanding of the term *"emotion"*. As described by Dixon (2012) *"emotion"* is a key word in modern psychology but is also a key word that is in crisis. However, there does appear to be a prevailing view that emotions include the appraisal of self-relevant experiences (Arnold, 1960; Tomaka, Blascovich, Kibler and Ernst, 1997).

Emotions are often regarded as episodic. However, we experience emotions on a continuous basis that are a response to life's experiences. More recently, emotions are described as a dynamic process rather than a state (Smith and Kemp-Wheeler, 1996). It is a two-way process that includes the environmental stressor and the response given by the person. Primary appraisal includes judgement of how stressful the experience is. For example, is it controllable, positive or, negative? Secondary appraisal is how the experience is coped with.

Lazarus (1991b) does not provide an explanation as to the term *"appraisal"*, however, Ekman (1999) suggests that appraisal is not just a consequence of biology but includes social learning as well. In their discussion paper on appraisal theory of emotion, Moors, Ellsworth, Scherer and Frijda (2013) refer to appraisal as a process that can detect and assess the impact of the environment on well-being. The process involves appraisal of information associated with: context of event, history and background, personal concerns and sensitivities. Moors et al. (2013) add that appraisal incorporates the evaluation and personal interaction with the environment, motivational content and, biological reaction. For example, feeling angry is because you have just been in discussion with a troublesome teen for not cleaning their bedroom. The event is caused by the teen's lack of action and apathy. This causes you to feel frustrated. The teen does not respond to initial requests. This leads to increased heart rate and blood pressure and, "*seeing red*". Anger is felt as an emotion. Moors et al. (2013) point out that appraisal of an event can occur in response to what another person may or may not do and whether or not the perceiver has previous knowledge. Strong emotions demand focus on that being experienced and can limit the extent a person is able to pay attention to what is going on elsewhere. Therefore, understanding and appreciation of how we feel can improve self-awareness and resilience when faced with challenging experiences.

This chapter discusses different theories associated with emotion and reflects upon the importance of understanding your own emotions and those in others. This chapter also reflects upon teaching with emotional intelligence. Those in the caring profession, that include the teachers, appear to be more successful when they have higher levels of emotional intelligence and can be an effective tool in helping improve the student learning experience. This chapter also includes sections on learned optimism and learned helplessness where focus is given to engaging in optimistic thoughts and feelings. Bullying and harassment can occur in any organisation and what is perceived as bullying or harassment by one person may be considered as good management style by another. Developing emotional intelligence skills can help staff members to cope with such experiences. Discussion is then made over to examples of therapy that can be used to help support those experiencing challenging experiences that may include interpersonal conflict. As advised several times in this chapter, it is important that professional support be sought and to use this text as a guide to help inform.

Different emotions

People experience the world in different ways, undergoing different emotional and social reactions and feelings. Emotions are not just biologically determined. They are also formed as a response to environmental factors (nature and nurture). They define us as human beings that allow us to understand the world around us and for others to understand how we feel. Emotions can be an internal experience that incorporate the mental state and physiological state. The mental state includes emotions such as: anger, hate, love, fear, anxiety. The sensations the body experiences are associated with the physiological state that include increased heart rate, increased sweating, and reddening of the face. It does appear that some emotions are universal such as *"fight or flight"* and may be associated with biology and genes inherited from our parents. However, some emotions are learned that can vary depending on culture. Furthermore, in the West high arousal emotions are valued. In the East, low arousal emotions are valued (Lim, 2016). There have been several attempts to define and explain what emotions are and how they are experienced. The table below provides examples of theories put forward.

Table 3.1. Theories of emotion.

	Examples of theories	Explanation	Sources
1	Evolutionary emotions theory(s)	This theory is associated evolution where the emotion evolves to help people respond/ act in order to survive. It is where with an event or experience triggers an emotion that leads to physiological responses.	Darwin (1872); Ekman (1992, 1999, 2003); Izard (1977, 1992)
2	James- Lang Theory	William James and Carl Lang came up with this theory about the same time. Hence the James- Lang theory. In contrast with the evolutionary theory James-Lange theory suggests that it is where the body responds to the experience that generates the emotion.	James (1890)
3	Two-factor theory	Similar to James- Lange theory, emotions are experienced due to physiological arousal. However, Schachter and Singer (1962) adds to the theory by suggesting that the emotion that is experienced is dependent on two factors: Physiological arousal and cognitive interpretation. When a person experiences physiological arousal when being in a particular environment, they then seek an explanation for the arousal.	Schachter and Singer (1962)
4	Appraisal theory(s) of emotion	This theory is associated with the appraisal of an experience; where emotions are experienced as a result of interpretation of the circumstances which the person in. Lazarus (1991a,b) adds to the theory by including cognition; where thinking should precede the arousal and emotion.	Arnold (1960), Lazarus (1991a,b); Scherer (1984, 1994, 2001, 2009)

5	Theory of constructed emotion	Barrett (2006, 2017) puts forward the theory of constructed emotion where the emotional concepts that are experienced lead to the formation of the emotion experienced. It is where the brain uses past experiences that are organised into concepts that guide actions, giving meaning to sensations.	Barrett (2006, 2017),

In the late nineteenth century, James-Lange put forward that emotions are governed by the way the human body responds. For example: when faced with a lion, we are frightened and then run; we are fearful because we are faced with the lion. Later on, Schachter and Singer (1962) introduce the two-factor theory that includes physiological arousal and cognitive interpretation. They argue that emotions are the result of physiological arousal together with a belief around its cause. For example: being at a concert and listening to music can lead to physiological arousal: clapping, singing, feeling generally uplifted. Others at the concert feel the same leading to *emotional contagion.*

The appraisal theory is where emotions that are experienced result from circumstances in which the person faces (Arnold, 1960; Lazarus, 1991a, b; Scherer,1984, 2001, 2009). For example: When at a football match there is a feeling of expectation and confidence that your team will win. When the opposition score, interpretation may then be given to the possibility of your team losing. This then gives rise to pessimism and fear. Lazarus (1999) brings in to the theory the term "*cognition*". For example: after the opposition scores a goal, you begin to think that your team is going to lose the game and these thoughts compound the emotions. This is supported by Barrett (2017), who suggests that past experiences influence the emotions experienced. Meaning is placed behind the emotion. For example: past experience of visiting a landmark brings back pleasant memories and this gives rise to feelings of contentment and satisfaction.

To add to the mix within the discussion around emotions, Davidson and Begley (2012) puts forward the term "*emotional style*", which is the way we respond to experiences that influences emotional traits, moods and states. Each person has individual emotional styles that lie within a continuum, as summarised in the table below.

Table 3.2. Emotional style.

	Style	Description
1	Resilience	The speed it takes for someone to recover from challenging experiences.
2	Outlook	How long positive emotions are sustained.
3	Social intuition	The ability to identify and relate with others.
4	Self-awareness	The ability to pick up feelings and using them to make decisions.
5	Sensitivity to context	Regulation of emotions taking into consideration the context.
6	Attention	Clarity and sharpness of the emotion experienced.
		Source: Adapted from: Davidson and Begley (2012).

Davidson and Begley (2012) come about the term *"emotional style"* following studies into brain imaging that show that emotions trigger patterns of biological brain activity within the prefrontal cortex and cerebral cortex as well as the limbic system. For example, Kim and Whalen (2009) find that the less the white matter (nerve fibres- axons- connecting nerve cells-neurons) the fewer connections there are, from the prefrontal cortex to the amygdala. In another study associated with self-awareness, Craig (2002, 2004) finds that those who are more self-aware experience greater activity in the insula (an area located in the cerebral cortex. In other studies, the amygdala appears to have a much bigger role than previously thought, allowing emotions to take control of our actions and rational thought (LeDoux, 1999, 2003, 2019). No matter how emotions are categorised or measured, theory and findings add to the complexity of information available. Emotions appear to have a much bigger role in forming behaviour and thinking, suggesting that all parts of the brain may have a role that is influenced and affected by emotions. What is apparent is that emotions are part of what makes us human, helping us to make sense of the world around us and to communicate to others how we feel.

Understanding your own emotions and those in others

Each person may see the world from his or her own understanding, background and experience. Furthermore, emotions are key to how we think and interact with others. It is, therefore, important to be able to understand your own emotions, those in others (and this includes empathy) and to manage those emotions. Emotions are made up of expressive components, physiological components and, subjective components. They provide information about how you are feeling and what is being experienced and to inform others as to how you feel. Being emotionally aware is developed from when we are infants and early experiences can influence subsequent behaviour and feelings later in life. If you are bullied in school and have to face the same physical, emotional and psychological abuse on a frequent basis, this can influence you, in later life, when you may have to face a manager or co-workers who may harass or bully you. To cope with this, you may feel fear and dread. "*Fight or flight*" may kick in. It is therefore helpful to understand your own emotions and how you respond to emotions experienced in others. Sometimes, showing feelings can be useful. On other occasions, it may be circumspect to suppress those emotions. A person with higher levels of emotional intelligence is more inclined to have greater empathy, and has a positive effect on mental, physical, and social well-being (Brackett, Mayer and Warner, 2004; Morrison, 2007). Those in the caring profession, that include teaching management and sales, appear to be more successful when they have high levels of interpersonal intelligence; understanding the working style, motivating factors and cooperation amongst colleagues.

Empathy also appears to be an important factor associated with emotional intelligence and interpersonal relationships, however, there appears to be influencing factors such as context, culture, background/ experience and workload pressure. There is also an acknowledgement that too much empathising could impact upon well-being. For example, engaging sympathy with a colleague or student emotions can be absorbed into the inner self, affecting how we feel, and creating pessimistic mood and thought. When feeling positive and good, it is easier to throw off the challenges and pressures experienced with daily life. When feeling sad and low, it is harder to adjust to the challenges and this can build up into feelings of stress and anxiety that in turn may lead to psychological and physical illnesses that can be debilitating, affecting performance both at home and work together with overall well-being. It is, therefore, helpful to identify the emotions experienced. Being emotionally aware is an integral skill in developing emotional intelligence and can be helpful and supportive when faced with challenging situations and experiences. Being aware of how we feel can also help address interpersonal conflict and how to move on from challenging situations. Being aware of other people's feelings and emotions is also a skill that can be developed that can include an understanding of verbal and non-verbal signals. It is the ability to empathise and to recognise the effects that emotions and behaviour may have. It is the ability to engage/ disengage with other people's emotions when required. The ability to manage emotions. Building emotional intelligence can, therefore, help oneself to be more resilient and more able to cope with personal interaction.

Emotional intelligence includes a set of inter and intrapersonal capabilities that are beneficial to those with higher emotional intelligence that can help manage stress and emotions in others. It enables a person to detect emotions in others, control their own emotions, and to deal with social interaction. Higher emotional intelligence is also beneficial to all parties concerned in managing emotions and that this is supported by positive associations being found with life satisfaction, happiness, social network quality and size and psychological health (For example, Austin, Saklofske and Egan, 2005; Day, Therrien and Carroll, 2005; Extremera and Fernandez-Berrocal, 2002; Furnham and Petrides, 2003). Studies also suggest that those who experience positive psychological well-being are likely to be healthier and to live longer (for example: Chida and Steptoe, 2008; Christensen, Doblhammer, Rau and Vuupel, 2009; Ostir, Markides, Black and Goodwin, 2000; Ostir, et al, 2001; Sadler, Miller, Christensen and McGue, 2011).

Teaching and emotional intelligence

To improve levels of emotional intelligence of students requires the teacher to be knowledgeable and skilled in understanding its inclusion in primary and secondary education that could reduce behavioural and emotional challenges (Cohen, 1999). Similar findings are expected for those at college and university (Hawkins, Von Cleave and Catalano, 1991). Having a rapport and relationship with students enhances the learning experience that students have. Emotional intelligence can have a positive impact upon teaching satisfaction and is an essential part of education for teachers (Mortiboys, 2012). Those with higher emotional intelligence can cope better with the interpersonal relationships. Can you imagine being in a bad mood and then having to deliver a workshop to students? Students may pick up on this and it may affect their learning. Nieto (2005) suggests that highly effective teachers are likely to be more self-aware, are resilient to challenging situations and connect with students. In other words, they are likely to be more emotionally intelligent. The table below provides examples of characteristics that Nieto (2005) associates with highly effective teaching.

Table 3.3. Characteristics of highly effective teachers.

	Characteristics
1	The ability to identify with student's life.
2	Placing high expectations on all students.
3	Commitment, in face of challenges and pressure commitment.

4	High value placed on students characteristics and personality that includes: language, race, experience culture, and gender.
5	Stakeholders (for example, community and parents) are included in the student learning experience.
6	Maintaining a safe and secure learning environment.
7	Prepared to challenge bureaucratic processes and procedures.
8	Able to be resilient to challenging experiences.
9	Engage with active blended learning.
10	Ability to experiment and to make quick decisions.
11	Commitment to lifelong learning
12	Respect and commitment to students.

Source: Adapted from Nieto (2005).

Whereas the above is associated with those who teach in schools, the content can be applied to those in higher education, including university level. Teachers with higher emotional intelligence are more likely to have greater self-esteem, empathy and leadership skills and are more inclined to experience greater teaching effectiveness and be more caring towards the students (Hwang, 2006, Ramana, 2013). Mortiboys (2012) explains that teachers who are more emotionally intelligent put as much energy into their expertise in their subject area as they do with developing their emotional intelligence. It also appears that emotional intelligence has a positive impact upon teaching satisfaction (For example: Yin, Lee, Zhang and Jin, 2013; Yin, 2015). This links to mindfulness which, is a subset of the socio-emotional behaviour that is associated with emotional intelligence (Mayer and Ciarrochi, 2006). It can provide the teacher with emotional stability helping them become more aware of their own feeling and thoughts (Zeidner et al. 2012). It is also *how* the teacher relates to others.

Daniel Goleman (1998) defines self-awareness as knowing what is being felt in the moment and using them to make decisions. It is knowing the internal states. Therefore, being aware of one's inner self (self-awareness) is fundamental to emotional intelligence. It is also having the qualities to be socially aware together with social skills as well as being able to empathise with others and understand how they may feel. Emotional intelligence, that includes emotional self-awareness, emotional self-control, expression, and self-management, are central to resilience and coping (Armstrong, Galligan and Critchley, 2011). A person who is more resilient is more likely to recover from stressful experiences more quickly and efficiently (For example: Carver, 1998;

Lazarus, 1993a). Having to cope with so many different demands within the workplace can give rise to negative feelings and emotions. It is, therefore, helpful to self-regulate the emotions, recognising when negative emotions emerge and to manage them accordingly. The absence of stress and negative emotions is associated with well-being (Little, 2014). It is maintaining control under pressurised situations.

Teachers who are successful are able to demonstrate emotions to reflect the emotional climate of the class and this could include empathy and kindness and also anger (Paulle, 2005). However, teachers may need to hide or suppress negative feelings such as anger, and disappointment. They may, therefore, need to pretend, act or exaggerate an emotion and experience emotional dissonance (Ogbonna and Harris, 2004). Examples of those who may need to demonstrate pretend or exaggerate emotions on a regular basis include: bill collectors being hostile, funeral home directors being sombre, and health service workers displaying a nurturing and caring nature (Abraham, 1998a, b, 1999). This may require the use of emotional labour; the need to fake or suppress emotion and to make use of negative and positive emotional displays (Ashforth and Humphrey, 1993; Glome and Tews, 2004). Hebson, Earnshaw and Marchington (2007) comment that teachers are expected to perform emotional labour that can lead to a negative impact upon the person's commitment, enthusiasm and performance (Philipp and Schupbach, 2010), alienating a person as he/ she tries to reconcile the challenges- emotional dissonance (Zembylas, 2002). Zembylas (2005) advises too strong and too weak emotions should be avoided in the teaching environment as emotional dissonance can have long term negative consequences including stress, burnout, job exhaustion (Dworkin, 1987; Erickson and Ritter, 2001; Erickson and Wharton, 1997; Wharton, 1993) and as a consequence may lose contact with true feelings (Diefendorff, Croyle and Gosserand, 2005). The above discussion relates to research undertaken within the school/ teacher environment. However, the experiences teachers have may not be too dissimilar to academics at university. Those who do engage with emotional dissonance can experience psychological and physical illness (Brennan, 2006; Kokkinos, 2007). Therefore, too strong and too weak emotions should be avoided in the teaching environment as emotional dissonance can have long term negative consequences including stress, burnout, job exhaustion. This can result in a loss of contact with true feelings, where emotions expressed do not correlate with those felt. Emotional dissonance can impact upon motivation when delivering workshops and seminars. Teacher motivation is intrinsic to delivering an excellent session for students. Students are likely to see through the act if there is a lack of motivation. Extrinsic motivational factors can also influence teacher performance. For example, constructive input from peers and line managers can reinforce a positive and constructive motivational approach to delivering workshops and seminars. Negative feedback can be destructive, leaving the teacher with reduced motivation and affecting their performance and service delivery. The manager providing the feedback may feel that they are "*saying it like it is*" and that it is their role to reinforce negative criticism. However, this approach can be highly destructive, especially with recipients who are highly self-critical and sensitive. It can destroy confidence and damage motivational levels that can lead to those in the teaching profession being disheartened to such an extent that they may take time off from work or even leave the profession.

Teaching with emotional intelligence can have beneficial results for both the teacher and the student. This includes being an active listener that creates genuine communication between teacher and student. It is not just *hearing* what is being said, it is engaging with the content of the communication allowing the speaker to finish talking and to incorporate suitable body language. It is important to "*listen*" not just what others say but also to what your body is telling you.

Empathy is an important factor in engaging with colleagues and students. It is crucial in creating team cohesion and bonding with students that in turn can improve performance and service delivery. It is making people feel part of the wider community. Managing interpersonal relationships can add to the bonding between colleagues and students. It helps create effective and dynamic relationships that can enhance the learning experience. There may be occasions where there is a breakdown of communication that lead to misunderstanding and confusion. The emotions felt, because of the breakdown of communication, can be fed back into the learning environment that in turn, can affect student learning experience. It is, therefore, important to manage interpersonal relationships to avoid possible breakdown of communication. It is also important to manage your own feelings and emotions to avoid emotional dissonance.

Learned optimism and learned helplessness

Studies discussed in this book suggest that mismanaging negative emotions can cause physical and psychological illness and yet we give focus to the negative thoughts and emotions much more than maybe we should. It is an evolutionary thing we have learned and adapted from our ancestors, *fight or flight*. Those who are prone to dwelling upon negative emotions are more inclined to experience depression that can be episodic lasting months at a time that includes feelings of worthlessness and guilt. The DSM-5 (Diagnostic and Statistical Manual) identify criteria associated with major depressive disorder(s) (MDD) that

Understanding and processing emotions

should include the presence of five (5) of the following during the same two-week time period of which one must be a depressed mood or loss of interest:

Table 3.4. Criteria for major depressive disorder.

1	Depressive mood/ irritable nearly every day.
2	Loss of interest/ pleasure in all or most day to day activities.
3	Change in appetite/ significant weight change (5%) over a period of one month.
4	Insomnia/ excessive sleep nearly every day.
5	Slow thought or movement/ psychomotor agitation nearly every day.
6	Energy loss/ fatigue nearly every day.
7	Feeling worthless and inappropriate guilt.
8	Reduced ability to concentrate, to think clearly, indecisiveness nearly every day.
9	Thoughts of suicide/ death.
	Source: DSM-5.

The DSM-5 divide the above into two columns "A" and "B" in which they identify the severity of the depressive episode.

Table 3.5. The DSM-5 criteria for major depressive disorder (MDD).

	Column A At least two or three symptoms should be present	Column B Symptoms from the list below should be present to add up to at least four
1	Depressed mood, largely uninfluenced by circumstances and sustained for at least two weeks	Loss of self-esteem and confidence
2	Loss of interest and enjoyment in usual activities	Ideas of inappropriate guilt and feelings of self-reproach
3	Reduced energy/ fatigue	Recurrent thoughts of death/ suicide
4		Reduced ability to concentrate/ think, indecisiveness/ vacillation
5		Change in psychomotor activity (Movement/ balance/ coordination)
6		Sleep disturbance
7		Increase/ decrease in appetite. Weight change
	Source: (The) American Academy of Professional Coders (AAPC) (2013).	

Seligman (1991) identifies that we are experiencing an epidemic of depression; ten (10) times what it was fifty (50) years earlier. This was reported in 1991. We are faced with increasing challenges in the twenty-first (21st) century. The Mental Health Foundation found that in 2014, 19.7% of people over the age of sixteen (16) experience anxiety or depression. Mental illness is reported to be the largest factor that causes disability with approximately 75% of people receiving no treatment (Annual report of the Chief Medical officer, 2013). The challenges of the modern workplace bring additional pressure and stress. Major depression has now become the second highest cause of disability, second only to lower back pain (Whiteford, Degenhardt, Rehm, Baxter, Ferrari et al., 2013). The World Health Organisation adds that there are three hundred million (300,000,000) people in the world that experience depression and nearly eight hundred thousand (800,000) people who commit suicide each year (WHO, 2018). It has become the predominant mental health issue worldwide and yet fewer than 10% receive treatment.

Those who are prone to pessimism and depression may be more inclined to be affected by the pressures and stress. Pressure is placed upon managers to obtain more from their team members and to be more productive. Pressure is placed on learning new skills to improve output and service delivery. Managers may revert to negative reinforcement, thinking that this can motivate the staff member to perform more effectively and efficiently. If the staff member is already a pessimist and experiences depression, the negative reinforcement can exacerbate the feelings of stress and helplessness that can in turn affect psychological and physical well-being. The negative reinforcement and feedback can severely impact upon the recipient. It can be corrosive and if experienced over time can lead to chronic stress. Staff members can become less motivated and feel disengaged with the whole learning process. Negative emotions experienced can build to such an extent, that this materialises in physical and psychological illnesses that can be reflected into their personal lives affecting others around them.

Organisations can have their own policies and procedures to help protect staff members. However, this may not be enough. What one person considers to be highly stressful, another may regard it as mild pressure. It is how we each respond to an experience. We can be our own worst enemy, sometimes, as we dwell on experiences and thoughts that reinforces negative emotions. We may not need to have someone tell us that we are underperforming or not behaving in the way that is expected of us. When in a pessimistic state, it is very easy to experience low self-esteem and to blame yourself when things go wrong. The added burden, of another person building on what may already be a fragile temperament, can lead to an imbalance of not being able to cope. As human beings, we can be conditioned to expect discomfort, pain and suffering and to think and behave as if we have no control over what is occurring and how we react. Even when we have the opportunity to extract ourselves from the cause, we continue to accept what is happening. We may just give up. Seligman and Maier (1967) describe this as learned helplessness. It is associated with depression (Seligman, 1974; Maier and Seligman, 2016; Seligman, 1991; Seligman and Maier, 1967). Some people are more resistant to the pressures and stresses placed upon them, while others less so. Some people are pessimists and others are optimists. The pessimist believes that bad events may last a long time, criticise and blame themselves when things go wrong. The inner voice undermines their actions and thoughts sending them further into pessimistic thoughts and behaviour. The optimist is more resilient to the challenges they experience. They see challenges as short term and temporary and causes are associated with each case. Whether pessimists or optimists, it is helpful to develop and improve resilience to the negative inner voices and external influences. Pessimism may appear to be deep-rooted and permanent. However, we can learn to control what happens to us.

We can learn to be optimistic, breaking the loop of pessimistic thinking. We can learn to take control. We can help change how we feel, improving psychological and physiological health, and generally making us feel happier. If a person develops their psychological resources, making use of positive emotions, it can improve a person's emotional well-being. For example: those who demonstrate higher levels of positive emotion are less likely to develop a cold and have greater resilience to recover from stressful experiences more quickly and efficiently and can help self-efficacy (Cohen et al., 2003; Fredrickson, 2000; Sutton and Wheatley, 2003). Those who express lower levels of positive emotions are more likely to have a stroke (Ostir et al., 2001).

> **Reflection: Coping**
> To help cope, externalise the experience. Place it outside yourself. When things go well, internalise them. Feel good and absorb the positive feelings associated with the event.

Using positive emotions and feedback to tasks well done can reinforce feelings of satisfaction and this can in turn reflect back into feelings of wellbeing. Feelings of contentment and happiness can improve commitment and motivate staff members to be more creative and involved in the organisation. Staff members may be less likely to take time off from work, reducing absenteeism and improving productivity and output. The emotions felt can be shared with friends and family. It is easy to recommend and suggest that positive emotions be developed and improved upon. However, when faced with regular negative reinforcement, from the inner voice and then from an external source such as a line manager, damage can become irreparable. The inner self may no longer be able to tolerate the pressures and stressors. Staying at the organisation may lead to further negative experiences increasing harm on psychological and physical well-being. Saying and doing nothing may be one option. *Positive action is needed.* Try meditation, mindfulness, or physical exercise. Try socialising, talking with friends. Maybe explain to your line manager how you are feeling. See if this works. However, that may not resolve the problem. It is possible to stand up and fight. This can lead to confrontation and fall out between you and the manager that could add to the negative emotions experienced. It could lead to a grievance being taken out against the manager. In turn, the manager could take out capability procedures against you. Are you willing for possible confrontation? Are you willing and able to defend yourself? It may be over a protracted period, possibly years, increasing problems associated with psychological and physical well-being that lead to lifelong illnesses.

Looking at the world with a different way of thinking can be helpful, refocusing the mind away from the pessimist to having a more optimistic way of assessing and evaluating experiences. The table below is adapted from Martin Seligman's (1991) book *"Learned optimism: How to change your mind and your life"*. He explains that the benefit of being optimistic is that there is likely to be greater resilience in the face of setbacks. Credit may be taken for success but little blame when there are failures. However, those with exaggerated optimism may be less aware of risks compared with those who are more timid (Kahneman, 2011).

Table 3.6. Permanent (Pessimistic) verses Temporary (Optimistic).

	Permanent (Pessimistic)	**Temporary (Optimistic)**
1	I am always feeling tired.	I sometimes feel tired and exhausted.
2	I've tried loads of diets, but none seems to work.	I need to eat out less than I do if this diet is to work.
3	You are always telling me off.	You tell me off if I don't clean my room.
4	I hate my boss.	My boss is appears to be in a bad mood but that will pass.
5	You never seem to talk to me.	You have been very quiet today. Share your thoughts with me.
6	I have to work with my boss indefinitely.	I think my boss may find a new job elsewhere or may even retire shortly.

| 7 | I see no way out and I am going to have to work in this place until the day I retire. | I am looking for a new role elsewhere and will move on within the next few months. |

Source: Adapted from: Seligman (1991).

The pessimist sees things as *"permanent"* while the optimist sees things as *"temporary"*. The focus is *"always"* and *"never"* associated with the pessimist, and *"sometimes"* associated with the optimist. The idea is to develop a permanent optimistic approach and see pessimism as a temporary/ episodic event. Reframing the way the mind thinks can be challenging, especially when immersed in a long term pervasive, depressive, state. Try and see things from a specific optimistic viewpoint and regard the experience as temporary; it will pass. Try and avoid generalisation where the experience becomes embedded as being long term and permanent. Refocus the thinking to see that these experiences are temporary and can be overcome. If the culture of the organisation, or the management style, is not going to change, there may not be another option other than to leave and find a job elsewhere. It may mean leaving a job that provides regular and good income. It may mean jumping into the unknown. Feelings of negative emotions can affect self-worth and confidence in making that jump. However, to stay could mean further health issues that could lead to going off work permanently. *Positive action is needed.* Have confidence. Do not give up. Feel good about yourself.

Bullying and harassment

Bullying and harassment appears to take the guise of different forms. It doesn't just happen in the school playground. It can be framed as management role and responsibilities. For example, insults and belittling comments may be made; unrealistic time frames set; and confusion created when unnecessary. The intent is to try and make the staff member feel small while hiding their own inadequacies and insecurities. The Advisory, Conciliation and Arbitration Service (UK) (ACAS, 2018) define bullying as behaviour that is felt to be intimidating, humiliating, insulting, offensive or malicious. It includes possible abuse of power that can injure the person emotionally and/ or physically." Bullying does not have a legal definition. However, the term *"harassment"* is used, that includes bullying behaviour, that falls under the U.K. Equality Act (2010). It is defined as *"unwanted conduct related to a relevant <u>characteristic</u>, which has the purpose or effect of violating an individual's dignity or creating intimidating, hostile, degrading, humiliating or offensive environment for that individual"*. The characteristics referred to include: age, sex, race, disability, religion, sexual orientation. Dweck (2017) comments that "*bullies judge*" while "*victims take it in*". If it remains inside it can lead to suicide and depression and possibly lead to violence.

Bullying and harassment happens around the world and this includes universities. In the Australian "*The Conversation*" dated 1st July 2018, they report that sexual abuse, harassment and discrimination is rife among Australian academics. This is supported by the headline in The Guardian (UK), dated 28th September 2018, that states that there are hundreds (100s) of university academics that have been accused of bullying students and colleagues. It comments that dozens of academics have reported experiencing career sabotage, extreme pressure and aggressive behaviour and that human resource managers appear to be more concerned with avoiding negativity rather than trying to protect staff. It appears to be ingrained into the culture. One former PhD student reports that they had experienced post-traumatic stress disorder. In another instance, a lecturer felt that she had been pushed into resigning saying that not only had she lost her job, she also lost the sole family income and nearly her sanity.

Interestingly, in a study undertaken by Giorgi (2012), bullying is considered to be a "*cause*" rather than a "*consequence*" of the organisational climate. Organisations can have policies and procedures associated with bullying and harassment. Organisations may also make it clear that bullying and harassment will not be tolerated. However, bullying and harassment seems to be part of the work-life experience and appears to continue and possibly thrive in places that you would think would have greater disapproval and better work ethic.

It may be helpful to introduce emotional intelligence training to all members of staff to help inform them and, develop greater resilience to the emotional upheaval that bullying, and harassment may have on them. It may be helpful to simply have a zero tolerance for bullying and harassment, allowing staff members to work in a safe and secure environment. It may be helpful to engage in therapy that can help place emotions in context.

Therapy

Emotions can help us understand what is going on in the environment around us and to help us interpret the experience. Emotions can be experienced as primary or secondary. Primary emotions are those that are experienced as an immediate reaction to an event. The emotion doesn't rely upon thinking about it. Secondary emotions are those that require a little thought and cognitive processing and follow primary emotions. Emotions can be triggered by the smallest thing sending people into overwhelming, uncontrollable rage and anger that is accompanied by threatening body language and vocal outbursts. Efforts can be made to control the emotions. It may be as a result of an immediate reaction. This anger may be suppressed and internalised in fear of possible reaction from others. Depression, or feelings of hopelessness, can then be felt as a secondary emotion so as to avoid the primary emotion of anger. Instrumental emotions can be learned from a very young age. If a child throws a tantrum or becomes angry, they may get the attention of the parent. The intention is to manipulate the parent with the intention of getting their own way. If it works once, or twice the behaviour may continue and ultimately transferred into adult behaviour. This behaviour may be shown in management style and approach to staff members, believing that this approach "*gets things done*" but simply distances the staff member that may make the manager even more irritable and angry.

Toleration of negative emotions

It is possible to become emotionally tolerant, helping us to cope with feelings of short and long-term pain and distress. Distress toleration is associated with avoidant coping strategies, suppressing the emotion. There are two (2) components to distress tolerance. The first (1st) is associated with the ability to cope with negative emotions. The second (2nd) is the behavioural response to the emotion. It is the ability to cope with an uncomfortable emotional experience without developing what would otherwise be "*normal*" emotional symptoms that are associated with mental health disorders (Greene, Grasso and Ford, 2014; Oldham, Skodol and Bender, 2014) For example:

- Borderline personality disorder (instability in mood, interpersonal relationships, self-image and impulsivity),

- Post-traumatic stress disorder (an experience of a traumatic event in which there is a threat of death or the person is faced with the possibility of grievous bodily harm),

- Substance abuse/ dependency (recurrent use of drugs that impairs the significant impairment of being able to work, attend school or carry out normal living arrangements).

There are different approaches that are available to help and support those with mental health issues that include emotion tolerance. Please note that where there is deep-seated anxiety, post-traumatic stress or other underlying psychological/ medical symptoms, it is recommended that professional advice be sought from those who are medically trained. The information provided here is given in good faith to provide a little light into the different therapies that are available. Here are a few examples.

Emotion-focused therapy

Emotion-focused therapy regards emotions as a foundation and integral to who we are as human beings. The main principles are intrapersonal emotion awareness, emotion regulation and transformation where the therapy helps the person become aware, accept and to make sense of the emotion(s) they are experiencing. It places emotion at the centre of the therapy. Those with depression or anxiety may find ways to avoid interpersonal relationships that cause worry and fear. They suppress and internalise the emotion. The role of the therapist is to listen, and to ask questions to help the person understand their emotions more clearly. This therapy is helpful to those who may experience depression, anxiety, borderline personality and interpersonal relationships. The therapist focuses on the present to help change how the person feels so as to form a healthier and more positive relationship. Greenberg (2004) points out that a major premise to this therapy is it is not possible to leave a place until the person has arrived there. The role of the person being counselled is to be honest and open when in a counselling session. There are three main stages that include:

a. Deescalating of the negative interaction between interpersonal relationships and to understand what is happening.

b. Discussion of fears within the relationship helping the person to be more responsive and open.

c. Helping the person to understand how the negative experiences arose and how to change that understanding that can be embedded in future interpersonal relationships.

The caveat with this therapy is that it is short term and may not be suitable for those who have more deep-seated mental health problems.

Emotion-processing therapy

Emotion processing therapy was developed by Foa and Kozak (1986) who explain that this therapy is associated with cognitive processes being used to generate emotions in response to experiences that we have. There are occasions where there appears to be an irrational reason for emotions that can develop into phobias. A fear of flying, spiders, creepy crawlies, unlucky numbers. In most of us, we cope with the experience. In others, it can cause anxiety, distress and depression. The phobias can be overpowering where they dominate, and control lives.

Emotion processing therapy recognises that there is thought behind the emotion. We think of an experience and that generates the emotion. It is the inability to process the emotion and as such, the emotion remains heightened even when there is no reason for it. This therapy uses exposure to help reduce the feelings of anxiety and fear. There are several steps that can be taken to help cope with this irrational emotion that are discussed below.

> **Reflection:**
> - Step 1: Be aware of the emotion when it occurs. Acknowledge that this is not normal. Take a few deep breaths try a little Mindfulness.
> - Step 2: Talk to yourself, aloud. Say how you are feeling. Say what emotion you are feeling. Now say that this is not normal. Again, take a few deep breaths and try a little Mindfulness.
> - Step 3: Again, talk to yourself. Acknowledging the emotion being felt, say to yourself that this doesn't matter. Say that there is no rational reason for the emotion. Your other voice may be saying that there is a reason. Allow it to speak. Now say again, "*there is no rational reason for the emotion. I am in a safe and secure place physically and emotionally*". Allow both voices to speak and as in steps 1 and 2, take a few deep breaths and try a little mindfulness.
>
> It can take time, however, with practice feelings such as anxiety and fear can be placed into a rational and "*normal*" state.

Cognitive Behavioural therapy

Cognitive behavioural therapy (CBT) focuses on solutions. It is where the client talks through their problems, helping to manage and modify the way to think and behave. It encourages us to think about the world and those in it. Whereas it can be used in other mental health disorders it is commonly and effectively used to help those who experience depression and anxiety. The therapy helps break down, what may be regarded as, insurmountable problems into smaller manageable parts that can include: Emotions, feelings, actions and thoughts. A good example is where someone purposely tries to avoid another person. Avoiding personal contact could develop into someone dwelling on negative emotions that they experienced in earlier meetings. These emotions could develop into a feeling of stress, anxiety and possibly depression. Not engaging with the other person could exacerbate an already challenging and stressful interpersonal relationship. This could lead to deeper psychological and physical ailments. It could lead to taking time off from work. It creates a vicious circle that is hard to break. Reading self-help books may be helpful. However, the problem may be deep-seated and may require the support from an experienced councillor. CBT involves:

- Replacing upsetting and self-critical thoughts with those that are helpful and realistic.

- Finding ways of doing something more constructive and helpful to overcome the problem.

CBT may not be suitable for everyone. It may be that CBT or other therapies are insufficient on their own and anti-depressants are needed. It is recommended that taking professional advice from a medical practitioner can help find the best therapy that may include the use of anti-depressants.

For those interested, the British Association for Behavioural and Cognitive Psychotherapies has an excellent web site at: https://www.babcp.com/Default.aspx. A caveat with CBT is that it is not short term. It can take weeks and possibly months before there are changes to the thinking and behaviour.

Summing up

This chapter has reflected upon different emotions that are experienced. Emotions such as anger and joy may be experienced differently. For example, anger over a particular event may lead one person to *"throw their toys out of the pram"* while swearing and shouting at the same time. Another person may feel slightly irritated over the same experience and show little outward signs of the emotion. Developing our understanding of our own emotions can be learned. It is recognising and acknowledging them and to regulate and control them as part of our daily lives. Understanding our own emotions is part of improving and developing emotional intelligence. Managing and regulating emotions can be challenging and sometimes it is helpful to have professional advice to help support and underpin emotional foundations. As you develop and improve emotional intelligence you may be better prepared and able to cope with an experience when someone else says or does something that upsets you. Developing and incorporating emotional intelligence into the teaching environment can be beneficial for both the teacher and the student. This can be supported by organisational policies and procedures that are enforced effectively to all members of staff. It is also important to be an active listener, engaging empathically with colleagues and students. It can help build team cohesion and bonding that in turn can improve performance and service delivery.

It is also helpful to look at the world through an optimistic lens, refocusing the way the mind dwells on negative experiences, feelings and, emotions that may appear permanent. Try and avoid the negative experiences becoming embedded as long term and permanent. Look at things as being temporary that can be overcome. Legislation is there to help protect staff members, however, this may not be sufficient. Organisations may have a zero tolerance for bullying encouraging a safe and secure environment to work in. Organisations may have their own policies and procedures; however, bullying and harassment appears to occur in all parts of life, including universities and can affect anyone.

Perception is influential in how a person experiences bullying and harassment. What is interpreted by one person as good management style (such as assertive behaviour) may be felt by another as bullying and harassment. Training people in emotional intelligence can help staff members become more resilient. This can help staff members cope with challenging experiences. This chapter also reflects on emotion-focused, emotion processing and cognitive behaviour therapy. Each type of therapy helps focus the mind and to understand more clearly how and why these emotions and feelings occur. Negative emotions and feelings can be associated with deep-seated psychological and physiological reasons that need counselling and support that books such as this may not provide. It is important to take professional advice and guidance.

Chapter 4

Coping

Stress is complex, and people experience stress from their own perspective and understanding. The person may also cope with the stressful event in a different way when compared to others. He/she may also cope differently depending upon context, and how they are feeling at the time. When reflecting on these stressful experiences the person may not clearly remember the feelings and how they coped. Being able to identify how and what people remember, can therefore be complex, adding to the challenges of measuring and assessing ways in which people cope. Furthermore, across culture, emotions may be culturally dependent (Zeidner et al., 2012). Cultural differences may also have an influence on how people cope as well as personality (For example: Connor-Smith and Calvete, 2004; Sica, Novara, Dorz and Sanavio, 1997; Wadsworth, Rieckmann, Benson and Compas, 2004). Compas, Connor-Smith, Saltzman, Thomsen, et al. (2001) refer to coping as the efforts to reduce or prevent threat, loss or harm so as to reduce the associated distress. Lazarus and Folkman (1984) define coping as the cognitive and behavioural efforts to enable a person to manage internal and external demands that are perceived to be taxing or exceeding the ability of the person to cope. Weiten and Lloyd (2003) define the term *coping stress* as the efforts that individuals make to reduce, master and tolerate demands that are created by stressful experiences. A challenge is to identify where stress ends, and coping begins (Sontag and Graber, 2010). To try and gain an insight into how academics cope with interpersonal relationships this chapter discusses how academics perceive how they cope emotionally with interpersonal relationships within higher education (*University*). Discussion is supported by information gained from a study undertaken by Bowen, Rose and Pilkington, (2018), using the coping strategies identified by Carver, Scheier and Weintraub (1989) as subheadings.

Coping strategies

Krohne (2002) argues that it is important to define the central person specific goals associated with coping. This is also referred to as *"reference values"* which make up the core of personality, enabling the person to understand stress and the ability to cope (Karoly, 1999). Krohne (2002) takes the explanation of stress a little further. He states that external demands (stressors) and that experienced by the body (stress) can be placed into two categories:

1) **Systematic stress** that is associated with physiological or psychobiology factors.

2) **Psychological stress** that is associated with cognitive psychology. Psychological stress can occur when the demands on well-being exceed the ability to cope. This is summarised in the table below.

Table 4.1. Types of stress.

No	Category	Associated with	Examples of researchers
1	Systematic stress	Physiological or psychobiology	Selye, (1956,1976).
2	Psychological stress	Cognitive psychology	Lazarus, (1966; 1991); Lazarus and Folkman, (1984).

As discussed earlier in this book, there appears to be three main ways of experiencing stress:

1) **Stimulus** (Masuda and Holmes, 1967; Holmes and Rahe, 1967);

2) **Response** (Selye, 1956, 1976); and

3) **Interactional** (Lazarus, 1966, 1982, 1990, 1991, 1993, 2006; Lazarus and Folkman, 1984,1986; Lazarus and Launier, 1978).

Masuda and Holmes (1967) refer to *"things"* that cause stress while Selye (1956) refers to the *"response"* given when the person experiences the stress. Lazarus (1966) refers to the *"imbalance"* between the ability and demands of coping. There are three categories associated with coping. These are:

1) **Problem-focused coping** – where a person solves a problem and removes the stressor.

2) **Emotion-focused coping** – where the person channels or reduces the emotion (For example: seeking support from others).

3) **Avoidance coping** – where the person avoids the problem (For example: watching television).

Lazarus (2006) argues that problem-focused strategy and emotion-focused strategy should be considered compatible with each other. For example, problem-focused coping, that is effective, can reduce the perceived threat and can also reduce the distress experienced while emotion-focused coping can enable the person to reflect on the experience more calmly. Those who experience greater stress are more inclined to make use of problem-solving (Quayhagen and Quayhagen, 1982). Problem-focused coping and engagement coping are more associated with better psychological and physical health; whereas emotion-focused coping and disengagement coping are associated with poorer psychological and physical health (Compas et al. 2001). Emotion-focused may involve denial and negative outcomes and problem-focused may have positive outcomes. Studies undertaken suggest that emotion-focused coping can help cope successfully with health problems (For example: Bishop, 1994; Goldberger and Breznitz, 1993; Snyder, 1999). However, other research suggests that emotion-focused coping is less effective (For example: Mackenzie, Wiprzycka, Hasher and Goldstein, 2008). Categorising into problem and emotional-focused coping is likely to be too simplistic as there appear to be more ways in which people cope (Aldwin, Folkman Schaefer, Coyne et al., 1980; Aldwin and Park, 2004; Folkman and Lazarus, 1980; 1985; Scheier, Weintraub and Carver, 1986). It is apparent that further research is recommended. As described by Lazarus (1966, 1982, 1990, 2006), the transactional model of stress is the relationship between the person and the environment and their ability to cope with a stressful experience. An imbalance between the stressor and the ability to cope leads to feelings of stress. The research associated with transactional stress has been developed, by Carver et al. (1989), into the assessment of coping strategies from which they devise a questionnaire. The coping mechanisms identified by Carver et al. (1989) are summarised in the table below.

Table 4.2. Coping mechanisms (Carver et al., 1989).

Problem-focused	Emotion-focused	Dysfunctional
Active coping	Seeking social support	Venting of emotions
Planning	Positive reinforcement	Behavioural disengagement
Suppression of competing activities	Acceptance	Mental disengagement
Restraint coping	Religion	Substance use
Social support/ instrumental reasons	Humour	Denial

Methodological study of how academic cope

Bowen, Rose, and Pilkington (2018) undertake a study into the coping strategies undertaken by academics to help them cope with stressful experiences. Bowen et al. (2018) us a mixed explanatory sequential methodology. A questionnaire is undertaken first, followed by semi-structured interviews that help explain and contextualise the findings. It brings together two types of data providing greater understanding and insight into the research topics that may not have been obtained analysing and evaluating data separately.

Mixed methodology is described as "*the third paradigm*" or "*third methodological movement*" (Johnson and Onwuegbuzie, 2004; Teddlie and Tashakkori, 2009). Whereas it can be time-consuming, it is considered as an intuitive way of undertaking research that is reflected within everyday life (Creswell and Plano Clark, 2011). It is now regarded as a methodology, which Greene (2007) defines as multiple ways of making sense of the world around us. It no longer restricts the researcher to particular paradigms that has been traditionally the case and has become a legitimate means of undertaking social and human research that helps to address broader questions adding insight, and generating new knowledge, that could otherwise have been missed (Creswell and Plano Clark, 2011, Stange, 2006). Rather than limiting research, the mixed approach is a creative and expansive approach to research Johnson and Onwuegbuzi, 2004). It provides a valuable tool for those researching in areas such as psychology (Bartholomew and Brown, 2012).

The mixed methodological approach used in this study helps to inform and contribute validity (Bazeley, 2002; Denzin, 1978; Gladding, 1984). While providing more evidence, it helps to understand the topic area in greater depth increasing confidence in findings (Albert, Trochelman, Meyer and Nutter, 2009; Creswell and Plano Clark, 2011; Hoover and Krishnamurti, 2010; Tashakkori and Creswell, 2008). The mixed methodological approach also offsets possible shortcomings from using a single approach (Caruth, 2013). This study adds to existing research, informing those undertaking future research the value associated with using the mixed methods approach. This study also contributes to the existing literature, in particular that associated with mixed methodology.

Academic sample

The sample used in this study are academics (those employed by a university full time, part time, and hourly and who may be lecturers, tutors, instructors, researchers) To gain access to the academics, around the world, the professional contact/ networking site, LinkedIn, is used providing access to potential participants. It is regarded as an excellent means of accessing people that may otherwise not be possible using traditional methods (Alter, 2015). Academics could therefore be contacted at universities around the world, creating links to allow two-way communication. The sample chosen has expertise and experience of being academics. The sample is directed to an online questionnaire via the online message. The online questionnaire allows for academics to be contacted that would not be possible with the traditional pen-paper approach. The drawback to this approach is that it is necessary that participants have access to computer hardware and software. Three thousand nine hundred (3,900) potential participants are contacted via LinkedIn. A reasonable figure of five hundred and forty-three (543) people respond to the questionnaire. Six (6) (1.10%) advise that they are students, and four (4) (0.74%) hold administrative roles at University; a total of 10 people (1.84%). Whereas it is appreciated they participated, to avoid confusion and to avoid misinterpretation of data, the information uploaded by the aforementioned ten (10) people is removed from the data. Therefore, the analysis and evaluation undertaken in this study is associated with five hundred and thirty-three (533) (100%) academics from universities around the world.

Designation of the participants are summarised below:

- 2.6% (N = 14) are grouped as associate lecturers or similar;

- 44.8% (N = 239) are grouped as Lecturer/ tutor or similar;

- 4.1% (N = 22) are researchers or similar;

- 29.3% (N = 156) are professors or similar;

- 1.5% (N = 8) are heads of department or similar;

- 1.1% (N = 6) are heads of schools or similar;

- 1.3% (N = 7) are directors or similar;

- 0.6% (N = 3) are chancellors or similar;

- 14.6% (N =78) of participants do not provide their job title;

- 45.8% (N = 244) are male with a mean age of 48.78 (SD = 10.9) and median of 48; and

- 54.2% (N = 289) are female with a mean age of 47.29 (SD = 9.78) and median of 48.

This study does acknowledge that job descriptions may vary from one country to another and from one university to another. The categories chosen identifies different levels of responsibility. For example: the associate lecturer may also work elsewhere or be undertaking research at the same time as teaching at the university. The lecturer/ tutor may be more likely to be responsible for teaching but less likely to have formal line management responsibility. The researcher could have a different role focusing more on research and less on the teaching. Those identified as a professor are likely to be those with PhD, have publications in their name, and regarded as experts within their field. Heads of Department included those who may have line management responsibility. The findings suggest that there is a reasonable sample across each job type that could be applied to a larger sample, from which fuzzy generalisations can be made. The table below identifies each of the coping strategies that Carver et al. (1989) describe and are used in this study.

Table 4.3. Coping strategies.

No	Coping strategy	Description
1	Self-distraction	Trying to take one's mind off it
2	Active coping	Concentrating on doing something about it
3	Denial	Refusing to believe it's real
4	Substance use	Use of alcohol/ drugs to make things better
5	Emotional support	Gaining comfort from someone else
6	Instrumental support	Gaining advice from others
7	Behavioural disengagement	Given up trying to deal with it
8	Planning	Coming up with a way to deal with it
9	Venting	Expressing negative feelings
10	Positive reframing	Seeing things from a positive point of view
11	Humour	Making jokes/ fun of it
12	Acceptance	Accepting that it has happened and live with it
13	Religion	Finding comfort in religion or spiritual beliefs
14	Self-blame	Blaming oneself

Source: Carver et al. (1989).

The findings from the questionnaire are analysed using specialised software (Statistical Package for Social Science- SPSS) that helps handle a large amount of data. It also provides tools to analyse the evaluation data that includes graphics such as histograms, scatterplots and boxplots The table below provides a summary of the findings from the questionnaire/ survey associated with the coping strategies identified by Carver et al. (1989).

Table 4.4. Coping (Carver et al., 1989) (Summary of items). Totals.

Coping strategies	Item	Don't do this at all	Do this a little bit	Do this a medium amount	Do this a lot
Self-distraction	Sub total	24%	34%	27%	15%
Active coping	Sub total	11%	21%	35%	33%
Denial	Sub total	72%	18%	7%	3%
Substance use	Sub total	76%	17%	5%	2%
Emotional support	Sub total	16%	34%	34%	16%
Instrumental support	Sub total	17%	34%	35%	14%
Behavioural disengagement	Sub total	67%	20%	9%	4%
Venting	Sub total	26%	37%	27%	10%
Positive reframing	Sub total	11%	31%	38%	20%
Planning	Sub total	9%	17%	39%	35%
Humour	Sub total	23%	35%	27%	15%
Acceptance	Sub total	10%	25%	40%	25%
Religion	Sub total	59%	15%	11%	13%
Self-blame	Sub total	31%	37%	20%	12%

Each of the coping strategies are placed in order, identifying the highest to lowest percentage of those who respond to: "*do this a medium amount*", and "*do this a lot*". The table below shows the findings.

Table 4.5. Coping strategies (Summary of do this a lot and a medium amount).

No	Coping strategies	Do this a medium amount	Do this a lot	Totals
1	Planning	39%	35%	76%

2	Active coping	35%	33%	68%
3	Acceptance	40%	25%	65%
4	Positive reframing	38%	20%	58%
5	Emotional support	34%	16%	50%
6	Instrumental support	35%	14%	49%
7	Self-distraction	27%	15%	42%
8	Humour	27%	15%	42%
9	Venting	27%	10%	37%
10	Self-blame	20%	12%	32%
11	Religion	11%	13%	24%
12	Behavioural disengagement	9%	4%	11%
13	Denial	7%	3%	10%
14	Substance use	5%	2%	7%

The highest shown is *"planning"* at 76% followed by *"active coping"* at 68%. *"Acceptance"* is a close third with a total of 65%. Two coping strategies associated with interpersonal relationships are emotional and instrumental support. Emotional support is where a person gains comfort from someone else and instrumental support is where advice is gained from others. The findings from the questionnaire are summarised in the tables below.

Table 4.6. Emotional and instrumental support (Responses).

Coping strategies	Item	Don't do this at all	Do this a little bit	Do this a medium amount	Do this a lot
Emotional support	I've been getting emotional support from others	17%	36%	'4%	14%
	I've been getting comfort and understanding from someone.	15%	32%	35%	17%
Instrumental support	I've been getting help and advice from other people.	15%	34%	37%	14%

	I've been trying to get advice or help from other people about what to do.	18%	34%	33%	15%

Table 4.7. Emotional and instrumental support (Summary of paired items).

Coping strategies	Item	Don't do this at all	Do this a little bit	Do this a medium amount	Do this a lot
Emotional support	Sub total	16%	34%	34%	16%
Instrumental support	Sub total	17%	34%	35%	14%

Qualitative research has become a prominent approach when undertaking social science research and interviews are essential to provide knowledge of the social world (King and Horrocks, 2010; Kvale, 1996). Qualitative research is concerned with the meaning and how others make sense of the world around them (Willig, 2008). To gain in-depth analysis of a person's thoughts and views, case studies should be carried out by means of carrying out interviews (Smith, Flowers and Larkin, 2013; Yin, 2003). Whereas research associated with qualitative data is associated with subjectivity, the objective is not to predict but to explain and describe events and experiences (Willig, 2008). The purpose of undertaking qualitative research is to delve deeper into how people cope with particular experiences and to find out how they think and feel. Kahn and Cannell (1957) state that interviews are a purposeful discussion between two or more people. It allows the researcher to gain an insight into how another person feels and thinks. The research allows categories to emerge that can be evaluated against the context from which they come enriching the findings (Smith, 1996).

Semi-structured interviews are undertaken in this study, as structured interviews would neither allow sufficient flexibility nor give sufficient depth of information. It is also felt that unstructured interviews would be too flexible and there would be insufficient control. Questions are mainly open-ended and the style of the interview non-directive, the purpose being to elicit the participant's own story. The questions are designed to be as short as possible to maximise the time for participants to respond. Invitations are sent out to participate in semi-structured interviews, via LinkedIn, at the same time as invites to participate in the questionnaire. A database is set up of those wishing to participate and they are contacted again via email prior to interviews being undertaken.

Pilot interviews are first undertaken person to person, on the university campus, where body language could be seen by interviewer and interviewee. The drawback of person to person interviews is that no matter which location is used to undertake the pilot interviews, interruptions are experienced. For example: people came in the room, the landline phone rang, and other work-related matters distracted the participant. Noise is also experienced from students and colleagues from outside the room and this appeared to cause distraction. The lesson learned from this is that interviews need to be carried out in a peaceful environment, possibly away from the university. Note taking is also undertaken in the pilot interviews. However, at times, the interviewer's focus is directed to note-taking rather than on the participant. It is felt that greater eye contact could be made, providing greater attention to the participant. Note taking is, therefore, discontinued giving the participant full attention of that being communicated. Those who participate in semi-structured interviews are summarised below. Names have been changed and means of identification have been removed maintaining confidentiality and anonymity.

Table 4.8. Information of those interviewed.

Stage and case study number	Pseudo-nym	Gender	Length of experience (years)	Age/ age group (where provided)	Full time/ part time	Current role/ job	Stage and case study number
Pilot interview 1	Jamie	Female		51 to 65	Full time	Lecturer	Pilot interview 1
Pilot interview 2	Sandra	Male		51 to 65	Full time	Lecturer	Pilot interview 2
Pilot interview 3	Petra	Female			Full time	Lecturer	Pilot interview 3
Pilot interview 4	Andrea	Female			Full time	Lecturer	Pilot interview 4
1.1	Simon	Male	3		Full time	Lecturer	1.1
1.2	Elizabeth	Female	11	40	Full time	Head of Department	1.2
1.3	David	Male	6	58	Full time	Lecturer	1.3

1.4	Robert	Male	31	57	Full time	Head of Department	1.4
1.5	Trevor	Male	2	29	Full time	Lecturer	1.5
1.6	John	Male	8	39	Full time	Associate Professor	1.6
1.7	Tina	Female	6	46	Full time	Lecturer	1.7
1.8	Mary	Female	25 approx. (with time out for family)	57	Adjunct/ part time/ temporary	Lecturer	1.8
1.9	Sally	Female	10 approx. (with time out for family)	46	Part time/ temporary	Associate Lecturer	1.9
1.10	Kelly	Female	7		Full time	Lecturer	1.10
1.11	Diane	Female	7	54	Full time	Lecturer	1.11

The table below provides a summary of the data associated with those interviewed.

Table 4.9. Summary of those interviewed.

Item	Total
People interviewed	11
Length of interviews	23.06 minutes to 1 hour and 11 minutes
Average length of interview	43 minutes
Ages of those interviewed	29 to 58 (2 people did not provide age)
Average age	47 (2 people did not provide age)
Male/ female	5 males. 6 females
Full time/ part time	9 full time. 2-part time/ temporary
Roles	2 Head of Department; 1 professor; 8 lecturers
Participants location when interviewed	8 UK, 1 Portugal, 1 USA, 1 Germany

Brocki and Wearden (2005) provide examples where, in one (1) study, one (1) participant is interviewed (Robson, 2002). In another study, thirty (30) people are interviewed (Collins and Nicolson, 2002). The largest number of transcripts identified is forty-eight (48) (Clare, 2002, 2003). Smith and Osborn (2003) advise that there is no correct sample size. However, there does appear to be a consensus where smaller sizes are emerging (Brocki and Wearden, 2005; Reid, Flowers and Larkin, 2005; Smith, 2004). As advised by Smith and Osborn (2003), a smaller sized sample can provide sufficient perspective subject to adequate contextualisation been given.

Interviews are carried out using Skype or landline telephone as the participants are located in different parts of the world and meeting them could be costly and time-consuming. The landline telephone is used in one (1) interview. The advantage with using the telephone is that the participant could be contacted without them having to be next to a Personal computer (P.C.) or mobile device. Interviews are undertaken where both parties are at home and/or outside normal office hours so as not to be disturbed by extraneous factors. The interviews are recorded using two hand held digital devices and one software device. Within forty-eight (48) hours of each interview, the recording is transcribed while fresh in the memory, and a copy is sent to the participant for them to check and amend. Pseudonyms are used to protect the identity of each participant. Data is held securely and stored on a username/ password protected P.C. NVivo software helps to manage the data more effectively when compared with manual analysis and evaluation or by spreadsheets. The transcripts are then imported into NVivo software programme that allows for the collection and handling of information to include categorisation of themes and coding of the interview transcripts.

Each of the case studies discussed below provide quotes and information from the semi-structured interviews undertaken by Bowen et al. (2018).

Planning

Planning is finding ways to cope with a challenging experience. In this study, planning is shown to have the highest response. When given the statement: "*I've been coming up with a strategy about what to do*" 37% said that they "*do this a lot*". A further 40% advised that they did this "*a medium amount*" (a total of 77%). When given the statement "*I've been thinking hard about what steps to take*" 33% responded that they "*do this a lot*" and 37% said that they "*do this a medium amount*" (a total of 87%).

Coping planning focuses on reducing and normalising stress while helping to improve regulation of the emotions. The idea is to change behaviour and focus on negative thoughts. Planning actions and setting goals can therefore be a constructive means in coping with challenging demands and expectations. As an academic, pressures and stresses can be experienced from different sides. For example, Management may demand changes to programmes and module content, new hardware and software may require knowledge and skill-based training and, undertaking research including writing academic papers. Student's expectations may place further pressure on the academic all of which needs to be undertaken within limited time frames and by deadlines. Creating an action plan can be a valuable tool in helping academics cope and to manage their workload. It is providing a plan that identifies actions that can help achieve particular objectives and goals, prioritising the workload and focusing on what is needed first. A line manager from many years ago informed me that that there were *"urgent, priority and, do now"* deadlines. There were also the *"panic"* items; those that were very, very urgent. His team of about fifteen (15) people were required to work under this system year after year. As you can imagine, it caused a little uncertainty and anxiety.

It is helpful to delve into the findings from the interviews and to consider how participants feel about their own experiences.

Planning does seem to be an integral requirement of the role of the academic. Tina comments that *"what I tend to do if something does upset me, I'll go away and think about it and think about it and plan a good way of managing it rather than allowing emotions to spill over where I get angry or that person gets angry and upset."* One of the challenges of working in such a highly dynamic and pressurised environment is the ability to switch off from work. Even when Mary is away from the university, she advises that *"I didn't have a vacation because I was doing all the planning, all the cooking, all the packing, all the driving."*

Diane refers to the term *"optimism"* and the need to *"constantly reflect on what I did, how I did it; what kind of feedback do I get, what feedback for feedback. Then I review that against what I've done, and [....], hope that it's ok and wait for feedback (laughs). Constant optimist. Optimism".*

As each person experiences the world from his/her own perspective it does raise the question as to the interpretation of the term *"planning"*. One person may feel that planning something is simply thinking about a wide generalised objective which they seek to obtain. Others may regard planning as meticulously arranging detailed action so as to achieve an objective. The findings from this questionnaire identify how challenging it can be to be able to generalise as each person makes sense of the world from their own understanding that include a multitude of variables including: culture and background.

Active coping

Active coping is to concentrate on doing something about the challenging experience. After planning this the second highest response with 68% of people saying that they did this "*a lot*" or "*a medium amount.*" Trevor says that the way he copes is "*Not letting it get to me. Certainly not taking it personally. Recognising that it is only a job. It isn't me completely.*" Simon comments that "*the way I coped with* [problems experienced at an earlier university] *that was look, it's not the best but it was like the motivation, the focus was on the end goal. You're getting the experience, you know, fill the job apps, you're getting the experience. You're acquiring the experience you need in order to go elsewhere. So what got me through that was the motivation that if I don't get a job here then I will get one elsewhere with the experience that I'd be acquiring. So that was very much how I managed that. It was just to keep my eye on the end goal, at the time, to secure a permanent post.*" Simon adds that he is "*always reviewing how I do things. I don't like to think I'm settled in my ways. So I try to take a pragmatic approach. I just thing, Ok, you know, it's gone wrong this time. If I'm going to run this course again next year, just have a think how I'm going to improve it so this it doesn't happen and so that, you know somewhere down the line, I'll hit the winning formula, I will have to change it. I will manage it, so again, the way I am dealing with frustration is let's have a look as to what's causing it, how can we alleviate it for the future. So I am trying to be as pragmatic as I can.*"

David explains that "*The last twelve months have been a challenge due to the intense pressure of work and part-time work, coupled with developmental work there never seems to have been a time of calm and consolidation. I have given up a lot of my own and family time to work and study, this was not a good idea. I did lose the ability to compartmentalise work and leisure, something I have been very good at in the past and so despite a challenging and demanding role something I would normally be delighted with) I began to lose sight of life away from work. I'm sure that this pressure on time is normal in teaching but the ability to step back is vital.*" David feels that *in the last twelve months* [work] *was very, very intrusive and, and that's why I've[....] had to come to this decision to say right there are certain things that aren't going to be done and I am now off for the weekend and so, [....] I do lots of sailing, competitive sailing but I was just missing races because I had [....] academic work to do at the weekend.* David goes on to say that in the twelve months he is making "*a positive effort to say right, finish, I'm not going to do anything today and get on with leisure and social life and particularly with the extra study with the PhD. We're not going to see the grandkids this weekend because I'm too busy and perhaps I need to recognise actually that life is a bit too short to do that.*"

In her book "*Mindset*", Carol Dweck (2017) points out the way we view ourselves can affect the way we lead our lives. She suggests that mindset can be seen from two points of view. Those who have a fixed mindset believe that personal qualities cannot be change. It is then a matter of having to continually convince yourself as to whether you succeed, look smart, be accepted or feel like being a winner. Those with the growth mindset acknowledge and recognise that basic qualities can be developed, and aspirations achieved through training and learning. The growth mindset can be best described as someone who has the passion and commitment to seeing something through even in the most challenging of circumstances. They continually stretch to improve themselves by seeking new challenges. It is important to recognise that mindsets can be changed. Actively engaging with changing the mindset can lead to changes in the way you live your life. It is important not to take things personally. However, this can be difficult to manage if the mindset is framed by negative emotions and feeling. Thinking about work when trying to relax or engage in other interests can preoccupy the mind to such an extent that trying to relax can be stressful in itself. It is, therefore, helpful to find an interest that allows the mind to refocus. For example, concentrating on sailing, or learning a musical instrument can allow the mind to regain control and to relax a little. However, engaging in such interests can take time that could be used to undertake work. It is a challenging dilemma that can take time.

Acceptance

Acceptance is where a person resigns themselves to what is happening. In this study 65% of participants say that they do this "*a lot*" or "*a medium amount.*" Trevor comments that he does make the effort so as not to let "*things get to me too much and doing all I can sometimes accepting that's all that can be done.*" Whereas, David doesn't "*accept change is for change's sake. We need to, [....] look at change and examine the analytical but [....] there are times when I just might want to stand up at a meeting and say this is a load of cobblers but that's not going to get anybody anywhere*". David laughs at this point but makes an interesting and valid point. Robert feel confident within his team of "*four people. With them I can be really open and say what I feel and they understand my points of view and sometimes I'd say even question me and make me come to some sort of sense because what they tell me actually makes sense and I'm wrong. I accept it and change my mind and so no problem at all.*" Whereas it is good to share feelings and thoughts with others, sometimes it may be better to hold your own counsel and to keep thoughts, feelings and emotions to oneself. Information that is shared may be passed on to others who may misunderstand or misuse it. Information that is shared may be used against you giving rise to feelings of increased stress and anxiety. It is therefore helpful to recognise that context and being able to trust others are important factors. As Robert adds "*it depends on the person I am talking to and this is a question of power of relationships.*"

Positive reframing

Positive reframing is where a person sees things from a positive viewpoint. In the study 58% of participants say that they do this "*a lot*" or "*a medium amount*" Diane advises that she allows herself to "*work in the evenings and I do allow myself to work at weekends sometimes because it's necessary to get the work done and so it does interfere with work/life balance*". However, Diane explains that she puts aside "*two nights a week where [....] I work with my partner teaching dance but that's my pleasure. That's me demarcating time for me to have pleasure and so when I demarcate time for a pleasure activity, I safeguard that, [....] balance.*" Diane is new to undergraduate teaching and uses escape mechanisms such as allocating time to focus on teaching dance with their partner. Similarly, David came to higher education after a career with the Police. When he is asked "*To what extent do you think your emotion management skills have changed as you have gained experience/ age, through your career?*" David responds by saying that "*generally they develop well.*" However, in the last "*maybe knocked back a little bit*" He adds that "*being able to recognise this, and I think having to two careers, has helped but [....] there is an awful lot of [....] growing up to do within that career and almost teen angst at the ripe old age really.*" It does appear that there is an overlap between coping strategies. Diane and David both appear to use active coping and positive reframing. Diane uses dancing and David sailing.

To help her relax, Mary finds it helpful to sit down with "*a silly sci-fi novel and a glass of wine, umm, but I really start unwinding when I start cooking dinner*". She adds that she is now "*I'm in my 50's and just [....] think that's just the reality and I'm[....] accepted of that so unwind, unwind, I really unwind.*" What is apparent is the effort that is given to separating work from home life, making time to spend on interests such as dancing, sailing, reading a novel and cooking a meal.

Emotional support

Emotional support is where a person seeks comfort from someone else. In the questionnaire/ survey participants are given the statement "*I've been getting emotional support from others.*" 14% advise they do this "*a lot*" and 34% confirm they do this a "*medium amount*" (total 48%). They are also given the statement "*I've been getting comfort and understanding from someone.*" 17% advise that they do this "*a lot*" and 35% advise that they do this a "*medium amount*" (a total of 52%). This suggests that approximately 50% of academics gain comfort from others using emotional support. A really good example of this is from John who explained that *"I don't like complaining really. So I don't, complain to colleagues, [....] well certainly not to my manager, [....] but I [....] take it home with me, [....] where my wife gets a ear full. That's [....] a problem and then [....] on the way to work [....] kind of ruminating over things and just can never let it go and you know, it's quite, quite stressful really."*

As well as emotional support, John also appears to gain instrumental support. Seeking emotional support from his wife, rather than colleagues, suggests that emotional and instrumental support is important to John. It may be that John is concerned with possible reaction and impact on professional relationships and career prospects and prefers to seek emotional support at home and away from the workplace. He may prefer to express their emotions with someone he feels that they can trust and that there will be no professional impact on their career. It does, however, raise the question as to how strong and resilient the personal marital relationship needs to be to withstand the emotional outpourings that may occur. The findings suggest that academics experience ways of coping that may be context dependent. For example: where one spouse or work colleague may listen, another may not wish/ be prepared to.

When married to her former spouse, Mary feels it really challenging to have any form of social engagement as he has a *"narcissistic personality disorder and also had sociopathic tendencies"*. After years away from academia, Mary is now back at university as an *"adjunct, temporary, part time, low end of the totem pole, because I've changed organisations so often, I feel like I'm always a satellite. I'm always peripheral. I'm never a member of the in group and so that gets very frustrating. I'm [....] very anxious to achieve a position where people will listen to me and pay attention to me and recognise that I have something to offer. [....] I've been really marginalised [....] I don't think I'm being hypersensitive about it."* Mary adds that *"I think I've really honestly have been marginalised in the last 15 years. [....] I was marginalised in my science and, and I'm an outsider coming in to education and having to thread that path, I'm not really certain yet"*.

Mary also finds it difficult to gain emotional support as she does not have a close family member to whom she can share her feelings. Being in a position of someone who is temporary, she may be reticent in, or not able to, seek emotional support from work colleagues. Mary adds that *"it's not something I can deal with right now and so it just gets put away [....] If I dwell on that too much [....] I get just frozen because so much of that is outside of my control at this point."* To help them cope Mary advises that she has *"a glass of wine and* [read] *very silly novels"*.

Litman and Lunsford (2009) find that coping includes both problem-focused coping and emotion-focused coping. In other words, where a person seeks support from others using emotional support, as in the instance of John who seeks emotional support from his wife, he also appears to show restraint within the workplace suggesting that he also uses problem-focused coping. Whereas Lazarus and Folkman (1984) refer to an imbalance between the ability and demands of coping it is still necessary to use problem-focused coping to help respond to stressful experiences.

Instrumental support

Instrumental support is where advice is gained from others. Approximately 50% of the participants who respond to the questionnaire/ survey say that they did this. The findings show that when provided with the statement that "*I've been getting help and advice from other people*," 51% of participants respond saying that they either did this "*a lot*" or "*a medium amount*". When given the statement "*I've been trying to get advice or help from other people about what to do,*" 48% of people respond by saying that they did this "*a lot*" or a "*medium amount*".

Tina identifies a challenging experience they have experienced with colleagues "*where my ideas were being blocked in a meeting consistently. I did speak up and say that I was unhappy about only the chair person's ideas being accepted and this was unacceptable. I wasn't happy about this. I was glad I spoke up there and then as this influenced the meeting but then I heard later that the chair person had been upset that I had spoken up. However, I think that this is a manipulative way of getting their own way and I know I was right to intervene.*" Tina points out that she is "*quite assertive [....] but that doesn't [....] stop the good relationship with that person and with other people in the team.*" She adds that she is not confrontational and prefers to ""*go away and think about it [....] and plan a good way of managing it rather than allowing emotions to spill over where I get angry or that person gets angry and upset*".

Simon relates a problem where he feels that he could not seek support from his line manager. This followed a complaint raised by a student. Simon comments that the manager "*was willing to give, [....] the students free for all [....] they haven't got my back here so if I have a problem I wouldn't have felt comfortable going to them*" suggesting their way of coping was *avoidance* and a feeling of *helplessness*, where he is unable to do anything about the situation (Argyris, 1957; Seligman, 1974). Simon subsequently left this university and, in their new place of work, they "*feel quite comfortable*". He adds that *"If everyone gets on fairly well which I think we do it can work quite well because if there is a problem, everyone backs you and you know everyone is aware of it whereas with a closed office you tend to be, you know it tends to be a little cliquey.*" This implies that interpersonal relationships and the need to vent emotions are important in helping Simon cope and this is supported by comments made later on in the interview where he comments that: *"Even when I was working at* (company named -before they became an academic) *sometimes looking back I was doing some of the things I did at the time at my previous university, [....] I was venting. [....] if there was something I felt, [....] was really inefficient. [....] I was thinking, why do we have to do this? [....] if there was something there that wound me up I tend to vent and as I [....] became more and more aware of this as we were going along, [....] when it got to the point, [....] some people were noticing it that's when I thought, [....] I think you need to [....] work on calming down and think of how you can manage this a bit better. [....] when someone says to you, I think that you are coming across as a bit angry."*

David is someone who came into academia late in their career, after 30 years in the police. He points out that *"when I first [....] started in academia as a [....] lecturer I was very over awed by the academic stature of colleagues and, and was quite in awe of somebody [....] who's title was doctor or professor and [I] tended to be very quiet and not say much but then I, [....] realised that [....] I was employed because of my particular expertise and my knowledge and that the knowledge is the important thing so, [....] I then started to speak, much more prepared to speak out at meetings and [....] actually people were listening to me, that we all in life have our specialities and our areas of knowledge and the fact that somebody has professor or doctor or whatever or something in front of their name doesn't mean they understand your subject. You know, [....] they're ordinary people."* David advises that to help him cope with interpersonal and stressful experiences: *"I walk into work through a fairly [....] deprived area; when I come into work every morning there are people sleeping in doorways and it's freezing cold. Now that to me is' when life's getting really bad."* David adds that *"So sometimes it's very difficult to understand why I and myself feel like that when probably, you know, one of those people in the door way has a lot more to worry about, all I have to do is worry about thinking about getting the marking finished I feel quite good about it."*

Tina is in a similar situation to David; someone who came to academia late in their career. Within a few days of them starting their new job at the university they *"remember talking to, [....] our manager at the time and he said you know are you ok, is it all working out ok? And I said oh yes we can do this, you know, it'll be fine. Umm, and, and teaching or maybe I'm a bit naive as well, umm teaching on subjects that I hadn't taught on before umm but just working hard to be able to try to make everything work and really having a sense of responsibility for making it all work and disappointment as well that students weren't happy"*. Advising management that they are under stress or complaining and expressing to management that they can't cope, could be regarded as a slight on professional integrity, suggesting that the academic may lack the strengths required that is expected of them in their role. However, when the academic seeks support from managers the experience could lead to *"a loss [....] of caution; the kind of trust that we have for the university as a bigger organisation and our management structures" (Tina).* In this instance, Tina is not able to express her true feelings suggesting that instrumental support needs to be two way which would necessitate each person being willing to speak and to listen. However, this may not have been appropriate, as Simon points out whereas they could vent problems to close colleagues, *"there are obviously some people I felt I didn't, I felt that I couldn't do that and my boss at my previous university and my boss here. If I've got problems then I felt like, I could vent, I felt that I could vent them and could discuss them constructively."*

The caution that Tina gives to seeking support is understandable. It does appear that context is a factor in gaining instrumental support. However, it also appears dependent upon trust. In other words, the academic can trust that the person they seek support from is going to deal with the matter in a considered and thoughtful manner –that emotional intelligence is demonstrated within the instrumental support. As Simon points out, seeking instrumental support appears to depend *"*[up]*on the context, [....] how well do you know the culture, how well do you know your colleagues, and what your colleagues are like".*

Robert is head of a department and comments that *"Teachers are not just that. They're persons. They're people with wives of their own which are mostly concealed from the community and you just look at them as Professor x or Professor y and Professor z and they have names, they have children, they have husbands, they have mates, they have a preferred bar where they go to. They have their own community of friends. That is one of the things I try to do: it's to know the people I work with."* It may be that Robert has more experience than Tina and Simon and at a position in the university that provides him with greater confidence and assurance to engage with colleagues. It may be that it is in his nature and part of personality. The point Simon makes about context does appear valid as different circumstances/ situations can give rise to feelings of frustrations. The lack of support and trust by management means that Simon could vent his frustrations with colleagues who may then need to cope with the matter themselves. This could have negative repercussion where colleagues feel uncomfortable listening and empathising, when they have their own pressures and stresses to cope with. However, there could be a reciprocal approach where others are like minded and instrumental support is shared. This supports the findings of Gillespie, Walsh, Winefield, Dua and Stough (2001) in which they find support from colleagues is an important factor to help them cope.

The findings from the questionnaire/ survey suggest that, of the 50% who advise that they gained instrumental support, it could have been with friends, colleagues and/ or line manager. Detail is lacking. This is the advantage of undertaking semi-structured interviews that give rise to factors that may otherwise have not been identified. It doesn't just appear to be context that is an important factor. Trust also appears to be significant. It is having trust in the person from whom instrumental support is sought. The trust being to provide empathetic understanding and to deal with the matter in a sensitive and considered manner.

Self-distraction

Self-distraction is where a person tries to take their mind off the problem. In the questionnaire/ survey, 42% of participants use self-distraction "*a lot*" or "*a medium amount*". David copes with challenging situations, including interpersonal relationships by exercising. He explains that "*I run and I walk and I do mountain biking. [....] I am more productive coming back when I have spent the day on the hills.*" Elizabeth copes with confrontational challenges with senior managers that when she comes home she "*deliberately did things to bring my adrenalin levels down. So I, [....] I started drawing again and went out for nice lunches. I put more effort in not being at work and making not being at work nice and distracting*".

Humour

Humour is simply making fun of the experience Robert is a long-established member of the university faculty who has risen to head of department. He explains that his wife is "*also a teacher here so [....] in terms of conversation we try not to talk about professional issues, but they always come 'p and that's also an element of friction and [....]'because we're not happy [....] our children tend to just go away as soon as we start talking about work because they know that something is about to go bad. So [....] that is not a very nice feeling and anguish of having to work in these conditions is stressful to the point of feeling that you [n]either have a social life or a family life.........*" To help them cope, Robert comments that *"I'm the sort of guy who actually tries to do a lot of humour...........trying to build some sort of fantasy around it so you can actually cope"*.

Venting

In the questionnaire/ survey, 37% of participants advised that they used venting as a coping strategy "*a lot*" or "*a medium amount*". Venting occurs where a person expresses negative feelings and emotions. As discussed above, Simon vents but only with colleagues that he can trust. This suggests that Simon may seek both emotional and instrumental support. However, it is apparent that reflecting on experience. Simon also uses planning and positive reframing to help cope, as shortly after the challenging experience he moves to another university.

Rather than venting in company of others, Robert confirms that he regulates his emotions by "*having a piece of paper and I start doodling. Sometimes, I just keep silent. Most of the times I close my eyes and pretend I'm not affected,* [and] *to calm myself down, think of what I'm going to say and how I'm going to say it. Sometimes, I make an excuse and say If you don't mind, I need to go to the toilet or I'll be back in a second. Sometimes, I even look at my cell phone and say, whoops, I've got a problem to solve and will be back. Most of the times I regulate emotions that are negative that way.*" Robert expands by explaining that *"I try and go out and explode either in the bathroom or somewhere else or by making drawings that would probably be un proper to show to people because I express those people in terms of drawing. [....] Sometimes, I even write what I would like to tell people, or what I'd like to call that person. Well, I'm getting a bit, how do you say, intimate with you. Sometimes I even write you (expletive used) exclamation mark. You know, what the hell are you talking about, I just write it for myself and that's the way of regulating my emotions and say "what a load of* (expletive used)*"*.

When asked "*What type of situations at work tend to challenge your emotion management skills?*" John responds by saying that he bottles up "*my emotions, well making sure they don't, [....] spill over really, which they do. I'm very good* [keeping] *feelings inside and not[....] venting my frustration, [....], in meetings really. [....] I won't use foul language ....*" John prefers to bottle things up and then vent his frustration, with his wife when he arrives home. He comments that "*I just tell my wife about it really and she's very patient and [....] she listens but not really much she can do about it, but apart from that I think it's just trying to think of ways of improving my situation really [....] surely other people must be recognising the unfairness's [....], the disparities, in the work place and yet people seem to be gliding, you know, happy, or at least when I see them people don't seem to be complaining as much as I do.*"

Being able to trust in work colleagues appears to be an influencing factor as to whether or not a person is able to vent and express feelings, thoughts and emotions within the workplace. Variables such as cultural context and background may influence how and from whom support is sought. For example: it may not be considered acceptable to complain/ to vent or to seek support and advice from managers. It may be seen as a sign of weakness. It is therefore understandable that academics may seek emotional and instrumental support from those he/ she feels closer to, as in John's example where he seeks support from his wife.

Self-blame

Self-blame is where a person blames themselves for the problem. It may arise following childhood experience where pressure is placed on the child to be perfect and is also associated where the child is blamed when things don't go in the way the parent wants or expects. When compared with other coping strategies, self-blame comes lower down with 32% of participants advising that they do this *"a lot"* and a *"medium amount."* Anxiety may influence how a person responds and rather than externalising the problem, it is internalised leading to greater anxiety and stress. However, none of those interviewed use the term "self-blame" or refer to it. However, Tina explains that she *"had a very hard, heavy workload [....] making it difficult to [....] manage the emotional demands. Oh my gosh there might be, there might be a complaint. My name might be mentioned in the complaint and that's going to look really bad for me."* Tina adds that *"I think quite anxious actually and a little [....] paranoid and wary that I may not be supported. I was aware that [....] my thoughts were becoming quite catastrophic about the incident or this kind of accusation, [....] that I hadn't been supportive. I think what's difficult is because I'm a therapist by background, the idea that I wouldn't be supportive to a student is umm. It's an interesting thing because as a therapist you would be supportive, but as a lecturer, you know, I'm not the student's therapist so there is a line there and there's a boundary to keep there as well."*

Religion

Many people take comfort in having a strong religious conviction that can help them cope with challenging experiences. 24% of participants said that they used religion to help them cope *"a lot"* and *"a medium amount"*. This was also lower when compared with other coping strategies. In the study undertaken by Perez, et al. (2015) of Latino adults in the USA, 58% of participants said that they used religion to help them cope. This is an interesting finding and may be cultural dependent reflecting on the percentage of people who attend church. For example, in an informal gathering, I was in discussion with a group of Muslim students in the United Arab Emirates about coping strategies they use and what they felt about such tools as mindfulness and meditation. One student asks, *"Why do we need things like mindfulness" when we have Allah"*. It does appear that religion is used as a coping strategy and may be more associated with those who have a greater commitment to their faith.

As well as context-dependent, it also appears that culture and background may also be important factors to consider and care should be given to generalise findings to a wider population.

Behavioural disengagement

Lazarus (1966) refers to problem focused (engagement) coping and, emotion-focused (disengagement) coping. Behavioural disengagement occurs when a person gives up trying to cope with a problem and is associated with emotion-focused coping. A total of 11% of participants said that they did this "*a lot*" or "*a medium amount*". None of those interviewed identified this within discussions. In an anecdote given to me while at a conference, I was informed by a senior lecturer, that relationships between him and his line manager had become strained and difficult to handle as he was unsure how the manager would act and respond. On occasions the manager was an attentive listener and on other occasions there was confrontation to such a point that the manager raised their voice, using language that the senior lecturer felt was bullying and intimidating. The line manager criticised him for a number of work and personal related matters that included the content of his workshops and also for his grammar and spelling. As well as being emotionally affected the senior lecturer also experienced physical illnesses that he had not faced previously. The senior lecturer tried to address the matter with his line manager explaining how and what they were feeling. However, the confrontational management style continued to cause stress and anxiety to such a point that it developed into feelings of depression. The relationship appeared to become more fragmented and the senior lecturer felt that the best recourse of action was to minimise contact with his line manager as much as possible. Unfortunately, meetings with the line manager continued to be fractious and after approximately twelve months it came to the point that the senior lecturer left the university.

Maybe this senior lecturer could have tried to be more self-assured and to try and resolve the matter by discussion. However, he informed me that after several meetings with his line manager that his self-esteem was "*shattered*". He had to interact with students and colleagues and his enthusiasm and positive nature was severely affected by continuous thoughts and negative emotions brought on by the about comments made to him during the meetings with his line manager. Leaving the university may have been a big decision; leaving a career that he had built up over the previous twenty (20) years or so. However, it was very clear that continuing was intolerable and likely lead to greater psychological and physical illnesses. When I met him, he advised that since leaving the university, his negative emotions had been reduced and he no longer had physical nor psychological illnesses, including feelings of depression.

Denial

Denial is refusing to believe that something has happened. 10% of participants confirm that they do this "*a lot*" or a "*medium amount*" whereas 90% feel that they "*don't do this at all*" or only "*a little bit*". Only one participant in the interviews felt that she may engage in denial. Tina relates a story where she felt that she was on "*a treadmill*"…...*I really was on a treadmill [....]. I've got a family, children, [I]t was a case of going from one moment to the next trying to keep afloat, [I]t was a very strong sense of [....] just keep going, just keep going, [I]t's quite interesting really when you look back at times like that as I'm not sure how in tune I was with my feelings or my emotions or how aware I was of being stressed. I remember talking to, [....] our manager at the time and he said you know are you ok, is it all working out ok? And I said oh yes we can do this, you know, it'll be fine. [....] maybe I was a bit naive as well, [....] teaching on subjects that I hadn't taught on before [....] but just working hard to be able to try to make everything work and really having a sense of responsibility for making it all work and disappointment as well that students weren't happy.*" Tina adds that this experience was close to when she started work at the university. Having now been at the university for "*six years if I had that situation to manage, I would be a lot more able to manage it.*"

The challenge with denial is that the person needs to remember that they refused to believe that something happened (Marks, Murray, Evans and Estacio, 2015). Denying something that has happened suggests that they seek to forget. How can you *purposefully* forget something? Furthermore, an academic may be in denial but not recognise it. The question may be more inclined to suggest that participants place the event to one side in preference of another option. Maybe the word denial is too strong a word as it does raise difficulties in interpreting the question.

Substance use

Substance use is where a person uses drugs or alcohol to help them cope. When given the statement "*I've been using alcohol or other drugs to help me through it*" 78% of participants advise that they "*don't do this at all*" and a further 15% said that they "*do this a little bit*" (a total of 93%).

In response to the statement "*I've been using alcohol or other drugs to make myself feel better*" 74% advise that they "*don't do this at all*" and 19% say that that they "*do this a little bit*" (a total of 93%).

The initial thought when looking at the data is that it is heartening to see that very few participants fall back on substance use. However, it doesn't necessarily mean that everyone is being honest and maybe under/ over exaggerating. The findings also show that 7% (37 people) used substances a "*me-

dium amount" or "*a lot*". Whereas this was considered to be a reasonably small percentage/number it is an interesting finding. The challenge is that well-being may be perceived from a subjective viewpoint, the hedonistic internalised view of the world, with each person having their own thoughts and perspectives of well-being or; from a more objective eudaimonic perspective where assessment is outside looking in at the person. This then gives rise to challenges as to assessing, evaluating and measuring well-being and the challenges of being able to generalise from the findings. Substance use may not be considered, by the person responding, as having a negative impact on their well-being (hedonistic viewpoint). However, there may be personal consequences of substance use that are not being acknowledged and accepted by the participant that can be observed by colleagues, friends and family (eudaimonic viewpoint).

The table below provides examples and summary of ways in which interview participants cope.

Table 4.10. Examples of how those interviewed cope.

No	Name	Years of experience	Observation	Feelings	Emotion Carver et al., 1989)	Ways participants cope
1	Simon	3	Dependent of culture, context and colleagues	Anger	(Lack of) Instrumental support venting	Physical activity
2	Trevor	2	Out of their control	Frustration	Active coping	Finding places to go (escaping)
3	John	8	Doesn't like complaining	Frustration	Venting	With wife
4	David	6	Volume of work	Frustration	Active coping	Physical activity
5	Tina	6	Emotional response appeared to be consciously aware after the experience	Frustration	Initial denial, positive reframing	Physical activity, talking to family and friends
6	Diane	7	"everybody being at the end of their tether"	Tired, upset, disappointed	Acceptance	Physical activity (dancing, walking)

| 7 | Mary | 25 (time out for family) | A feeling of being marginalised | Anxious, angry, frustration | Acceptance, self-distraction | *"my teaching, my writing, my studies"* |
| 8 | Robert | 31 | Management responsibility brings different and potentially greater emotionally challenging experiences | Anxious, worried | Humour, Instrumental support | Creating *"networks of people who support you in all respects in terms of what goes on with you as a professional"* |

Diane is new to undergraduate teaching and uses coping mechanisms such as allocating time to focus on teaching dance with their partner. Similarly, David, who came to higher education after a career with the Police, appears to separate work from their home life, making time to spend on interests such as sailing, and using positive reframing to help them cope. Mary also appears to do this. However, she also suggests that they have become *"emotionally shielded and maybe it's just age"*. The interesting finding that comes out of this study is that each person appears to have their own strategy of coping and that coping strategies may overlap with each other. Furthermore, there appear to be factors that influence the way participants cope that include experience, context, and trust in colleagues/ line manager.

The table below provides a summary of the main findings identifying overlapping coping strategies that participants use.

Table 4.11. Examples of coping strategies used by those interviewed.

	Interview participant	Coping strategy	Coping strategy	Coping strategy	Coping strategy
1	David	Active coping	Positive reframing		
2	Simon	Emotional support	Positive reframing	Instrumental support	Planning
3	Tina	Denial	Self-distraction		
4	Robert	Humour	Acceptance		
5	Mary	Acceptance	Positive reframing		
6	Trevor	Active coping	Positive reframing		

| 7 | John | Venting | Emotional support |
| 8 | Diane | Acceptance | Self-distraction |

The table below provides examples of where there is an overlap where, for example, a participant may use dysfunctional coping such as venting while at the same time seek instrumental support.

Table 4.12. Coping with interpersonal relationships (interviews).

Participant	Coping strategy (emotional/ instrumental)	Comments	Approach (overlap) to coping	Participant
Mary	Emotional support	Adjunct/ temporary	Always a satellite	Outside my control/ put it away (Denial)
Robert	Emotional/ Instrumental support		Teachers are not just that. They're persons.	Humour *Empathy (Interviewers observation)*
Tina	Instrumental support	New to job	Loss of trust	Acceptance
Simon	Instrumental support	Context	Close colleagues	Venting
David	Instrumental support	New to job	In awe of colleagues	Acceptance
John	Emotional support	Take it home	Wife gets an ear full	Ruminates (venting)

The examples shown are only a few but highlight the variations in circumstances, experience and context that each academic finds themselves in. This could apply to every one of those who completed the questionnaire/ survey. It also identifies the challenges when undertaking research in social science.

Comparison between studies

In a study of two hundred (200) Latino adults in the USA, Perez, Gavin and Diaz (2015), find that the most frequently used coping mechanism are: active coping (70%), planning (64%), acceptance (58%), religion (58%) and reframing (57%). Most participants appear to respond to stressors using adaptive and maladaptive coping mechanisms. In comparison to Perez et al. 's (2015) study, the findings from this study show the following: active coping 68%, planning 74%, acceptance 65%, religion 24%, reframing 58%. Planning being the highest. The findings suggest similarity where active coping, planning and acceptance are the highest three (3). The biggest difference is religion, where Perez et al. (2015)

report 58% use religion to help them cope. In this study, 24% of the sample use religion to help them cope. This difference could be explained by different sample population influenced by culture, background and environment.

Summing up

Each person appears to have their own strategy of coping and that coping strategies may overlap with each other. The findings from the questionnaire show that the coping strategy that participants use a lot or a medium amount, is planning (76%) and active coping (68%). Acceptance is third with 65%. Denial and substance use is the lowest with 10% and 7% respectively. This suggests that of the five hundred and thirty-three (533) participants approximately thirty-seven (37) use substances "*a lot*" or "*a medium amount*". These are academics who are likely to have regular contact with students and colleagues which raises interesting questions as to how well they are able to function when under substance influence.

The interview data provides valuable insight into individual experiences, which have been exemplified in this chapter. It reveals information that may not have been identified using a questionnaire alone. Each academic appears to have their individual experiences when coping with stressful experiences and this is highlighted in the examples discussed in this chapter.

It does appear that to cope more successfully, academics should find ways of improving the way they cope with stressful experiences that could, in turn, help improve work/life balance. For example, academics could participate in physical activity or simply engage with family members allowing them to focus on other interests besides work. However, disengaging from work can be extremely challenging.

The findings from the interview data suggest that each person has their own ways of coping, depending on the context and, the way that they cope may differ. It is apparent that they do not use one particular coping strategy but may engage in several where one may overlap with another. This concurs with the findings from other studies, that coping is individual to the person and their personality (for example: Bolger and Zuckerman, 1995; Gomez, Bounds, Holmberg, Fullarton and Gomez, 1999; Gomez, Holmberg, Bounds, Fullarton and Gomez, 1999; Moos and Holahan, 2013).

Chapter 5

Personality and individual differences

This chapter builds on earlier chapters and discusses the relationship personality has with emotional intelligence, coping and stress personality. Notwithstanding the studies undertaken, only part is understood about emotional intelligence, stress and coping. Similarly, debate exists as to exactly what personality is. Carver and Connor-Smith (2010) point out that individual differences make up each person's personality. Personality traits can influence the way a person copes and is an imperative part of being able to cope (Bolger and Zuckerman, 1995; De Longis and Holtzman, 2005; Khan, Siraj, and Li, 2011). It can also have an influence on outcomes (Strelau, 2001). However, it is dependent upon the individual; how they perceive, and react to stressful experiences (Terry, 1994). It is what makes each person differ from one another. In his book *"Personality- a psychological interpretation"*, Gordon Allport (1937) identifies fifty (50) possible definitions. The pragmatic view put forward by William James (1907) is that the definition of personality is dependent upon the setting. Sigmund Freud (1923, 1933) adds to the discussion, suggesting that personality is made up of the id, ego and superego. The id being the childlike self; the ego that deals with reality and; the superego is knowing what is right and what is wrong- the social conscience. There are, therefore, different views and understanding as to what personality is. To try and reduce the definition of personality into a few words is understandably challenging. However, personality appears to be internal states of mind that include thoughts and emotions, that may help explain behaviour.

Background

Allport and Odbert (1936) studied the English dictionary to find approximately eighteen thousand (18,000) words believing that personality characteristics/ traits are included into the English language. A trait being characteristics of the personality. This may be an interesting exercise, however there are significant drawbacks. For example, it is almost impossible to comprehend due to the volume. Furthermore, words may be used in other languages to describe personality traits that are not included in the English dictionary. Cattell (1947) follows up this study by reducing the list of traits to sixteen (16) dimensions, as shown in the table below.

Table 5.1. Cattell's sixteen dimensions of personality.

1	Cool/ warm
2	Reasoning- concrete/ abstract thinking
3	Sensitive- affected by feelings
4	Emotional stability
5	Submissive/ dominant
6	Liveliness- sober/ enthusiastic
7	Rule conscious- expedient/ conscientiousness
8	Social- shy/ bold, tough/ tender
9	Vigilance- trusting/ suspicious
10	Abstractedness- practical/ imaginative
11	Forthright/ shrewd
12	Self-assured/ apprehensive
13	Open to change- conservative/ experimenter
14	Self-reliance- group orientated/ self-sufficient
15	Perfectionism -undisciplined/ controlled
16	Tension- relaxed/ tense

Source: Cattell (1947).

Eysenck (1947) applies a similar approach, reducing the dimensions to three (3): extrovert, neurotic and, psychotic. Later, Tupes and Christal (1961) pulls together data sets from different sources, including Cattell, and identifies five (5) dimensions as shown in the table below.

Table 5.2. Tupes and Christal's five dimensions.

	Factor	Dimension
1	i.	Surgency
2	ii.	Agreeableness
3	iii.	Dependability
4	iv.	Emotional stability
5	v.	Culture

Source: Tupes and Christal (1961).

Around the same time, Norman (1963) undertakes his own study and obtains similar findings. Following a review of existing literature, Lewis Goldberg (1990, 1992) provides an alternative description of personality and is the first to refer to the *"big 5"* factor structure. It is he, together with Digman (1990), who revive the research into personality traits. Digman (1997) introduces the two higher meta traits *"factor alpha"* and *"factor Beta"* that are subsequently described by DeYoung (2006) as *"stability"* (factor Alpha) and *"plasticity"* (factor Beta). Costa and McCrae's (1992) subsequently develop the *"big five"* personality traits into those summarised in the table below.

Table 5.3. The *big five*.

No	Digman's Factor	Dimensions	Trait facets
1	Factor Beta	Extroversion	Warmth, gregariousness, assertiveness, activity, excitement seeking, positive emotions
2	Factor Beta	Openness	Fantasy, aesthetics, feelings, actions, idea, values
3	Factor Alpha	Agreeableness	Trust, straightforwardness, altruism, compliance, modesty, tender mindedness
4	Factor Alpha	Conscientiousness	Competence, order, dutifulness, achievement striving, self-discipline, deliberation
5	Factor Alpha	Neuroticism	Anxiety, angry, hostility, depression, self-consciousness, impulsiveness, vulnerability
		Source: Adapted from Digman (1997) and Costa and McCrae (1992).	

The traits identified by Costa and McCrae should be seen as dimensions, along which a person can be placed rather than clearly identifying them as being of a particular personality type. Like many other studies associated with social science, this instrument is self-report and gives rise to challenges of reliability. For example, each person may have a different perspective and understanding of terms such as happiness, well-being and worry. Their overall temperament may influence how they score. Furthermore, scores may vary depending on how the person is feeling when they take the report. If they are having a *"bad day"* they may score lower than if they were having a *"great day"*. The challenge is that the base level differs for each person. It is not an exact science, and this is often the case when undertaking social studies. However, Costa and McCrae's *"big five"* has been tested and studies suggest that it stands up to reliability and validity.

Emotions and emotional intelligence may be part of personality but there are different views and opinions and a lack of consensual agreement. Different models and theories have been put forward to measure emotional intelligence. As discussed in an earlier chapter, Salovey and Mayer (1990) regard emotional intelligence as being an ability that is associated with cognition. The mixed model put forward by Goleman (1995) and Bar-On (1997) include personality traits into their models. Petrides (2009) and Petrides and Furnham (2001) directly link trait emotional intelligence with Costa and McCrae's (1992) *"big five"* personality traits. There is a lack of consensus. There are distinct approaches to measuring emotional intelligence, however, it is apparent from the academic studies undertaken on the topic that there is evidence to suggest that it does exist. The studies also suggest that it is possible to identify personality traits, in particular, the *big 5*. For example, Eysenck (1965,1991) provides an interesting slant where he suggests that smokers can be identified from non-smokers by their personality type. He finds that heavier smokers are more likely to be more extrovert. They crave excitement, take chances and are more impulsive. He also adds that those who are extrovert are more inclined to lose their temper more quickly, tend to be aggressive and not always reliable. Vollrath and Torgersen (2000) argues that those with a more positive and outgoing personality are more inclined towards positive psychological health. Whereas, those with more of a negative personality are more inclined towards distress. Those who are more inclined towards neuroticism are likely to experience stress from interpersonal interactions and regard such experiences as potentially threatening (Penley and Tomaka, 2002).

Personality and coping

Lazarus and Folkman (1984) argue that coping is a conscious and intentional response to stressors. However, there appears to be a difference of opinion. For example, Eisenberg, Fabes, and Guthrie (1997) consider that coping is associated with involuntary responses, in other words- part of a person's make up or personality, suggesting that there is a link/ correlation between personality and coping. If coping and personality are related, personality can influence the particular coping strategy selected and also influence the outcome (Vollrath, 2001). Therefore, coping should be redefined and regarded as a personality process (For example: Kato and Pedersen, 2005; Fickova, 2001; McWilliams, Cox, and Enns, 2003). The table below provides examples of studies undertaken that either associate coping as being innate (part of personality) or learned (a conscious and intentional response).

Table 5.4. Personality and coping.

1	**Innate** (part of personality)	<ul><li>Bolger and Zuckerman, 1995;</li><li>De Longis and Holtzman, 2005;</li><li>Eisenberg, Fabes, and Guthrie (1997);</li><li>Fickova, 2001;</li><li>Kato and Pedersen, 2005;</li><li>Khan, Siraj, and Li, 2011</li><li>McWilliams, Cox, and Enns, 2003;</li><li>Skinner, 1995).</li></ul>
2	**Learned** (a conscious and intentional response to stressors)	Lazarus and Folkman (1984)

Positive psychological strength and the *big 5* personality dimensions appear to be significantly related to the way people cope (Costa and McCrae, 1992). For example, those with high extroversion, openness and conscientiousness are more likely to engage with problem-focused coping and regard an experience as a challenge rather than a threat. Neuroticism is an exception, as those who are more inclined towards neuroticism are less engaged with the coping mechanism. He/ she is likely to experience stress from interpersonal interactions and regard such experiences as potentially threatening. There is also a greater relationship between personality and coping in those who experience high or chronic stress (Connor-Smith and Flachsbart, 2007; Moos and Holahan, 2003). The table below provides examples of researchers and their findings associated with personality types.

Table 5.5. Examples of research undertaken on personality type.

No	Personality type (Costa and McCrae (1992)	Findings	Examples of researchers
1	Extroversion	Better Physical health	Carver and Connor-Smith (2010)
2	Extroversion	Greater well being	DeNeve and Cooper (1998); Steel, Schmidt and Shultz (2008)
3	Conscientiousness	Less likely to externalise or internalise problems	Malouff, Thorsteinsson and Schutte (2006)
4	Neuroticism	Lower coping strengths; more inclined to interpersonal stress and regard potential stressful experiences as threatening	Penley and Tomaka (2002); Deary, Egan, Gibson, Austin, Brand and Kellaghan, (1996)

5	Neuroticism	People are more inclined towards anxiety and depression	Malouff et al. (2006)
6	Neuroticism	More inclined towards poor health	Chida and Hamer (2008)
7	Openness	Those in old age experienced loss of openness to feelings	Terracciano, McCrae, Brant and Costa (2005)

Using the brief COPE scale (Carver, 1997) on a sample of two hundred (200) Malaysian students, Khan et al. (2011) finds that positive psychological strength and the *big 5* personality dimensions (Costa and McCrae, 1992) are significantly related to the way people cope. For example: those with high extroversion, openness and conscientiousness are more likely to engage with problem-focused coping while those who are more inclined towards neuroticism are less engaged with the coping mechanism. Using the COPE inventory, Samms and Friedel (2013) argue that there are numerous factors that can influence a student's learning including: motivation, attitude towards learning, disability, ability, learning environment and teaching methods. They explain that each person is different and learns in a different way and each new situation experienced can develop a new way of coping. This may be achieved where the student builds on their knowledge and ability to solve problems. They also point out that a tutor's learning style may differ to that of the student and each new situation may lead to another way of coping. Empathy, and interpersonal relationship, between teacher and student is therefore an important factor to engender greater interest in that discussed in lessons/lectures/seminars the in turn can help the student to develop their skills and abilities.

Personality and stress

People differ in how they experience and cope with a stressful event. Maybe people are born with the ability or maybe it is a learned skill. We inherit genetic makeup from our parents and we learn from experience. We may inherit traits from our parents that predispose us to acting and feeling in particular ways. The genetics may predispose us to fight or flight when faced with a challenging experience. We learn to either avoid them or to face up to the possible conflict that may in turn add to feelings of stress and anxiety. Eysenck (1990) suggests that environmental factors have a small influence on personality differences while Bouchard and Loehlin (2001) point out that there is substantial evidence to suggest that personality traits are influenced by the genes inherited from our parents. This is supported by Pinker (2003) in his book, "*The blank slate: the modern denial of human nature*", in which he argues that human behaviour is shaped by evolutionary psychological traits, psychological advantages that are passed down from our ancestors. However, there are other non-shared characteristics that can also influence personality, for example: cultural influences, group relationships and socialisation. This is exemplified by Raby, Roisman, Fraley and Simpson (2014) who suggest that the emotional support experienced by a child in the first three and a half (3.5) years effects their social life, romantic relationships and education twenty (20) to thirty (30) years later on in life. This suggests that whereas genes do have a strong role to play in influencing human behaviour, our environment and social interactions with others also have influence. The complexity of unravelling, where nurture ends, and nature begins, continues to challenge research undertaken in this area.

The "*big five*" allow for analysis and categorisation of the personality type we are. However, personality could be a little like peeling an onion. On the surface and overall there is one personality, but as you peel the onion, there may be other more complex layers beneath. The surface layer may suggest that there is resilience and strength within the personality when faced with challenging emotional experiences. However, just below the surface, there may be sensitive spots or layers that may become evident once the surface layer is peeled back. For example, one confrontation meeting with a line manager may have insignificant affect and the person is able to cope with experience. There may be a handful of confrontational meetings that eventually lead to the person breaking down that in turn leads to high levels of stress and the feeling of not being able to cope. For example, anxiety may emerge where there is anticipation of waiting for the next confrontational meeting. It materialises within the *big 5* as neuroticism. To a greater or lesser degree, we are all likely to have neuroticism within our makeup. However, some people are more prone to it than others. Under normal circumstances, the person may be quite able to cope with the stressful experience. Neuroticism may be at low levels. However, with repeated and regular exposure to stress, the level of neuroticism may rise and become a much more dominant trait than maybe it had been earlier. If neuroticism is high on personality traits, it may lead to much greater anxiety, stress and depression than that experienced by another person who is low in neuroticism. Furthermore, if there are two or more stressors pulling and pushing the person, the psychological strain may be too great to cope with and the stress levels are magnified accordingly, leading to psychological and physical ailments.

Millward- Brown (1996) identifies that over 50% of academics and researchers feel that their jobs cause them stress all or most of the time. Research undertaken by Tytherleigh Webb, Cooper and Ricketts, (2005) also finds that the factor that worries people most is job security and that stress experienced by university staff appears widespread. These are just a couple of examples from the 1990s and 2000s. Stress in the teaching environment does not appear to be declining. Indeed, the findings show that the pressure of work and feelings of stress remain increasingly high. The days of the traditional view of university teaching, where it is considered a low-stress job, appears to be long gone (Fisher, 1994). Having a personality that is low in neuroticism may therefore be an advantage enabling the person to cope with stress.

Personality (The "big five") and job performance

The *"big five"* personality traits have become a means of predicting job performance, in particular, if the job context is taken into consideration. In a meta-analysis undertaken by Barrick, Mount and Judge (2001), findings suggest that conscientiousness is important in job performance. Ozer and Benet-Martinez (2005) also find that extroversion and emotional stability (inverse of neuroticism) are important factors in predicting performance, but not in all occupations.

Studies have been undertaken of university teachers that show that demonstration of more positive aspects of the *big 5* personality traits can lead them to be more effective in managing students and lecturing (Attar, Ather and Bano, 2013; Vandervoort, 2006). The conclusions that Attar et al. (2013) arrive at is that there is a positive correlation with extroversion, conscientiousness, openness to experience and a significant inverse correlation with neuroticism. These findings are supported by Hogan and Holland (2003) who suggest that personality traits are important, dependent on the job, and are influential in how a person copes with challenging experiences. As described by Lord and Rust (2003), the *"big five"* has become the linchpin holding personality assessment together within the work environment.

Personality (The "big five") and trait emotional intelligence

Studies about the relationship between the *"big five"* and emotional intelligence have been undertaken in English speaking countries and those that do not have English as their first language. What does appear to come out from these studies is that there is a correlation. For example, Petrides, Vernon, Schermer, Ligthart, Boomsma and Veselka (2010) look at two (2) samples from the Netherlands. The robustness of trait emotional intelligence is also tested on a sample of seven hundred and thirty-seven (737) Italian children by Russo, Mancini, Trombini, Baldaro, Mavroveli and Petrides (2012). The findings confirm consistency with earlier studies that show an overlap between trait emotional intelligence and the *"big five"*.

Personality (The "big one") and trait emotional intelligence

Musek (2007) first put forward empirical data in support of a General Factor of Personality (GFP) that has become known as the *big one*. It is where the *big five* are drawn together under a single factor. For example, a person low on neuroticism and high on other factors, in the *"big five"*, would have a high GFP score. Whereas not all academics agree that a single factor can be derived from the *"big five"*, studies suggest that there is a relationship between the GFP and trait emotional intelligence. In a meta-analysis, Van der Linden, te Nijenhuis and Bakker (2010) find that there is an overlap between GFP and trait emotional intelligence. Van der Linden, Schermer, de Zeeuw, Dunkel, Pekaar, et al. (2018) also support this finding. However, it is worth adding a few words of caution. There appear to be multiple ways of evaluating GFP (Revelle and Wilt, 2013). It is, therefore, important that when undertaking a study that similar measures/ tools/ instruments be used. Notwithstanding the criticism and different measures used, there does appear to be evidence to suggest that GFP does exist.

Summing up

The English dictionary is made up of many words associated with personality traits as identified by Allport and Odbert in 1936. Goldberg reduces the number of traits to what has become known as the *"big five"*. Personality may be made up of different layers and may be much more complicated. To categorise a person with a single or a handful of personality traits may not clearly explain who they are. For example, context, background and external factors may influence a person to demonstrate particular personality traits. Studies have been undertaken affirming the presence of the *"big five"* personality traits and linking them to emotional intelligence. Studies also suggest the existence of a single general factor (GFP). It is, therefore, acknowledged that personality traits do exist and can be measured.

There appears to be a difference of opinion as to whether coping with a stressful experience is a conscious decision or if it is built in as an innate reaction. Each has its supporters. The findings from this chapter suggest that personality traits can influence how a person copes. For example, a person who is more inclined to neuroticism may regard challenging situations more threatening and stressful. Their ability to cope is affected that in turn can lead to depression, anxiety and poorer psychological and physical health when compared to someone who may be more of an extrovert.

Personality traits can also influence how successful a person performs in a job. For example, a teacher may need to demonstrate extrovert behaviour as well as emotional stability when engaged with students. Their effectiveness can be influenced depending on the personality traits (Attar, Ather and Bano, 2013; Vandervoort, 2006).

Studies also suggest a relationship between personality (the "*big five*") and emotional intelligence. A number of authors have gone as far as to suggest that it is possible to identify a single "*general factor of personality*" (GFP), the *big one* that correlates to trait emotional intelligence (Musek, 2007; Van der Linden, et al, 2018; Van der Linden, te Nijenhuis and Bakker, 2010). However, as with different approaches to the measurement of emotional intelligence, there appears to be differing views and means of measuring the GFP (Revelle and Wilt, 2013). A digital photograph relies on the number of pixels that provide detail. Each year further studies are undertaken, adding further pixilation. The more pixels, the greater the detail. Studies, undertaken, also provide further depth and explanation of existing theoretical approaches and a greater understanding of the topic area. However, it would be helpful if researchers agreed to clear definitions and one approach to measurement.

Chapter 6

Intelligence and groups

This chapter begins with a conversion around the term intelligence and the difference of opinions as to what intelligence is. Definitions and explanations are wide. It is therefore helpful to delve into the topic. This chapter also widens the discussion out, reflecting on how intelligence has been incorporated into studies around groups.

We are influenced by others around us whether we like it or not. We seek others who are like-minded and support our own views, views that can be hardened by influence; the consequences of which can have a dramatic impact upon our lives especially in the social network era that we are now in. We share our thoughts and views with others reaching a much wider audience than we have in the past. Information can be passed around the world in split seconds that used to take weeks, months and possibly years. We are "*wired to connect*" yet, amongst all the noise, the feeling of loneliness continues to exist. Teams are the foundation of organisational success in which we work together in cohesive teams. Breakdown of relationships can damage the team's cohesiveness and its ability to function at its maximum productivity. If group intelligence exists, then it suggests that group emotional intelligence does as well. Having to conform to rules and rationalisation of how people work can give rise to feelings of stress that can be shared with fellow members of the group. Group psychological strain may occur where there is more than one stressor pulling the group in different directions. Therefore, developing and improving skills associated with emotional intelligence can help support team cohesiveness. Team members may come together to support each other, and to help the group cope, when faced with stressful experiences providing emotional and instrumental support. The final part of the chapter considers the relationship bees have in the beehive, where they work together to support the wider good of the colony. As human beings, we do seem to work in a similar manner; working for the common good. At the same time, we seek to maintain individual identity that may conflict with others in the group. The challenge we all have is to maintain our individuality while maintaining the cohesive work ethic sought by organisations to compete within the global marketplace.

Intelligence

In the early part of the twentieth century, a group was set up by the French Government that is called "*La Société libre pour l'étude psychologique de l'enfant."* The group is asked to find a way to identify children that may require alternative education to help them get back on track. One of this group is Alfred Binet (1916), who believes education can change intelligence. In collaboration with Simon, Binet develops the Binet-Simon (1911, 1916) intelligence scale that includes thirty (30) tasks such as: counting, number recall, following a lighted match, sentence completion and naming parts of the human body. Teachers are then asked to identify children in their classes that they feel are academically average for their age. These children are tested relative to their age, and findings compared with others. For example, a six (6) year-old child who passes the test meant for those aged five (5) would be given the mental age of the five (5) year-old. A seven (7) year-old child who passes the test for those aged eight (8) years of age would be given the mental age of an eight (8) year-old. The test is first given to those between three (3) and ten (10) years of age and subsequently expanded out to include children up to the age of fifteen (15) and later adults.

Terman (1916) finds that the Binet-Simon intelligence test does not work well on a sample of children in California, USA. He adapts the test to include forty (40) new items that can be used on children from the age of four (4) to fourteen (14). The test is described as the Stanford- Binet test and includes tasks such as finding shapes that match, awareness of dates, mental arithmetic, identifying the longer of two horizontal lines, copying shapes. Terman's sample is larger than that used by Binet and Simon, providing more accurate information that helps to standardise the test. Around the same time, a German Psychologist, William Stern (1914) builds on the work undertaken by Binet and Simon and identifies the intelligence quotient (IQ) which is the mental age divided by the actual age multiplied by 100.

$$(\text{Mental age}/ \text{actual age}) \times 100 = IQ.$$

Stern finds that the mental age is proportionate the actual age of the child. For example: When a child is tested at six (6) years of age, they may have a mental age of five (5). A one-year difference. When the child is ten (10), they have a mental age of eight (8). A two years difference. Terman utilises Stern's IQ calculation and applies it to the test he has developed.

In 1917 the USA enters into the first world war and the American Psychological Association set up a committee to find out how psychology could help the war effort. Binet and Simon's intelligence test has to be undertaken person to person and is found to be unsuitable for group participation, where there is one person administrating the test. As chair of the committee, Yerkes (1921) develops the army alpha and army beta group intelligence tests. The army alpha test is aimed at those who are literate that includes eight (8) tasks such as: following oral instructions, solving arithmetic problems, understanding and identifying similar and opposite words and, rearranging sentences so that they make sense. The army beta test is aimed at those who are illiterate or less than six (6) years speaking English. There are seven (7) tasks that include: completing a picture by adding items, rearranging geometrical components to construct a figure and, finding the best route to take in a picture of a maze. The findings from the sample of 1.75 million people led to Yerkes being asked to apply it to the general population. The advantage that Yerkes time limited IQ test has is that it can be administered by one person to a group of people allowing IQ scores to be compared and contrasted with others. The IQ test has become a staple part of recruitment and selection in many organisations.

Relying on an IQ test to heavily can have its drawbacks. A new recruit may gain a high IQ score but may be low in empathy and people management skills. They may receive a lower than average IQ score but may have excellent skills in recognising and analysing facial and body language. Each person may have individual characteristics associated with temperament and abilities. We learn and develop skills throughout life and our brains learn to adapt accordingly. Questions and arguments have been held over the twentieth century as to whether or not intelligence is associated with nature (genes) or nurture (environment). There is one argument that intelligence (IQ) is what we are born with and cannot be improved. There is the opposing argument, supported by Binet, that we can train and develop our intelligence. It is, therefore, important not to rely too heavily on the findings from an IQ test and to use it as part of a wider recruitment tool kit.

General intelligence

Around the same time that Binet and Simons are devising their intelligence scale with children, Charles Spearman (1904, 1927), an English psychologist, came up with the term general intelligence. The first part of the study involves intelligence tests on a group of children from his local school which he subsequently expands out to other schools in his area. He then undertakes factor analysis of the findings from the intelligence tests showing that if a child performs well on one intelligence test, they will likely to well in other tests. For example, spatial awareness, vocabulary, mathematics. He describes this positive correlation as *"positive manifold"* within a two-factor theory of intelligence. The first is specific abilities (s) that identifies the specific intelligence needed for the child to perform well on that test. The second is general intelligence (g), or mental energy, that underlies the specific intelligence that allows the child to understand the relationship between information, objectives and events.

Using Spearman's two-factor theory, David Wechsler (1939) devises the Wechsler- Belleview scale based upon a sample of one thousand five hundred

(1,500) adults. In 1955 he introduces separate tests for children (The Wechsler scale for children- WISC) and for adults (The Wechsler adult intelligence scale- WAIS). The same test could be taken by a person of any age. Calculation of the IQ no longer required using mental age and actual age of the person. It is now calculated dividing the test score by the score expected for that age and then multiplied by 100.

(test score/ expected score for that age) x 100= IQ.

Whereas they have been revised, these tests are being used into the twenty-first century.

Based upon Spearman's two-factor theory, John Raven (1938) devises his own matrices intelligence test made up of sixty (60) items. The difference between the tests is that Raven reduces the influence that language and culture may have on the overall score. The idea is to identify relationships between information, relying more on abstract thought than applied or practical thought (Raven, 1938, 1962).

Louie Thurstone (1927,1938,1953) undertakes his own appraisal of Spearman's two-factor approach and puts forward a different view of general intelligence (g). Spearman considers "g" as underlying intelligence. Thurstone (1938) suggests that rather than informing and supporting specific intelligence (s), "g" is arrived at as a consequence of seven (7) primary abilities, shown in the table below. This proposes that there are more than two (2) factors of intelligence, as identified by Spearman.

Table 6.1. Thurstone's seven (7) primary mental abilities.

	Primary mental ability	**Explanation**
1	Memory	Learning through repetition (rote learning), retrieve information
2	Number	Mathematical calculations
3	Perceptual speed	Visual- Analyse similar objects, detail
4	Reasoning	Able to apply logic
5	Spatial ability	Able to analyse objects (distance- near/ far)
6	Verbal comprehension	Able to read, understand words and, comprehension
7	Word fluency	Able to use words
		Source: Thurstone (1938).

Raymond Cattell acknowledges the work undertaken by Spearman that there is such a thing as general intelligence (g). However, in his article "*Theory of fluid and crystallised intelligence*" (1963), he builds on the theory suggesting that "*g*" can be divided into crystallised intelligence (Gc) and fluid intelligence (Gf). Crystallised intelligence is associated with the knowledge that is stored in the memory. Fluid intelligence is associated with the ability to reason and acquisition of information.

In his research, Guilford (1977) doesn't think that "*g*" exists and proposes that intelligence composes of one hundred and fifty (150) independent abilities that fall into three (3) dimensions: operations, content and products. These are summarised in the table below.

Table 6.2. Guilford's independent abilities.

	Dimension	Independent ability
1	Operations (Types of mental processing).	• Cognition. • Memory. • Evaluation. • Convergent production (able to bring together information into a single theme). • Divergent production (able to develop ideas from a single theme).
2	Contents (Ways in which operations apply).	• Semantic (Meaning: including written, oral, perception). • Symbolic (Meaning in symbols). • Visual. • Auditory. • Behavioural.
3	Products (Form in which information is stored).	• Units (For example unit of measurement: metre, inch; unit of currency: Euro, Dollar, Pound). • Transformation (Understanding of changes in information. For example: stocks and shares, currency exchange rates). • Implication (Understanding logic, and significance. For example: If I spend all the money in my pocket now, I may not be able to buy lunch tomorrow). • Relations (Understanding the relationship between two or more things. For example: The scaled down drawing of the building in front of me is 200 time smaller than it actually is). • Systems (Understanding the link between processes, procedures and people. For example: for a planning application to be approved it needs to be drawn up and submitted to the local authority for approval. It is only when it is approved that work should begin). • Classes (Items that share properties. For example: Students who receive grades C to A will pass. Those with F will fail).
		Source: Guilford (1977).

Guilford's model expands the understanding of intelligence further. Whereas, he identifies one hundred and fifty (150) independent abilities associated with those shown in the table above, it is much more challenging to manage and understand the whole model and apply it.

Vernon (1950) proposes an alternative to the models put forward by Thurstone and Spearman, suggesting that intelligence can be placed in a hierarchy with the highest intelligence being "*g*". At the lowest level, there are specific factors. Between them lie the major group factors and minor factors.

Table 6.3. Hierarchy of intelligence (Vernon, 1950).

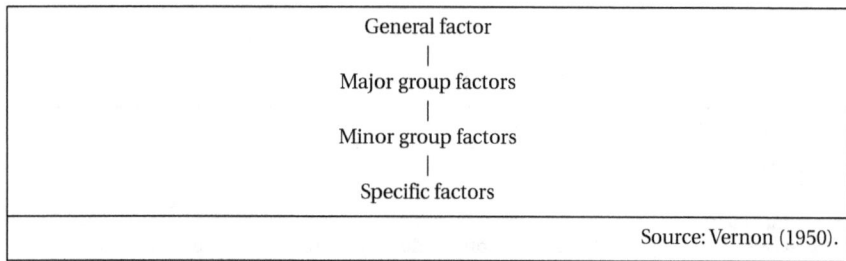

General factor
|
Major group factors
|
Minor group factors
|
Specific factors
Source: Vernon (1950).

Carroll (1982, 1993) pulls together much of the previous research placing intelligence into three (3) hierarchical levels (Stratum, I, II and, III).

Table 6.4. Carroll's three (3) stratum hierarchy.

Stratum I	Narrow	Specific levels of cognitive ability/ intelligences	
Stratum II	Broad	1	Fluid intelligence (Gf).
		2	Crystallised intelligence (Gc).
		3	Broad cognitive speed (Gs).
		4	Processing speed (Gs).
		5	Auditory perception (Gu).
		6	General memory (Gy).
		7	Visual perception (Gv).
		8	Ability to retrieve information (Gr).
Stratum III	General	General intellectual ability	
			Source: Carroll (1982, 1993).

Further studies by Horn and Cattell (1967) suggest that there are nine (9) broad dimensions to intelligence, as shown below.

Table 6.5. Cattell, Horn and Carroll theory.

	Dimension	Code
1	Tertiary storage and retrieval.	TSR/ Glm
2	Auditory processing.	Ga
3	Visual processing.	Gv
4	Processing speed.	Gs
5	Quantitative knowledge.	Gq
6	Decision speed.	CDS
7	Short term comprehension, grasp and ability to retrieve.	SAR
8	Fluid reasoning (To think in a flexible manner).	Gf
9	Knowledge intelligence (To adopt cultural traits of another group).	Gc

Source: Horn and Cattell (1967).

The above provides a short explanation of different ideas and thoughts that have been put forward in the twentieth century. IQ tests may measure aptitude that contributes to daily life. However, on its own, aptitude is not enough. Intelligence may include other factors such as being analytical, creative and practical (Sternberg, 1996, 2012). Reflecting on the content, it would be helpful to simplify to enable a clear definition of the term "*intelligence*" to emerge. However, this would not give acknowledgement to the in-depth studies undertaken and it may not be possible to simplify the term into a short definition. Whereas intelligence may depend upon variables including background, culture, and context, IQ tests have been undertaken in different geographical locations and appear to show consistency. The findings suggest that general intelligence may exist and that it is possible to measure intelligence by using IQ tests, devised and tested over recent generations. It is on this premise that intelligence can be explained and can be used to measure a person's level of intelligence.

If intelligence can be explained and measured within individuals, it may be possible to expand further and to apply the concept to groups. It provides a different perspective on how intelligence is understood. This is what is discussed in the following sections.

Groups and groupthink

As individuals, we have our own thoughts, views and understanding of the world around us. We have individual differences. Tom Boyce (2019) provides an excellent explanation as to the individual difference in his book *"The orchid and the dandelion"*. Organisations need dandelions to provide stability. Conforming to norms and organisational demands may come at ease to the dandelion and they can thrive in any environment. The orchid needs a more exacting growing environment and may find that they are unable to meet the organisational demands and fail. Orchids are more inclined to be thrill and novelty seekers. Boyce (2019) points out that organisations need both the dandelion and the orchid that gives the organisation adaptive flexibility. However, policies and procedures are often written to apply to all members of staff notwithstanding individual differences. Similarly, management style is often applied to individual performance and outputs. At work, we have to interact with colleagues and are required to conform to norms that include the way we dress, speak and behave. Outside work or school, we meet people with similar interests. It may be a football team or a book club. Again, we need to conform to that which is expected of us in that context. Whether it is at work or at home, as human beings, we tend to engage in groups and teams. I discussed this with students in one of my leadership and management workshops a few years ago. One student, who was studying banking, stood out amongst the rest- twenty (20) something with an attitude. He lived at home with his parents in a respectable suburb of the city. He always had a Mohican haircut and dressed in punk attire. He made it clear that he did not conform. He didn't like rules regulations. Nor did he like being told what to do and what to wear. He never voted and didn't believe that politicians should "*interfere*" with his life. He was an *"individual"*. When asked what he did on the weekend, he commented that he visited the local pub where other punk aficionados attended. He always arrived around at 10.00pm when the headline act was due to perform. To get into the club, he had to pay at the door and was given a blue temporary entrance stamp on the back of his hand. He shared thoughts on fashion and music with his friends, who are also fond of punk music. He was reinforcing his own views and ideas with others with similar interests. Whether he liked it or not, he was conforming to the stereotype associated with his group. It is a common experience that we have as human beings. We seek individuality and at the same time seek to conform with our own group. We engage with those who are similar minded. We maintain allegiance to that group for as long as we feel committed to the ideals and views shared. However, we are influenced by what we see and what we read as well as shared experiences with others. We can be influenced to changing allegiances to another group that may be more aligned with our own thinking.

That group can reinforce its own rules and regulations that in turn, reinforce our own views, thoughts and indeed prejudices. This Banking student is now working in the city selling stocks, shares and commodities, and wears a three-piece suite every day. He is also an active member of local politics. Group allegiances can change.

Whereas belonging to a group can provide feelings of comfort and belonging, groups can be influenced by those who subvert the norms and can be influential in changing the group dynamics. From past experience, I am aware of a group, made up of year eight (8) children, that came together on the school playground to protect themselves from the bullying handed out by others. Within the school grounds, the social dynamic was to protect and support group members. They enjoyed talking about their local football team and became regular visits to the ground when the team played at home. There was a child, named Michael, who was proclaimed leader by the others and was often acceptant of differences of opinion and thoughts. It was agreed that the group would not engage in challenging the authority of the school and would not participate in activities such as smoking, bunking off lessons, and bullying other students. In the spring term, a new student, by the name of Tom, arrived and was enthusiastically welcomed into the group. Tom began to usurp the role of the leader in a very short time. At lunchtimes he went for a smoke behind one of the school outbuildings and made it clear of his dislike for the local football team while preferring to spend Saturday afternoons wandering around the town centre with students from his last school. Initially, the group held strength and tried to ignore Tom's behaviour. After a few weeks, one or two of the boys joined Tom on his regular Saturday outings and became friends with those from his old school. Cigarettes were exchanged and on occasions, cans of lager or cider were drunk surreptitiously in empty shop doorways. By the end of the Spring term, Tom had influenced the majority of the group to engage in smoking, drinking and other nefarious activities. Michael was expelled from the group as he wanted to maintain the original principles. He was followed by two (2) or three (3) others, leaving Tom to take overall control. Tom continued to maintain control after the students had left school. It is a sad story as most of this group did not receive good exam grades and went on to jobs that they held for very short periods of time. Within a year or two, a number became long term unemployed while others drifted from job to job. The aforementioned exemplifies the influence that one member can have on the overall group dynamic.

Other more well-known and extreme examples are those who become a self-proclaimed prophet and lead their members to their death. For example, Jim Jones, cult leader, who was responsible for the mass suicide of over nine hundred (900) of his followers, at Jonestown, Guyana, in 1978. Another example is the leader of Heaven's Gate religious group, Marshall Applewhite. In 1997. He led his followers to commit mass suicide in the belief that a spaceship would accompany the arrival of the comet Hale-Bopp and that their spirits would be taken on board to travel to another planet. It is amazing how we can be influenced into thinking and believing that which can be "*out this world.*" Popper (1962) identifies this *immodest* belief in superior intelligence as "*pseudo-rationalism*" that contrasts with Socrates "*true rationalism*" as recognising limitations in intellect and knowledge.

These examples are linked to groupthink, where a group of people seek to conform and minimise conflict, which leads to dysfunctional or irrational thinking. It is the desire to maintain an "*ingroup*" mentality. Groupthink is where irrational thoughts are shared by others in a group while maintaining consensus and harmony in that which is shared. This idea of groupthink is first put forward by Janis Irving (1973) in her book "*Victims of groupthink*". She explains that when like-minded people get together, their views and thoughts can become more polarised and extreme. In his book, "*You are not so smart,*" David McCraney (2012) points out that true groupthink is where a group of people like each other, they are in isolation of others and that there is a deadline for crucial decisions. He expands by explaining that the group defends its cohesion from harm by suppressing doubt and not raising alternatives that make the leader assume that everyone is in agreement with his/her viewpoint. Feelings and emotions are sometimes whipped up to such an extent that lead to community and social unrest. Indeed, groupthink can be highly dangerous where lives are threatened. For example, the Spanish Inquisition, that began in the late fifteenth (15th) century, led to tens of thousands of people being killed. Similarly, the Nazis gained support through ideological views. A more recent example is that of Brexit where the UK Government carried out a referendum in 2016 that narrowly supported to leave the European Union. The challenge is, which is better- to stay in or leave. Information is mainly given in sound bites. Strong views are held by the "*Brexiteers*" and the "*Remainers*". Who is right? Who is wrong? How does each side *really* know that their argument is correct? Can we really make decisions without engaging emotions? Whichever side chosen, there appears to be groupthink at work and groupthink influences our behaviour, whether we like it or not.

A nudge in the right direction

This leads on to Thaler and Sunstein (2009) nudge theory. They point out that, when making decisions, people think instinctively and irrationally rather than the traditional logical and rational approach. Nudge theory is based upon indirect suggestions and avoids direct enforcement or instruction. By making small suggestions together with positive reinforcements, it encourages positive *free* choice, helping people to make better decisions by changing behaviour. As explained by Thaler and Sunstein (2009), a nudge is placing fruit at eye level, encouraging them to engage in positive reinforcement. However, this theory also suggests that people can be influenced to support ideological thinking that can have a damaging impact upon society and people within it (for example, Jim Jones, Charles Manson). Nudge theory can be used to influence group and organisational behaviour, moving people to make decisions that they may not have done without that nudge. What may have been unacceptable a generation ago is now an accepted norm of society. It may be something that takes several years to change. It may be something that has an immediate effect. For example, between 2012 and 2017, the UK Government changed the legislation requiring organisations to automatically include members of staff into a pension plan. This has resulted in many more people saving for their old age. However, nudging can lead to social division, creating a stronger bias against opposing groups. For example, in the recent past, white nationalist sentiments, have been kept out of mainstream news. Access to their views and thoughts are now readily available at the click of the computer keyboard (Sunstein, 2019). In parts of the world, segregation of white and non-white was incorporated into legislation. It is now considered by many to be abhorrent. Nudge theory demonstrates how we can be influenced and persuaded to make choices that may not be rational and logical. It acknowledges that as human beings we make irrational decisions based upon how we feel. However, what is rational and logical to one person may not be to another. Who decides? Legislation is enforced by Government officials. Organisations have policies and procedures. Each of us has our own morals and ethical view of how we should live our lives. Who is right and who is wrong? (That questions again). Is it as clearly defined as right and wrong, and at what point is information sufficient to make an informed decision or choice? Furthermore, thoughts are influenced by emotions, and decisions are made, making us *think and believe* we have free choice. But we have to believe in something.

Social networking

No matter how much we think that we are individual and make our own decisions, we are influenced by those around us, by what we read and what we see and hear. A viewpoint may be held by a small committed group or individuals. They can communicate this viewpoint through social gatherings including social media. Reasoning and problem solving is becoming more shared, placing a different perspective on intelligence as a collective process. More recently, social network sites have become immensely popular. Information can be shared freely from restrictions of the physical world. It allows users to access information that was simply not possible just a few years ago. In higher education, technology and the use of social networks can enhance the student learning experience. Students can access information relating to their programme and module by a touch of the mouse and keyboard. They can interact with peers and lecturers via instant messaging services together with social networking sites such as LinkedIn, Twitter, and Facebook. Statista reports that in 2010 there were 0.97 billion social network users worldwide. In 2019, this rises to an estimated 2.77 billion users. The table below provides a summary of social network users between 2010 and 2021.

Table 6.6. The number of global social network users.

Year	Number (billions)
2010	0.97
2011	1.22
2012	1.40
2013	1.59
2014	1.91
2015	2.14
2016	2.28
2017	2.46
2018	2.62*
2019	2.77*
2020	2.90*
2021	2.21*

* estimate
Source: Statista (2018).

Users of social network sites are often faced with online advertisements. They are targeted by spammers who send out messages that can influence and possibly mislead the user into believing the content. At the time of writing this book, it is alleged that Russia influenced the 2016 election of the USA president, Donald Trump, by sending out false news messages on social networks. Individuals can influence others. Individuals can become minorities where those with likeminded views come together. There is a tipping point where the minority view gains traction and eventually become a majority approach to thinking (Gladwell, 2001). Gladwell, (2001) adds that simply manipulating the size of the group can improve how it receives new ideas. Furthermore, there can also be an "*illusion of explanatory depth*" where people think that they understand something in greater depth than they actually do (Rozenblit and Keil, 2002). Think about who you may vote for in the next general election. How do you make a decision? Is it based upon what you see on the television and in newspapers, or maybe social media? Do you have sufficient knowledge for you to make an informed decision? In their book, "*The knowledge Illusion*", Sloman and Fernbach (2017) suggest that people focus on what they believe without underpinning their views in rational and clear reasoning. They maintain a strong position based upon very little supporting information and do not consider causal explanation. Sloman and Fernbach add that illusions can be shattered, and strong views can be moderated by getting someone to think about the matter in greater depth. Unfortunately, politicians and journalists often use the tactic of underpinning statements with clichés and banal platitudes associated with revered and sacred values that reinforce views and thoughts without necessarily explaining content and consequences. However, it nudges the person a little closer to tipping over until they actually do. Exposing and shattering an illusion can upset people and maybe make them feel stupid. Trying to get the person to understand and explain their view may generate interpersonal friction and a hardening of views. It is, therefore, important to acknowledge that by doing so can lead to the person distancing themselves from others in the group, maybe forming a new group of their own with other similar likeminded people. As the digital age progresses, we become more influenced by content and views that invade daily lives. We seem to attach ourselves to memes, first put forward by Richard Dawkins (1976) in his book "*The selfish gene*". Memes include emails and social media, checking updates and placing our inner thoughts for others to see. Memes are also used in social media sites that connect us to ideas and thoughts that can influence our behaviour. Memes are also widespread ideas, thoughts and views that may be published on the internet in frequent blogs or websites. Having greater access to information on the internet may make us feel that we are better informed and that we can make better decisions. However, the use of social networking amplifies this information and is often too much to absorb. It is challenging to remember what we ate for dinner just a few days ago let alone trying to remember all the information that we see and hear. Our brains are not built to remember every detail of our daily experiences. Think about being at an airport waiting for your plane. People are milling around looking at the information board, others are shopping, or having a meal. A child is crying as she is tired and bored of waiting. You need to go to the checkout to book in your cases. It is all information. The information overload causes a cacophony of noise. It is why we are selective in that which our brains absorb. Some information remains very short term, other information medium term and then there is long term information that we keep stored in our brains for the rest of our lives. That is why we often see headlines and hear sound bites, while ignoring deeper content. As human beings, we seek to explain the world around us into a more condensed and simple manner as it is a lot easier than trying to remember everything. We have to make decisions, often life-changing decisions based on limited information, knowledge and understanding. The world is a complex place, as is the mind. It may be more helpful to acknowledge that we are simply ignorant of full data and knowledge. Now, where did I leave my mobile phone?

Social intelligence and loneliness

The term social intelligence is knowing yourself and others. It is having the ability to steer oneself in social settings and to build relationships. Daniel Goleman (2006) describes it as the *"new science of human relations"*. As human beings, we are *"wired to connect"* (Davidson, Gardner, Goleman, Siegel et al., 2012). There are times we may need our own space; a place to think on our own. However, we are built to interact with others and engage in social relationships. Our daily lives are affected by the strength/ weakness of the relationships that we have. We are not built to live alone. Indeed, there is strong evidence to show that loneliness can lead to a psychological illness that include personality disorders, depression and, alcohol abuse. Loneliness can also lead to physical illness such as diabetes, obesity and coronary disease. Selimi (2016) refers loneliness to the virus of our modern age. The *"Campaign to end loneliness"* goes as far as to say that loneliness can be as damaging as being a heavy smoker (smoking fifteen (15) cigarettes a day or more). Therefore, to engage in productive interpersonal relationships can have a beneficial effect on psychological and physical well-being. Developing social intelligence can help build and develop interpersonal relationships and can be a useful asset in improving psychological and physical well-being.

Group/ team/ intelligence

As the technological age advances, more and more collaborative teamwork is being undertaken. This includes studies into collective intelligence and behaviour where group/ team IQ is identified. In an article titled *"Group IQ"*, Johnson (2010), points out that groups have characteristics that are more than a summing up of the individual parts. Sloman and Fernbach (2017) book emphasise the power that collective wisdom has when compared to individual thought. This is supported by a study of social and cognitive characteristics undertaken by Williams and Sternberg (1988) who find that group products (made up of videotape ratings, written tests and group performance) are higher quality than that of the individual. In a further study, Woolley, Chabris,

Pentland, Hashmi, et al. (2010) use a sample of six hundred and ninety-nine (699) people. They are placed in teams of up to five (5) people and asked to undertake tasks such as puzzle solving, brainstorming and moral reasoning. The findings suggest that groups can have their IQ score that are independent of individual intelligence. It, therefore, points to the acknowledgment that collective wisdom and collective intelligence does exist. However, in another study by Bates and Gupta (2017), individual IQ levels are found to influence the group IQ. Notwithstanding the contrary findings, it appears that working cohesively in team roles can lead to better results than relying on the individual alone. Being prepared to share, support and be part of a group can help build interpersonal relationships enhancing team and organisation learning.

Group emotional intelligence

Emotional intelligence has been linked to the individual and has reflected on how important it is. It appears that emotional intelligence (EI) can be as critical to individual performance as IQ. As human beings, we engage in interpersonal relationships within society and within teams in organisations. Teams are the foundation for the success of an organisation. Without team collaboration and cohesive working relationships, breakdown of communication can occur, leading to fragmentation of overall organisational performance and output.

Group emotional intelligence emanates from Daniel Goleman's (1995) book *"emotional intelligence: why it can matter more than IQ"*. Studies do suggest the presence of team and group intelligence. If group intelligence does exist, then it follows that group emotional intelligence may also exist. Druskat and Wolff (2001) certainly finds this is the case. They point out that the importance of creating the conditions in which team members can build on group emotional intelligence. In his PhD dissertation, Hamme (2003) has gone as far as to develop an assessment instrument to measure group emotional intelligence. Wolff (2006) has also designed a technical manual on group emotional intelligence. Wolff (2006) explains that group emotional intelligence is where a group generates a set of norms that are guided by the interactions within individual level, at group level and between groups (cross-boundary). He identifies nine (9) norms that make up group emotional intelligence. At the individual level, he identifies: (1) interpersonal understanding with group awareness of members, (2) confronting members who break the rules and (3) caring behaviour that is associated with management of group members. At the group level, he identifies: (4) team self-evaluation with group self-awareness, (5) creating a positive working environment, (6) creating resources for working with emotion, and (7) proactive problem solving are associated with group self-management. At the cross-boundary level Wolff (2006) identifies: (8) organisational understanding and (9) building external relationships with group social awareness and external relationships. The success of the organisation depends on interpersonal relationships where team members create a sense of group identity, where they have greater understanding and trust amongst each other. The interpersonal relationships develop feelings of achievement and empathy where group members are willing and able to share their experiences. Rapisarda (2002) adds the empathy and achievement are positively related to team cohesiveness and performance. Norms are then created that members of the group can identify with. Developing group norms includes developing the belief that working in a team is more effective than working individually. The challenge with working with others is that personalities can conflict. There may be differences of opinion and team members may not be prepared to compromise. Rather than creating conflict, people can share views and concerns and build upon the differences to find common agreement, helping and strengthening relationships. Developing improved interpersonal relationships can help gain skills in negotiating challenging experiences. It may be that the team leader needs to act as an intermediary or to take control of the negotiation. The team leader needs skills in directing team members, removing unhealthy norms for those that are positive. However, this needs to be supported by team members who engage in positive team working norms as identified by Wolff (2006).

Reflection: Group emotional intelligence

To help build an emotionally intelligent team:
1. Create and develop confidence that views and thoughts can be shared amongst team members.
2. Be aware of your own and other team members habits and emotions.
3. Become more able in regulating your own emotions and managing emotions with others.
4. Where personalities dominate, include others into discussion.
5. Be aware of team members level well-being.
6. Trust team members and gain their trust in you. (If something is said in confidence, keep it that way)
7. Develop and build on sharing views thoughts and emotions within agreed parameters.
8. Allow for errors to happen and to learn from them.
9. Develop and build listening skills. Not just what the team member is saying but also what they are not.
10. Build upon understanding of team and organisational objectives and aims.

Management business perspective

Goleman (1995, 2006) points out that the competencies associated with emotional intelligence (motivation, self-regulation, self-awareness, empathy and social skills) are key to the success of being a successful leader. For example, a successful leader leads by example (demonstrating motivation); they are decisive and intuitive (demonstrating self-regulation); they are confident, consistent and honest (demonstrating self-awareness); they are able to relate to others (demonstrating empathy) and; they are good communicators and listeners (demonstrating social skills). While acknowledging that they may not be perfect, the successful leader is shown to be effective by demonstrating skills in leading themselves, leading others and leading the organisation. They continually challenge themselves and set themselves goals and objectives while mastering the skill to keep calm and focused. Druskat and Wolff (2001) explain that because a team is made up of those who are individually emotionally intelligent, does not necessarily mean that the group is emotionally intelligent. They suggest that the team needs to create emotionally intelligent norms associated with attitude and behaviour that ultimately become habits that encourage an atmosphere of team trust, identity and efficacy. This can then lead to greater skills in coping with emotionally challenging situations. This is exemplified in a study undertaken by Suifan, Abdallah and Sweis (2015) of one hundred and ninety-three (193) respondents in the insurance business in Jordan. They find that work outcomes are positively affected by emotional self-awareness, self-management, social awareness and relationship management. Emotional intelligence is associated with effective interpersonal relationships and intrapersonal skill, effective skills for leader when faced with increased challenges in the global market place. In 2011, a national study is undertaken in the USA by Harris Interactive (2011) of two thousand six hundred (2,600) managers and human resource professionals. They find that 71% of respondents value emotional intelligence more than IQ in an employee. The reason being is that those with higher levels of emotional intelligence are more likely to stay calm and have greater empathy with team members. They are more likely to lead by example and more capable of resolving conflict while making more thoughtful decisions.

In my long career, I remember watching a director of services standing over junior staff members shouting and screaming at them, then walking away smartly. On other occasions, she would pull in junior staff members and spend an hour or more telling them how *bad* they were. "*What you do is a mess! It's confusing! We are going to have complaints!*" I asked one of the junior staff members why they put up with it. The response was that they had been in the job for years, the director would likely move on after a year or two. They had no wish to uproot themselves nor their family in search of another job, nor had they intentions of causing possible conflict by trying to stand up to the director. There was an air of acceptance. Other members of staff who felt bullied and intimidated by the Director's abrupt manner decided to leave. A few gained similar jobs elsewhere. One or two left without another job to go to. A big decision to make when there are family commitments, including a large mortgage and school fees to pay. Complaints about the Director's behaviour appeared to fall on deaf years. One grievance was made by William, a very well thought of member of staff, who was highly skilled and knowledgeable. It required them to attend a senior management board meeting that the Head of Human Resource Management chaired. He was asked to explain the reason the grievance was brought. After William had been asked to leave the room, the Director was then invited to come in and explain their side of the story. Subsequently, William was called back in and a passing comment was made to him by the Head of Human Resource Management that it may be a good idea that they leave. Thinking that it meant to leave the room, William stood up and made one step towards the door. The Head of Human Resource Management called him back and whispered, *"leave the organisation"*. William took about three (3) months to find another job and left. Good people were leaving the organisation. It did appear that the Director liked to single out those who were passive, and, in her view, showed little sign of drive and motivation. When I asked why she raised her voice with colleagues, she responded by saying that it was because she shouted at them and gave them a *"good talking to"* that they delivered on projects within time and budget. *"Making errors is totally unacceptable. I just give them a motivational talk"*. Maybe these people would have delivered the projects on time and in budget even if she never raised her voice. This anecdote is similar to that of the football coach who shouts at his best striker to score goals. The more he shout, the more the striker scores goals. It doesn't seem to cross the coach's mind that the striker may score the goals because of their innate ability and skills and not because of the *"motivational talk"*. I learned that the director subsequently fell out with other senior members of staff and her contract was not renewed. She left after three (3) years. By then many members of staff had departed. There isn't just a human cost to this management style there is also a financial and human cost to the organisation. Recruiting and training new members of staff can cost thousands of pounds. Turnover means that there may be job vacancies that remain unfilled for weeks, possibly months. This means that either the work doesn't get done or pressure is placed upon other members of staff to meet the work demands. Output and performance may also be affected because of challenges associated with staff turnover. For example, those who leave may be taking expertise, knowledge and skills that may be difficult to replace The Director's reputation preceded her. Whereas she appeared to lack skills associated with emotional intelligence, she continued to get those high-level jobs. A few members of her Department continued in their roles for many years to come accepting whatever was thrown at them. Other colleagues who left found alternative employment. In one or two instances, it did take a year or so. People like this director may rise to their positions by stealth and guile. They may find ways of manipulating circumstances and prospective employers into believing that they have the requisite tools and skills to deliver on organisational objectives. They may read books and go on seminars to *"learn"* about topics such as emotional intelligence, motivation and leadership skills. However, they may revert to their *"old selves"* and their basic instincts.

The successful leader can accept that errors happen, and to learn from them. They are able to build skills and knowledge that can enhance their own learning and application. They have the ability to work with others, enhancing team cohesion and focus. They keep calm and focused when faced with challenges. They engage in empathic interpersonal relationships with staff members, building on cohesive teams and inspiring staff members to achieve personal demands. They are emotionally intelligent leaders creating an emotionally intelligent team.

Group stress and group psychological strain

Lazarus (1966) refers to stress as the imbalance between the ability to cope and the demands placed on the person. Public speaking is an excellent example where people find it really challenging to stand up in front of others and present. In the quiet of their own home, there are no problems. As soon as they are in front of others, the nerves start to jangle, beads of sweat appear on their forehead and they lose concentration. Other examples of where there is an imbalance between the ability to cope and demands include experiences where interpersonal skills can sometimes break down. There may be an overload of work. There may be a personality conflict. Some may feel that group working is not fair as they may have to do more than others. Leadership skills may not meet with the demands placed upon the manager. There may be external demands on the organisation; for example, competition from overseas where the service or product is being provided at a lower rate. The stress experienced may be external. Stress may be internal to organisation or group. The stress may be experienced individually by the members of the team. However, the feelings of stress can be shared throughout the whole team. Some may be more able to cope than others.

The pressure and stress being experienced in the workplace appears to be increasing. The success of the organisation depends on its service delivery, performance and, output. Organisations are having to compete in a global market place that, just a few years ago, was thought to be science fiction. The information technology (I.T.) revolution is being overtaken by the artificial intelligence (A.I.) revolution. Fewer people are needed for the job and greater pressure is being placed on remaining staff members to perform. Team members are having to learn new ways of working with new hardware and software. Furthermore, restructuring and reorganisation appear to be occurring on a regular basis. Organisational change is now continuous. The role of the team player is becoming even more important. Working together as a team can add strength to commitment and motivation. However, if mismanaged or poor controls are in place, the pressures placed upon teams can be overpowering affecting output performance and motivation. The stress caused by "*things*" can be amplified within a team and the *"response"* to the stressor can damage its cohesion and ability to function properly. The imbalance experienced can lead to *group stress* that can deplete the team of drive, motivation and cognitive strengths.

Whereas it may not be possible to completely remove a group stressor, it is important that it should be addressed by team members and team leader helping to understand the cause and to find out ways to ameliorate or remove it. Addressing the stressor can help pull team members closer together, knowing that each trust and depend on other team members. The danger is that team members may be affected to such an extent that they take absence from work or leave to work elsewhere, adding to existing stressors faced by the team. It adds to the human and financial costs.

To add to the mix, groups may experience *"psychological strain"*, where there is more than one stressor on the group. For example, competition from other organisations around the world may result in senior management feeling pressurised into placing more onerous responsibilities on staff members (external). Team members may become less supportive of colleagues and try minimising output to avoid personal stress levels (internal). This places more pressure on other members of staff who feel even less supportive of colleagues. Together with heavier workloads and demands, there is often limited time in which to deliver. The added stressors can affect the individual team member that is fed into the group performance and output. Increased stress can lead to group psychological strain. The problem becomes cyclic that can be difficult to break away from. It may be that management feels that being stressed encourages the member of staff and the group they are in to feel more motivated. Short periods of stress can be exhilarating and helpful in meeting deadlines. Team members and groups may perform and deliver good quality service/ product. There is a breaking point, though. Feeling permanently stressed can be debilitating not just for the individual but also the team. The group psychological strain can lead to lower performance and output that pulls in an opposite direction to group intelligence. Using group intelligence and emotional intelligence can also help overcome the psychological strain being experienced, placing the stressors in context. Also developing personal skills in emotional intelligence can be helpful. However, it is acknowledged that the strain may become prolonged and overbearing to such a point that it is no longer possible to cope with the strain. The diagram below illustrates the sources of stressors that may be internal or external to the team member and the group. The diagram also shows factors that can influence the team member and the group.

Diagram 6.1. Group psychological strain.

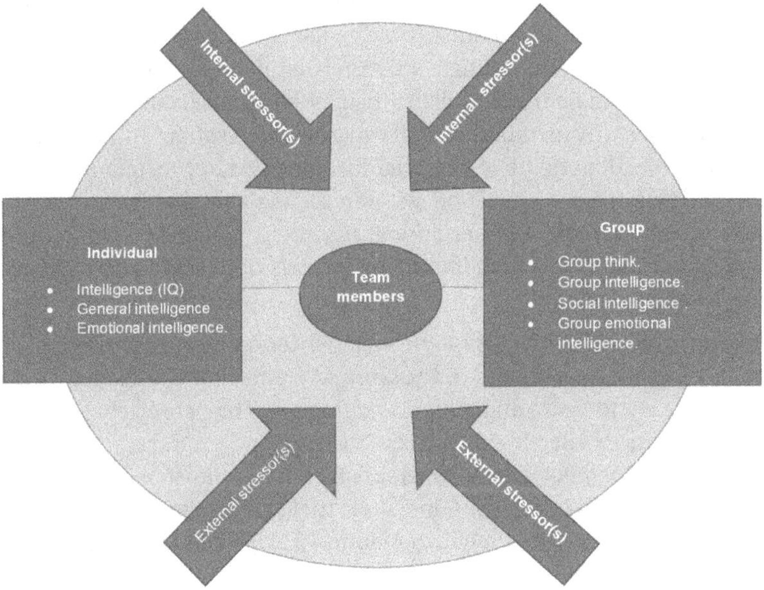

[Diagram showing Team members at center, with Internal stressor(s) arrows from above and External stressor(s) arrows from below. Individual box on left contains: Intelligence (IQ), General intelligence, Emotional intelligence. Group box on right contains: Group think, Group intelligence, Social intelligence, Group emotional intelligence.]

Financial cost

The human cost can be challenging to place in financial terms. How a person is feeling and how they cope with challenging experiences can be difficult to quantify. Furthermore, findings from qualitative studies may not provide sufficient evidence to implement action. It may be helpful if organisations built into their financial models the affect that stress has on individuals and teams and how it affects the organisation over the short, medium and long term. It could be reported in the organisation's public headline financial statement as a financial cost (C): the number of people absent due to stress-related causes (P(n)), multiplied by the number of weeks absent (W(n)) multiplied by the hourly rate for that job (H(rate)).

$$C = P(n) \times W(n) \times H(rate).$$

The above calculation helps focus on underlying costs that can be clearly seen by all stakeholders, in particular those who control the financial strings. It is easier to understand. More detailed figures could be provided for each department and team. Understandably, the accuracy of the data relies on the reliability and validity of reported content. It relies on temporal consistency as well as cross border consistency (comparing one group/department/organisation with another). This may encourage all staff members to be more cognisant of stress-related illnesses *before* it leads to absence from work. It is recommended that action is taken by management while staff members are at work. It may also help that independent assessments are regularly undertaken by an external consultant to assess and evaluate stress-related illnesses and absences from which a report can be made available to all members of staff. This could also include reasons why members of staff leave an organisation. To avoid possible bias and misleading findings, the brief for the external consultant should be open, allowing freedom to report without feeling shackled by restricted demands or expectations. Furthermore, it may help to reduce feelings of individual and group stress while improving feelings of physical and psychological well-being.

Pressure and stress are likely to be experienced in most organisations. It is how each person experiences it. Groups and teams that work together cohesively are likely to share and support colleagues. They are likely to be more resilient to the challenges they face. Discord and conflict between team members and line manager may increase feelings of pressure and stress pulling the group/ team in different directions that can damage motivation, aspiration and performance. It requires emotional skills and knowledge to manage and work with others. If the pressure and stress becomes intolerable and the team member is no longer able to cope, there may come a point that the only course of action is to leave the organisation and move on to pastures new. Reflections provided in the book are there to help prompt thought as to actions that can be taken.

Group coping

Group coping leads on from the last section on group stress. Group coping is where team members come together and support each other when the team is faced with challenging and stressful experiences. Group coping can be included under Carver et al. 's (1989) explanation of *"emotional support"* and *"instrumental support"*. Emotional support is where the person gains comfort from others and instrumental support is where advice is sought from others. The focus of Carver et al. 's (1989) explanation of emotional and instrumental support is associated with the individual and how they cope. If the teamwork together cohesively and uses group intelligence and group emotional intelligence the team may be more able to support individual members when faced with feelings of stress. Group coping focuses on the members of the group as a whole. Where feelings of group stress are felt such as: additional workload, excessive administrative work and interpersonal relationships, members of the team can come together to help and support the group as a whole. Group coping skills training can be provided to include the sharing of feelings, emotions and concerns, together with intervention skills. Group coping can provide the support that may not be available from individual members alone and sharing and supporting team members can become a valuable asset to help address pressure and stress.

Reflection: Group stress
- Within the group, there may be psychological strain where there is tension pulling the team and individuals in different directions. Rather than trying to avoid or deny it, engage with it and, try and understand the cause.
- Talk with others and write down thoughts.
- Be constructive and thoughtful, making yourself aware of your own emotions, emotions in others and managing the emotions.
- Avoid personal attacks and needless conflict.
- Identify three or four "action" points that can be taken to help address the feelings of group stress.
- Revisit the action points in four weeks and reflect upon how successful they have been.
- If there is feeling that actions have not been addressed sufficiently well enough, consider and write down reasons why. Rewrite actions. This is an iterative process that can include colleagues and family.

The beehive

The workplace can be compared to the beehive where there is the queen, the worker and, the drone. The hive is made up of individual bees, however, the hive works together as an integrated whole. At the centre of the hive is the queen. In an organisation, this may be the chairman, owner or, vice chancellor. The beehive requires workers who are central to the success or failure of the organisation. Like the worker bee, each of us has a role to play in society and in the workplace. We find a place within the hierarchy, understanding where we belong in relation to other members of the organisation. We have roles and responsibilities that fit within the wider organisational aims and objectives. Within the hive, there are the drones who are useful in fertilising the queen. Drones are useful when things are going well. When the temperature changes and there is less food, drones are expelled from the hive. In the twenty-first (21st) century, organisations face global competition. To maintain competitive, they may need to restructure, removing posts that are felt to be no longer viable. The drones can therefore be compared to those who are surplus to requirement. People are an important asset to the organisation (*as long as they are needed*).

The challenges of globalisation mean that organisations need to continually change. The change experienced means that new ways of working are introduced. Restructuring is carried out and this becomes a more regular occurrence. This change increases feelings of uncertainty. Furthermore, organisational change can lead to staff members feeling the pressure and stress as a consequence of increased demands placed upon them. This can be felt within the group and within each team member. It is therefore helpful if team members work together cohesively supporting each other in the face of increasing pressure and stress. As such, each member can be more effective and able to cope. This can help reduce absenteeism, improve performance and output, and most importantly, help motivation and commitment. We may be individuals with individual differences. However, we are also part of a hive where the whole is greater than the sum of the individuals.

Summing up

This chapter began by looking at the term intelligence and how studies have been undertaken that have led to means of measuring the intelligent quotient (IQ). The use of the IQ test has become a popular tool in recruitment and selection of potential candidates. However, a person may have a high IQ but score lowly in other tests such as spatial awareness and people management skills. The use of IQ tests should, therefore, be used together within a wider recruitment and selection too kit. This chapter goes on to consider the term "*general intelligence (g)*" pointing out that there appears to be a difference of opinion to exactly what it is. However, the studies undertaken over the last one hundred years do suggest that general intelligence does exist but there is no consensus as to its definition and means of measurement.

If intelligence does exist, then it may be possible to expand out to groups. Studies suggest the presence of groupthink where people can be influenced to think and behave in ways that they would not have done if it were not for the influence. We cannot avoid being influenced by outside stimuli such as TV and social media. We seek to reinforce our own ways of seeing the world and drift to those who are like minded. The world is a complicated place. Whereas, we are *"wired to connect"*, there is so much information that we are unable to absorb it all. Indeed, only a small part is picked up by our senses. We are social animals that are genetically created to interact with others. However, there appears to be a virus of loneliness in society that can severely deplete psychological and physical well-being (Selimi, 2016). Developing interpersonal relationships can reduce loneliness and improve well-being. It is, therefore, helpful to develop social intelligence by getting to know yourself and others.

The chapter then builds on the findings to discuss groups and teams pointing out that groups have characteristics that are more than a sum of the individual parts. Working as a cohesive whole, groups can be more successful than individuals acting alone. The studies undertaken show how important interpersonal relationships are in enhancing team and organisation learning. If group intelligence does exist, then it follows that group emotional intelligence may also exist. Group emotional intelligence is where a group of norms are generated within the group and between groups creating a sense of identity. Developing the group norms can improve interpersonal trust and understanding leading to greater team cohesiveness and performance.

The chapter continues to discuss how group stress can be caused by demands and expectations leading to threats on team cohesiveness and motivation. Group psychological strain is where there is more than one competing demand pulling the group in different directions. If the psychological strain is too much, it can lead to fragmentation and lower performance. Carver et al. (1989) identifies "*emotional support*" and "*instrumental support*" where the person seeks comfort from others or advice is sought. Group coping is where the group comes together in support of demands and pressures placed upon it. Sharing the pressure and stress with the group as a whole can help underpin motivation.

The chapter also suggests that organisations could report the financial cost that stress has on individuals and teams and how it affects the organisation over the short, medium and long term. This could be built into their financial models and reported in the organisation's public headline financial statement helping to focus minds on organisational strategies so that action is taken before it leads to absence from work. The chapter concludes by reflecting on how the workplace can be compared to a beehive. We are individuals and have individual differences. However, we have a role to play as part of the workplace and as part of society. Organisations have to compete in an increasingly globalised environment. Competition is no longer local or regional. It is, therefore, acknowledged that organisations feel the stress and strains of operating in this challenging market place that can lead to group psychological stress and strain. Organisation often creates internal barriers where one department/ section is placed in competition with others. Rather than having internal competition between sections and departments, it may be helpful to work more as a *cohesive body* enabling the organisation to effectively face the increasing challenges and continuous organisational change.

Chapter 7

Emotional intelligence and well-being

Discussion has been given to the impact that stress can have on organisations and staff members. Stress is linked to absenteeism from the workplace, loss of productivity, ill health, and death (for example: suicide, heart disease, cancer, liver disease, and lung ailments). Stress can also lead to mental illness, cognitive impairment and depression. Those who are stressed may be more inclined to snap at family members, friends and colleagues and to worry about things that others may see as trivial. Feeling stressed can become so debilitating that it overwhelms every moment we are awake affecting relationships and our ability to work in a productive manner. It creates conflict within us and also with those we most cherish. It can destroy relationships both at home and at work. Discussion has also been given to coping strategies that people use that can influence the outcomes related to work, health and marital relationships, together with finance, occupation and parental roles. (For example: Folkman and Lazarus, 1980; Goldberger and Breznitz, 1993; Pearlin and Schooler, 1978; Zeidner and Endler, 1996). The coping process is variable and complex. Crum, Salovey and Anchor (2013), point out that to avoid or reduce stress can be counterproductive. They argue that demands placed upon managing or avoiding stress could lead to increased stress. For example: avoiding paying the gas or electricity bills can lead to greater stress later on. The way of coping is to either deny that the bill has been received or acceptance that whether payment is due now or later there is likely to be challenges with finding the monies. It acknowledges that there is likely to be increased feelings of stress within the group that are either unable to afford or able to manage their personal finances. Context is an important factor and stress can emerge from the way we interact with the world around us. Coping with personal finances is something that most of us have to cope with. Some are less able to cope than others. To add to feelings of stress, the day also contains periods in which work dominates the mind. The day may be busy, and you are fully able to cope with the challenges. Then the line manager calls you in and, in no uncertain manner, berates you for a spelling or grammar error in a recent report. They then tell you that you are not working hard enough and that there are programmes to design and modules to populate online. They go over and over each point, making it clear that you are not meeting the organisation's expectations. After the hour-and-a-half meeting, you are now behind on the day's work that you had planned earlier that day. The outcome of the meeting has made you feel demotivated and you begin dwelling on how you are going to cope. Stress can also come from home life where there may be a conflict between family members. In the short term, trying to avoid or reduce stress may be a way of coping. In the medium and long term, it can lead to a build-up of pressure and stress that can be difficult to cope with. This may materialise in interpersonal relationships both at home and at work where tempers may become more frayed, and there is less tolerance to other views, actions and behaviours. This in turn can impact upon performance and output. The ability to cope varies, depending on each individual. However, experiences such as the aforementioned appear to occur in many workplace environments. It is, therefore, helpful to make use of effective coping strategies that can ameliorate the negative experiences of stress. However, it is important to recognise that coping strategies, such as denial or acceptance, may have the opposite effect. It is also helpful to delve into "*ways of coping*" a little more. Krohne (2002) explains that appraisal and coping are two concepts which are central to stress theory that are referred to as "*ways of coping*". Carver et al. (1989) go on to explain that within the "*ways of coping*" scale there are two types of coping 1) The first reflects on a person's ability to solve or do something that can alter the source of stress. 2) The second approach focuses upon the person's ability to manage the emotional stress experienced. The findings of research suggest that there is a correlation but varies across studies. This may be partly explained by the studies being spread across decades. The social and working environment at the time may differ to studies undertaken at other times. Other factors that may explain the variance include demographic and cultural changes, background and personal experience.

This chapter builds upon the findings from earlier chapters and begins by exploring in further depth the importance and relevance well-being has in the workplace and at home. Discussion is then given to the importance of thinking in a positive manner and to recognise that personality types such as being introvert can predispose the person to illness. Investigating is then given to the relationship between emotions, memory and creativity and the role that telomeres have. The chapter continues by identifying key mental illnesses that affect people around the world and then delves into the "*dark triad*" (narcissism, Machiavellian and psychopathic dispositions) where people use emotions to manipulate others while having self-centred, grandiose opinions of themselves. This chapter then considers the strong influence emotions have on the way we think and behave and reflects upon the role that cognitive thinking has in helping to learn and understand emotions. This chapter continues to explore the damage stress can have and how it can have a debilitating effect on physical and psychological well-being that can impact on the capacity to function at home and at work. The chapter concludes by explaining the importance that exercise has for both mind and body.

Emotional intelligence and well-being 137

Physical/ psychological well-being

The Chartered Institute of Personnel and Development (CIPD, 2007) define management of well-being as creating an environment that can promote a state of contentment allowing employees to reach their full potential that benefits both themselves and the organisation. They go on to say that it is more than just avoidance of becoming physically sick and that attention should be given to physical, social and mental health. Wilton (2013) adapts the CIPD (2007) sources to explain the five (5) domains of well-being that are shown in the table below:

Table 7.1. Five (5) domains of well-being.

Domain	Indicative element
Physical and mental health	Working environment, physical safety and security.
Values	Ethical values and standards; diversity and inclusion, psychological contract.
Personal development	Lifelong learning. Autonomy. Opportunity to be creative.
Emotional	Positive interpersonal relationships, emotional intelligence, social engagement.
Work/ organisation	Work/life balance. Engaged in organisational change.
	Source: Wilton (2013) adapted from CIPD (2007).

It is too simple to consider well-being in binary terms- feeling well or feeling unwell. As described by Travis and Ryan (2004), well-being should be considered along a continuum with illness at one end and growth at the other. In the middle, there is a neutral point within which there are no signs of either illness or wellness.

Diagram 7.1. Illness/wellness continuum.

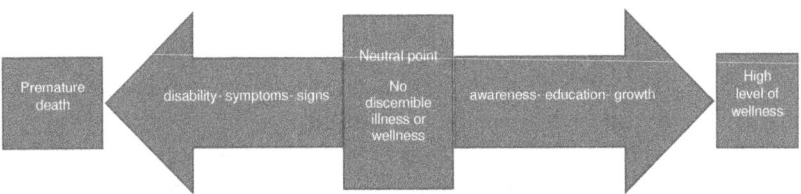

Source: after Travis and Ryan (2004).

Different coping mechanisms are used when coping with stress that includes social interaction with friends and family, watching TV and listening to music. The Anxiety and Depression Association of America (2018) report that participating in physical exercise can have a strong influence on well-being. Similar findings are found in studies that suggest that engaging in physical activity can have beneficial effects on well-being (Liao, Shonkoff and Dunton, 2015). For example, it can vary from doing vigorous exercise at the local gym, running and playing football, to more moderate exercise such as regular walking and gardening (The Mental Health Foundation, 2013). The table below provides a little more detail.

Table 7.2. Types of physical activity.

Activity	Explanation
Sport	Engaging in structured and competitive physical activity.
Exercise	Engaging in physical exercise to improve health and fitness.
Play	Engaging in unstructured physical activity for enjoyment and fun.
Daily physical activity	Daily activity that engages in physical activity. For example, walking to and from work; walking up and down stairs.
	Source: Adapted from Mental Health Foundation (2013).

Physical exercises vary. Walking up the stairs each time we go to bed is a physical exercise. However, that alone is unlikely to be enough in improving feelings of well-being. It is therefore helpful to categorise physical exercise. The Mental Health Foundation (2013) places physical exercise into groups: sport, exercise, play and, daily activity. It is not a matter of having to train to run a marathon or to join the local cycling team. The Mental Health Foundation (2013) comment that even short bursts of a ten-minute brisk walk can increase mental alertness positive mood states and energy. It is putting things in perspective and being sensible about the matter.

The Office for National Statistics (ONS) (2018) find that those between the age of sixteen (16) and twenty-four (24) are more likely to engage in physical activity when compared to other age groups. The UK's population of sixty-six (66) million (mid 2017) is getting older. In 2016, 18.2% people are over the age of sixty-five (65) and 2.4% over the age of eighty-five (85). In another twenty-five (25) years it is estimated that those over the age of sixty-five (65) will make up 25% of the population. Engaging in physical exercise can not only help physical well-being but also psychological well-being and can help support those in society as they enter the older age group. For example, in a meta-analysis undertaken by Stults-Kolehmainen and Sinha (2015), they find that in the majority of the studies analysed, stress impairs the ability to be physically active. This is supported by a study by Novakova, Blahutkova, Muchova and Lepkova (2016) who find that those between the age of sixty-four (64) and seventy-eight (78) years of age show less stress when they attend exercise classes. In the UK, the Department of Health (2011) adds that physical exercise can help reduce depression, stress and anxiety and yet as we get older we participate in less physical activity with those in lower socio-economic groups even less likely to participate. However, this finding does not appear to be consistent when compared to other countries. The World Health Organisation (2018a) point out, that worldwide, an average of 28% of adults (23% men and 32% women) aged eighteen (18) and above are not sufficiently active. Germany, Italy and the UK have similar socio-economic foundations and it would be expected that lack physical activity would be very similar. The UK is above the global average with 35.9% insufficient physical activity and is below countries such as Germany (42.2%), Italy (41.4%) and the USA (40%). However, countries such as France (29.3%) and Spain (26.8%) are well below the UK. It may not be a simple correlation of linking socioeconomic factors with lack of physical exercise. Kuwait is shown to have the highest level of 67% of physical inactivity closely followed by Saudi Arabia (53.1%) and, Iraq (52%). Uganda and Mozambique have the lowest figures of 5.5% and 5.6% respectively. There may be other influencing factors such as ethnographical factors including culture, religion, and background. Further study in this area would be helpful.

The table below provides examples of physical inactivity in selected countries.

Table 7.3. Examples of physical inactivity.

Country	Percentage of insufficient physical activity among adults aged eighteen and over
Kuwait	67%
Saudi Arabia	53.1%
Iraq	52%
Brazil	47%
Germany	42.2%
Italy	41.4%
USA	40%
Greece	37.7%
Japan	35.5%

UK	35.9%
India	34%
France	29.3%
Spain	26.8%
Russia Federation	17.1%
Kenya	15.4
Belarus	14.1%
China	14.1%
Jordan	11.9%
Lesotho	6.3%
Mozambique	5.6%
Uganda	5.5%
	Source: World Health Organisation (2018a).

Notwithstanding the differences in lack of physical activity from one country to another, studies undertaken do suggest that there is a relationship between feelings of depression, stress and anxiety with lack of physical activity. For example, the Anxiety and Depression Association of America find that only 14% of participants exercise to help them cope with stress. A similar study undertaken by Arthritis Research UK (2017) report that 18% of people exercise daily and, 17% say that they never do any form of exercise. The reasons given for not exercising range from not having enough time to feeling too tired. The demands placed upon us in daily lives and in the workplace can become overwhelming, affecting our ability to think clearly and to maintain focus. It appears that as we age, we exercise less, and this can impact upon the ability to cope with stressful experiences. Taking a short break can help recovery and can help improve performance and output. It is the ability to be able to take control and cope with the demands in a resourceful manner. Without it being made mandatory, it may be helpful if organisations made more commitment to staff well-being by engaging with them directly in encouraging physical activity. For example, within the working day, staff could be asked to go for regular and frequent ten (10) minute walks, allowing them time to gather thoughts and regain composure before returning back to the workspace. This may be seen as an added cost; however, the ten (10)-minute breaks may lead to improved motivation, drive and performance.

> **Reflection: No excuses!**
> - When you have completed a task, try and take a break from your workplace.
> - Take regular breaks. If possible at least five minutes in each hour.
> - Take a quick walk round the building and reflect on how you feel on your return.
> - Before and/ or after work take the opportunity to engage in some form of exercise. Go to the gym for half an hour. Go for a swim. Go for a longer walk and pick up the pace. Again, when you return to the workplace or home reflect how you feel.
> - Make time in your day to exercise and enjoy it.
> - Don't make excuses.

Having good social relationships with others can also have a positive influence on well-being that includes *"emotional support"* (gaining emotional support from others) and *"instrumental support"* (gaining advice from others). It is really important to share and engage with others. It helps improve physical and psychological well-being, making us feel happier and more content. The Mental Health Foundation (2016) describes it as the way in which two (2) or more people are connected, or the state of being connected. Studies show that a child that has a secure relationship helps them cope with stress in later life (Gunnar, 2016, Winston and Chicot, 2016). They have a higher positive self-worth and are more able to cope with challenges and change. Being overly critical can undermine a child's self-esteem and development. It can lead to self-doubt. When there is uncertainty and doubt, confidence can be impaired, dividing us into pessimists and optimists (Sigman, 2018). A child that feels insecure or rejected can affect parts of the brain that in later life impairs emotional management (Hart and Rubia, 2012; Oomen, Soeters, Audureau, Vermunt, van Hasselt, et al., 2010). Habits are formed that can be challenging to escape. For example: being excessively self-critical, fear of failure, worry and, low self-esteem. It is no wonder that as adults we are sensitive to criticism, especially when it is personal. Sigman (2018) suggests that there appears to be a link between frontal gyrus within the right hemisphere of the brain. Those who are inclined to be more pessimistic are likely to experience greater activity. Those who are optimistic are likely to see less activation. Sigman (2018) points out that it is not necessarily the capacity to evaluate what is good, but the ability to ignore and to forget what is. It, therefore, appears that there are physiological factors as well as psychological factors that influence how we see the world around us.

We are in a much more connected environment compared to earlier generations. We are now able to connect with people around the world that only a few years ago was regarded as science fiction. We video conference, email, text and share a space on social media. We are more *"wired together"* than ever before, sharing our thoughts and views. However, we may still feel lonely; what appears to be a product of modernity, as it does not appear in English before 1800. There is so much noise going on around us and yet we feel disconnected, and isolated, from true social interconnectedness where we can interact with friends and family. In collaboration with the Welcome Foundation, the BBC (2018) has undertaken a study where fifty-five thousand (55,000) people responded. They identify reasons that participants feel lonely: 1) having no one to talk to; 2) feeling disconnected; 3) feeling left out; 4) sadness and; 5) not feeling understood. The findings show that 40% of those between sixteen (16) and twenty-four (24) years of age feel lonely often or very often. This compares to 27% of participants over the age of seventy-five (75). Those under the age of twenty-four (24) are more likely to engage with social media and it would be expected that they would have more people to talk to, when compared to those over the age of seventy-five. It appears that it is personal interaction and true relationships that are important and not the number of *"friends"* we have on social media.

Loneliness and isolation can lead to long-lasting physical and psychological harm. Studies undertaken on children find that social exclusion can lead to problems later on in life such as self-harm, depression and anxiety and can lead children to using coping strategies such as comfort eating. Hawkley, Thisted, Masi and Cacioppo (2010) find that in a study of those in middle and old age, loneliness appears to predict increased blood pressure. Whether child or adult it is important that social interaction occurs to help develop and maintain healthy well-being (Holt-Lunstad, Smith, Baker, Harris, et al., 2015; Holt-Lunstad, Smith and Layton, 2010). The nature of engagement with others is an important factor and is described as *"social connectedness"*. It is enjoying good interpersonal relationships and having many friends. Sharing feelings and thoughts with others helps build social cohesion and includes emotional support together with material aid that creates a sense of value and belonging that can help reducethe feeling of stress and anxiety. It is important to place things in context. See how small things really are. Social connectedness does have its benefits.

Reflection: Social connectiveness
- Being on your own does not necessarily mean that you are lonely or lack *"social connectiveness"*. We all like time out and a place to think and do things on our own.
- Being in a crowd or a group of people doesn't mean that you are *"socially connecting"* with others. It may be that you are waiting for someone to talk to you. It can be daunting for many people, rather than wait, initiate a discussion.
- When at conferences I often see people, who do not know each other who engage in conversation. It is having the confidence to engage.
- *"Social connectiveness"* could lead to the next step in your career. The more and the better the connections the more likely it is that you can succeed.

Infection, illness, introversion and negative thinking

You may be susceptible to illnesses due to genetic inheritance. It may be that upsetting events from earlier in life that prompt mental illness such as depression. However, Cohen and Williamson (1991) report that when one hundred (100) people are introduced to a cold virus, not everyone becomes sick suggesting that there is likely to be something else that is causing people to become ill. It is not just the common cold making people sick. There is something more going on that appears to relate to personality type. For example, if you are introverted or a negative thinker, you are more likely to be susceptible to developing a cold (Cohen, Doyle, Turner, Alper et al., 2003).

The World Health Organisation (WHO, 2017) reports that depression is now the leading cause of disability and ill health worldwide A large study of nineteen thousand six hundred and forty-nine (19,649) participants show that in a follow up period of eight and a half (8.5) years, those who experience major depressive illness are just under three (3) times more likely to die from heart disease compared to those who did not experience depressive related illness. (Surtees, Wainwright, Luben, Wareham, Bingham and Khaw, 2008). In another study of ninety-six thousand three hundred and seventy-six (96,376) post-menopausal women, the findings show that depressive illness is associated with heart disease (Wassertheil-Smoller, Shumaker, Ockene, Talavera, Greenland et al., (2004). It does suggest that depression and anxiety are associated with heart disease. However, it doesn't necessarily mean that there is a causal relationship. The World Health Organisation (2017) add that between 2005 and 2015, there has been an increase in depression of more than 18% to three hundred million (300 million) people and those with depression are also likely to experience anxiety, change of appetite, energy loss and reduced energy. Further studies also suggest that if you experience bullying at school or experience difficult home life, it can predisposes you to illness as an adult that include: diabetes, cancer and heart disease (for example: Copeland, Wolfe, Angold and Costello, 2013; Copeland, Wolfe, Lereya, Shanahan, et al, 2014; Hemingway and Marmot, 1999; Miller and Chen, 2010; Repetti, Taylor and Seeman, 2002; Teicher and Samsung, 2016; Teicher, Samsung, Polcari and McGreenery, 2006). Emotional imbalance can also contribute to illness. For example, repressing or containing emotions can intensify if not dealt with in controlled measures.

The widening gap in inequality

Inequality is associated with unfairness where one person may have less opportunity than another. In the UK, The Equality Act (2010) was brought in to protect against discrimination, extending protection to include race, religion, gender, disability, age. However, inequality expands much further than income parity/ disparity. Inequality includes factors associated with income, wealth and consumption. This section discusses the affect that inequality is having on social cohesion and considers its effect upon psychological and physical well-being.

The Organisation for Economic Cooperation and Development (OECD, 2018) state that wealth inequality is twice that of income inequality. Zucman (2019) expands the discussion by explaining that in 1980, the combined share of wealth in China, USA and Europe, for the top 1% of the population, accounted for 28%. The latest figures suggest that this has increased to 33%. At the same time, the share of wealth for the bottom 75% of the population remains around 10%. However, measuring wealth at the top does have its limitations as financial globalisation increases challenges in identifying sources. For example, assets can be hidden in places such as tax havens (Zucman, 2019). Mayer and Sullivan (2018) suggest that economic well-being is more nuanced than simply using income as a measure of inequality and it may be more appropriate to use the term "consumption" When compared with income inequality, they suggest that there appears to be little evidence of rising consumption inequality among the bottom half of the population and more modest amongst the top half, especially since 2000. The challenge with measuring consumption is how and what data is collected. It requires consistent and reliable sources. Furthermore, the world population is increasing, and greater demands placed upon consumption. There are so many people who do not grow their own food. They may be subsistence farmers. Data, from such sources, may not be readily available. For the purposes of comparisons, levels of income may be a better means of measuring inequality as this information is more readily available.

The OECD (2019a) report that income inequality amongst the countries in the OECD is higher now than in the past fifty (50) years. The salary gap between the richest and poorest in countries such as the USA and UK has been increasing since the 1970s and is now at a similar level to that experienced in the early part of the twentieth (20th) century (DeNavas-Walt and Proctor, 2015; Wilkinson and Pickett, 2019). Whereas there has been growth in the world economy it is has been uneven. The OECD (2019a) comment that income for the richest 10% is now nine (9) times greater than the poorest 10%. The richest 1% (earning more than one million dollars) owns 45% of the global wealth. Those earning less than ten thousand (10,000) dollars, and make up 64% of global population, own less than 2% of global wealth (Credit Suisse, 2018).

The OECD (2019a) identify the main drivers of inequality to include globalisation, changes in countries policies and changes in skill-based technology. Income in equality impacts upon economic growth and social cohesion (OECD, 2015). The social divide associated with income inequality has been getting bigger over the last few decades and there does appear to be a relationship with health, income differences, inequality and well-being (Marmot, 2015; Pickett and Wilkinson, 2015; Wilkinson and Pickett, 2006; Wilkinson and Pickett, 2010).

The OECD (2019b) report that in 2017, countries with the highest levels of income inequality include South Africa, Costa Rica, Mexico, Chile and Turkey. The USA is sixth (6th). The Equality Trust (2019) report that, when compared to other developed countries, the UK has a very high level of inequality. The UK follows as the ninth (9th) most inequal society. Countries identified as having the highest levels of equality include Slovak Republic, Slovenia, Czech Republic, Iceland, Norway and Belgium.

In the "spirit level", Wilson and Pickett (2010) explain that in more inequal societies the hierarchy of status and income is greater, than in countries that are more equal, creating greater competition and insecurity in the population. Those at lower income are likely to experience greater financial stress; unable to pay the latest utility bill or school uniform. Inequality crosses boundaries such as gender, class, religion and background. It increases feelings of superiority and inferiority between groups in society in which one person compares their status to another. We need to fit in and find our place. The increasing levels of inequality mean that finding our place can result in increased levels of stress and anxiety. It can also lead to feelings of inadequacy. Stretching the hierarchy creates greater differentiation between those who have and those who don't. The effects of inequality therefore reach a wider part of society. It doesn't just impact upon the poorest. It limits social mobility and economic well-being.

Limitations are acknowledged in measuring levels of inequality whether this is by means of income, wealth or consumption. For example, Mayer and Sullivan (2018) point out that the official statistics may refer to pre-tax income and may not take into consideration factors such as tax credits, food stamps and housing benefits. Limitations may influence the analysis and evaluation of data. There are different approaches to measuring inequality (for example, income, wealth and consumption). Notwithstanding the limitations, there does appear to be supporting evidence to support the view that the difference between the lowest paid and the highest paid is increasing. This is leading to a steeper hierarchy in which members of society need to identify their position and status. They increasingly compare themselves with others, placing themselves under greater stress and anxiety. It increases the likelihood of interpersonal disagreement and conflict. It increases the likelihood of disharmony and discontent amongst society. It is apparent that income inequality is associated social cohesion. In such a society, it is likely to be easier to pit one group against another, to create infighting. While this goes on, those in the 1% increase their stake of income and wealth. Pickett and Wilkinson (2015) suggest that well-being and health would improve if the gap in inequality were narrowed. There would likely be greater cohesiveness in communities and greater social cohesion and trust (Paskov and Dewilde, 2012; Uslaner, 2012). There does appear to be a link between levels of mental illness and stress being experienced and the widening of social inequality. Pickett and Wilkinson (2010) point out that in countries such as Germany and Japan, where there are lower levels of inequality, approximately 10% of the population report experiencing a mental illness in the previous twelve (12) months. The findings from the USA show that mental illness accounts for 25% of the population. Similar findings are found in a meta-analysis undertaken by Ribeiro, Bauer, Andrade, York-Smith et al. (2017).

It is not just a matter of how the person copes with stress. There are wider issues that affect organisations, communities and countries that also need to be considered. Whereas it is important to address personal feelings of stress and anxiety, it is helpful to look at wider influences that affect how we experience and manage stress, not just from an individual point of view, but from a societal and organisational point of view as well. When addressing mental and/ or physical illness, it is important to look at who we are as a whole, and not just the individual, bringing the whole system back into balance (Barrett, 2017). Inequality damages society (Wilkinson and Pickett, 2019).

The latest figures (216/17) identified by the Social Metrics Commission (2019) identify 22% of the population in the UK are in poverty. This amounts to 14.2 million people, of which, 8.4 million are working age adults. The Social Metrics Commission (2019) define poverty as a family that receives 55% or less than that received by "*the median family*", the one in the middle. Whereas measurement of poverty is relative, maybe a more egalitarian approach would change the way we think, taking more time to recognise and include all members of society. Maybe, a more equal society would reduce poverty and improve social cohesion. It could improve feelings of psychological and physical well-being.

Passiveness and "*I can take it*" syndrome

Western thinking encourages the "*go getter*". The "*I can take it syndrome*". Western society appears to encourage the "*strong*" and the "*resilient*", where personality is associated with the individual. In Asian countries, personality is associated with the person being interdependent where there is greater personal interaction between people (Markus and Kitayama, 1998). Those who are inclined to have a passive personality are more likely to the associated with collective Eastern cultures, whereas in Western culture, it is seen as a negative (Sue and Sue, 1990; Triandis, 1996). It is, therefore, not unsurprising that Asian men experience difficulties in adapting to Western culture. Not everyone is made of the "*I can take it*" approach. Those in Western society who have a passive personality and are introverted may also experience difficulties in adapting. They may try to demonstrate the resilience that others around them show and that which is expected by the organisation. However, the demands placed upon them can conflict with their true self potentially giving rise to stress and anxiety. Staff members may suppress emotions and display others that do not accurately represent how they actually feel. It leads to emotional dissonance which is the conflict between emotions experienced and that required by the organisation.

Personality factors such as being introvert do appear to be a strong contributing factor that influences how people respond to stressful events. For example, having a passive personality does not necessarily help in coping with the demands placed on people in the working environment. The challenge that many people have is to cope with the daily challenges of life. The stresses experienced can impact upon the immune system. Predisposition to passivity and being introvert can place increased pressure on the body's immune system and can result in problems with health. Western culture may not be conducive to those with passive personality as those who are passive are more inclined to experience stress, experience distorted thinking and less able to deal with stressful problems (Smith, 2002). It may add to emotional dissonance contributing to feelings of job tension, emotional exhaustion, reduced self-esteem, stress and anxiety (Abraham, 1998; Indregard, Knardahl, and Nielson, 2018). It is not surprising that some people can say that "*I can take it*" while others find it challenging.

Emotions and memory

Emotions play an important role in cognitive processes. For example, attention, learning reasoning and memory. Emotions help encode, consolidate and, retrieve information.

Encoding is the perception and interpretation of stimuli by the senses that stored in the brain. The senses help encode the memory include: acoustic (hearing), visual (sight), tactile (touch) and is related with short term (working) memory (Kane and Engle, 2003). Individual differences and context also play a role that influences the meaning and understanding of the experience. Lindstrom and Bohlin (2011) carry out a "*two back test*" where they show a sample of fifty-two (52) adults highly negative stimuli involving violent death and highly arousing stimuli with sexual scenes. They find that the emotional stimuli help to improve response and reaction. In another study, Mackay and Ahmetzanov (2005) carry out a Stroop test where seventy-two (72) participants are given a colour naming task and location of a word and asked to ignore the word meaning. They find that attention enhances the overall location of the word and memory of the colour and that emotion enhances the memory for the location of the word but not the colour. This suggests that memories charged with emotion are not like photographs where there is a high density of pixels that provide detail. Memories appear to be constructed with less detail and fewer pixels making up a mental image very similar to a *fuzzy photograph*. However, there are exceptions. Brown and Kulik (1977) refer to the term *"flashbulb memory"* in which people are able to recall details where an event occurs that is significant to them. A good example is that of 9/11, where people remember vivid details of what they were doing at the time and how they were feeling. It suggests that the emotional state of how the person is feeling at the time influences whether or not the event is encoded into the memory and to how deep it is encoded. However, it appears to be dependent on the significance of the event.

Consolidation is where short-term memories are transferred to long term memory. Emotional memories are formed and consolidated following positive or negative experiences. Retrieval is where stored information is recalled. Recalling information repeatedly strengthens and reinforces neural pathways in long term memory. However, they do not necessarily become permanent. It is the process of recalling the memory that allows for its retention. Memories can be faulty, though. Information about the memory is stored in different parts of the brain and necessitates neural pathways delivering the information as it happens. However, it is not a simple act of recalling and replaying the experience. Opinions are formed, and judgements made as to whether or not we like something. Our very make up and understanding of the world around us can influence how and what is retrieved. Our bodily states and emotional values lead us to making decisions and to whether or not to approach or avoid something (Damasio, 1994). Taleb (2007) adds that we fool ourselves by constructing insubstantial and flimsy accounts of past events, believing that they are true. The whole experience may not be recalled or reconstructed. We may engage with negative emotions such as fear and anger. These can become recurring to such an extent that they can be overwhelming and debilitating. False memories can be formed and there can be the misinterpretation of the actual experience. This is when it is helpful to call on experts in the field to help replace and reconsolidate less harmful and threatening memories. New contexts can be formed and activated helping to place the experience in a different context.

Emotions and creativity

Fredrickson (2001) comments that positive emotions can be fundamental to human strength that involves creativity, while negative emotions can be detrimental to creativity. However, subsequent studies suggest that it is not necessarily the contrast between positive and negative emotions that relate to the level of creativity. It may be the degree (motivational intensity) as to how much a person is attracted to or seeks to avoid something. Kaufman (2015) adds that creativity comes from the ability to broaden attention and to narrow attention. Creative people appear to show greater connections between areas of the brain associated with spontaneous thought and cognitive control. It involves both rationality and calmness together with feelings of inspiration and euphoria. Creative people have the ability to mix what appear to be incompatible states (Beaty, Benedek, Kaufman, and Silvia, 2015). Further work undertaken by Ceci and Kumar (2015) finds that those who experience intense emotions score higher on creativity compared to those who just feel positive and negative emotions. Kaufman (2015) puts it succinctly; living life with intensity and passion, that includes experiencing full depth human experience, is conducive to creativity. He adds that the extent that a person is open to their emotions is a better predictor of creativity than IQ or intellectual engagement. He concludes by suggesting that managers could encourage a creative working environment in which staff members can embrace different feelings and emotions (emotional ambivalence) that can broaden or narrow focus (motivational intensity). For organisations to succeed in the global market place, creativity is needed. Creativity can help develop and improve ways of working and can result in improved output, motivation and performance. Furthermore, staff members, who work in a more creative environment where there is less stricture (control, criticism and restraint), may feel less pressured and stressed.

Self-help

As human beings, we have the ability to ruminate on experiences. While ruminating, it is possible to live through the emotions of the experience as well as the actual event. Indeed, it may be that the rumination of the event can lead to exaggerated feelings and emotions, increasing anxiety and emotional negativity. This can add to a feeling of already being overwhelmed placing greater stress on the body and mind. Alternatively, we may seek to try and suppress the memory and move on. However, in the back of our mind, the memory may create anchors that remain years and years after the event. It is only when a similar event occurs again that we react- while we may not remember the event itself. The complexity of the mind!

It may be helpful to reframe the way our minds pick up on the stressful event. However, by thinking of an experience allows us to dwell on it and this can increase the stress levels rather than reducing them. Distancing thoughts from emotion can alleviate the stress being experienced, where the person sees themselves as an observer looking in from an outside point. By doing so, it helps decrease emotional reaction. However, one person may be able to visualise themselves more effectively as an observer, while others may find it much more difficult.

> **Reflection: Two-week diary**
>
> Keep a two-week diary of what you do each day and include:
> - The time you go to bed and the time you wake up.
> - What you eat and when.
> - Travelling times.
> - Breaks during the day and what you do in those breaks.
> - What you do when you return from work.
> - Keep in tune with your emotions and write down what and how you are feeling.
> - What is the best thing that has happened during the time you have kept the diary.
>
> Having kept the diary review its contents and consider:
> - Are there events that could be better planned and organised?
> - Could you have dealt with particular experiences in a more focused way?
> - Are you getting enough sleep?
> - Are you eating enough and the right things?
> - Can you find more *"me"* time and accept *"things just happen"*?
> - Ask yourself *"Am I in tune with work and home life?"*
> - How did you feel when you experienced the best thing that happened to you while keeping the diary?
> - Reword challenging and demanding experiences that you have had in more positive terminology.
> - Now ask, what are you going to do about improving and developing your skills in addressing the challenges.
>
> This is a cyclic process that allows you to develop skills in managing time, events and most importantly you.
>
> **Remember:** Focus on the positives.

Telomeres

It is important for organisations and staff members to acknowledge and recognise that different personality types can influence how well pressure and stress is dealt with. At one end of the spectrum are those who are prone to pessimism and more likely to have shorter telomeres. They ruminate on negative experiences and outcomes that can be associated with depressive disorders including anxiety and depression (Nolen-Hoeksema, 2000). At the other end of the spectrum are those who have an optimistic view of life and focus on positive outcomes and experience. They face up to challenges as having little or no effect on their well-being. Telomeres are short lengths of DNA that protect the chromosomes and as we get older, the telomeres reduce. As long as telomeres function, cells in the human body continue to divide. However, a little bit of the telomere is lost each time a cell divided. As we get older, telomeres shorten, and cells stop dividing, leaking substances into the system that make us more susceptible to illness and disease. As we age, we get to the point where we leave the period of good health and enter age-related illness and disease that is referred to as *"senescence"*. Furthermore, each time we are stressed, ruminate, or try and suppress a negative experience, cortisol goes up, blood pressure goes up, and heart rate goes up, reducing the length of telomeres. As the telomeres wear down, they are unable to protect the chromosome, as well, and cells begin to malfunction. This creates the conditions in which the body is at increased risk of serious illness such as cancer and diabetes. Heavy workloads and demands, long working hours and, financial problems add to the pressure on physical and psychological well-being that can reduce the length of telomeres.

Stress appears to be directly associated with shorter telomeres. It is not just the actual event that can cause stress. Stress and impact upon the telomeres can occur worrying and thinking about something that is yet to happen. The greater the stress, the greater the impact there is on telomere. Reduction in telomeres leads to premature aging and the immune system becomes less able to cope with disease and illness such as cancer, diabetes, flu and, colds) (Basu, Skinner, Litzelman, Vanderboom et al., 2014; Cohen, Janicki-Deverts, Turner, Casselbrant et al., 2013).

It is an interesting observation that some people may look older than they actually are. Others appear to be a lot younger than they actually are. Admittedly, nature and nurture both have roles to play. However, it does appear that those who have a negative view about aging see others differently when compared to those who have a positive view. Furthermore, those who have a negative view may experience a greater decline in memory. They are more likely to have a heart attack and are likely to recover more slowly after an injury or falling ill (Levy, Slade, Murphy and Gill. 2012). It, therefore, follows that thinking of aging in a positive manner can lead to us living longer; possibly up to seven and half years longer than someone with negative thinking about age.

Sleep can also influence the length of telomeres. Those who sleep less than five (5) hours are likely to have shorter telomeres. Those who sleep seven (7) hours, or more are shown to have longer telomeres that help protect the immune system (Jackowska, Hammer, Carvalho, Erusalimsky et al., 2012). This is particularly helpful as we get older and less able to cope with serious illness (Cribbet, Carlisle, Cawthon, Uchino et al., 2014).

Education is recognised as a predictor of physical and psychological well-being and in studies undertaken it is found that those who have more education are likely to have longer telomeres (Adler, Boyce, Chesney, Cohen et al., 1994; Robertson, Batty, Der, Fenton et al., 2013). Studies also show that having the basic needs of life can influence the length of telomeres. Those who do not have enough money to afford the basic needs are more likely to have shorter telomeres. However, having more wealth does not necessarily mean that telomeres will be longer (Theal, Brett, Shirtcliff, Dunn et al., 2013). In a further study, those who are in white collared jobs are more likely to have longer telomeres when compared to those from blue collared jobs. This may be related to education, as those in white collared jobs are likely to have experienced higher levels of education, when compared to those who are in blue-collared jobs (Cherkas, Valdes, Hunkin, Gardner et al., 2006).

The blunt message is that keeping healthy can help manage stress and this can protect the telomeres. It reinforces the advice to exercise, to have a balanced diet and sleep pattern while maintaining a sensible work/ life balance.

Reflection: Three to five-minute break

Try and take a three to five-minute break each hour while focusing on your breathing.
- Breathe in through your nose from one to three.
- Breathe out through your mouth counting one to five.
- Repeat this exercise- remember: focus on the breathing and don't allow other thoughts to intrude.

The dark triad

One of the challenging areas of life is having to interact with someone who does not experience emotions as others may do. History is littered with people who have psychopathic tendencies, that can influence others, that in the end may end in destruction. They appear to be convincing but, underneath, there is no consciousness. As well as being psychopathic, there may also be evidence of narcissistic and Machiavellian behaviour which is described as *"the dark triad"* and can be partially inherited from our parents (Paulhus and Williams, 2002; Vernon, Villani, Vickers and Harris, 2008). Collectively, *"the dark triad"* is demonstrated in human behaviour as someone who acts in self-interest and uses antisocial approaches to achieve their objectives and goals both at home and at work (Jonason, Li, Webster and Schmitt, 2009; Jonason an O'Conner, 2017). While demonstrating spite and sadistic traits, they are motivated by power, focus on the present moment, and seek to dominate others. (Birkas and Csatho, 2015; Marcus, Zeigler-Hill, Mercer and Norris, 2014; Semenyna and Honey, 2015).

Babiak and Hare (2006) define psychopathy as a personality disorder where the person is without conscience and is incapable of loyalty, guilt or empathy except to themselves. There appears to be an insensitivity to emotional information. Vernon, Villani, Schermer and Petrides (2008) find that psychopathy is more likely to be influenced by heritable factors and less so by environmental factors when compared with Machiavellianism and narcissism.

Levenson, Kiehl, Cory et al. (1995) identifies two (2) subtypes of psychopathy. The first being *"primary psychopathy"* which is an interpersonal dimension that is characterised by traits such as cruelty and lack of conscience. They are interpersonally manipulative, are emotionally cold, and lack empathy. The second is *"secondary psychopathy"* which describes someone that may be socially deviant or as being irresponsible. A person high on the psychopathic scale is likely to experience low anxiety levels, be impulsive and a thrill seeker, engaging in anti-social behaviour. They are more inclined to be socially deviant and irresponsible. Babiak and Hare (2006) state that subclinical psychopathy includes cheating, plagiarism, bullying and drug use. Subclinical psychopathy is characterised by high impulsivity and thrill-seeking, paired with low anxiety and empathy (Hare, 1985). At the time of writing this book, Babiak and Hare (2016) are developing an instrument to measure attitudes, behaviour and judgments. They put forward a list of examples of leadership traits and psychopathic traits. For example, leadership traits may include someone who is charismatic, self-confident, able to persuade others, and is a visionary. In comparison, those with psychopathic traits include someone who lacks emotions, has superficial charm, is impulsive, has feelings of grandiosity and manipulates others for their own gain.

Using Levenson et al. (1995) self-report psychopathy scale, Dutton (2012) has undertaken his own study of psychopathic traits and which professions it appears more/ less prevalent. He finds that those with the greatest prevalence are Chief Executive Officers (CEO), lawyer, media (TV/ radio) and salesperson. Interestingly police came seventh (7th) on the most prevalent. Those who show the lowest levels of psychopathic traits include: care worker, nurse, therapist, craftsperson and beautician. Teachers came seventh (7th) on the least prevalent.

When thinking about the working environment, and those in it, there does appear to be a fine line between these traits. However, before coming to any conclusions about your line manager or colleagues, it is worth noting that it needs an expert to form a medical conclusion, but it does show how easy it is for someone to gain the trust of others and to manipulate them. The employer may have a person who is not necessarily the person that they thought or think they appointed. Self-report psychological tests are often relied upon within the working environment to assess a person's personality, attitudes and habits; for example, when a person applies for a job. This requires the person to be truthful and honest. Whereas the tests are designed to identify errors and possible lies, it is possible that a person can fake or slant the results and get away with it. Those with psychopathic tendencies can damage the working environment and customer relations and can impact upon the overall success of the organisation. It is sometimes better to move on than to face the *"devil"*. As Babiak and Hare (2006:313) explains the best solution is to put as much distance as possible between you and the psychopathic co-worker. If the situation becomes untenable, it may be necessary to consider a transfer away from the co-worker or to even leave the organisation completely.

Narcissism is where a person is egotistic and self-orientated (Raskin and Hall, 1979). They demonstrate high self-esteem, selfishness, and a feeling of grandiosity. They have feelings of self-importance and lack conventional morality while displaying manipulative behaviour with the intention of promoting their own interests. As well as being arrogant, they have feelings of entitlement and have a sense of superiority over others. It isn't just self-delusion; they really believe it. Craig Malkin (2015) delves much more deeply into spotting *"outsized egos"* in his book *"The Narcissist test"*.

A person with Machiavellianism tendencies is likely to be emotionally distant and detached in their interactions with others. They are inclined to be deceptive or cunning with the desire to gain advantage over others. They exploit others to achieve their own self-interest and have a lack of morality (Christie and Geis, 1970). The term Machiavellianism is derived from Machiavelli, a playwright, philosopher and politician who was born in Florence in 1469 and rose to become a diplomat in the Florentine republic. When he was dismissed from his role in 1512, he wrote *"The Prince"*, that points out the ruthlessness, guile and deceit used by politicians. It has come known as the *"handbook for politicians"* from which the term Machiavellianism has been derived.

Austin, Farrelly, Black, and Moore (2007) find that, whereas there is a positive correlation between Machiavellianism and emotional manipulation, there is a negative correlation between Machiavellianism and emotional intelligence and, there is a negative correlation between emotional manipulation and emotional intelligence. O'Boyle, Forsyth, Banks and McDaniel (2011) look at two hundred and forty-five (245) samples, in a meta-analysis, that include forty-three thousand nine hundred and seven (43,907) people and compare the dark triad with behaviour. They find a clear indication that the quality of the job performance is consistently associated with Machiavellianism and psychopathy and that counterproductive work behaviour is associated with increases in each of the components of the dark triad. The dark triad, that these people exhibit, can influence other people leading to damage to the organisation and impact the well-being of staff members. They may demonstrate the presence of high levels of emotional intelligence (when it may be superficial) using it to their own advantage and to the detriment of others. In other words, they can manipulate other people leading to stress, burnout or indeed, death in extreme circumstances.

Emotions and cognitive thinking and control

Being able to control how feelings are expressed can be challenging to many of us, especially when emotions are heightened. It may require steely determination not to say something. It may be having to say no to that chocolate cake placed in front of you. It may be associated with holding back views about others. It requires control, cognitive control, of how we behave. Cognitive control has benefits for society and those in it and this is reflected in the dualist way of separating emotions from rational thinking. Emotion is often regarded as the antithesis of cognitive control that undermines rational thought. However, as human beings, emotions are an integral part of our makeup. Emotions help us remember things. They help us store information in the memory. Suppressing emotions can suggest that we maintain calmness and cognitive control. However, to do so can have an adverse impact upon overall physical and psychological health. Suppressing emotions can also lead to mental fatigue and memory lapses. Over time it can result in chronic stress that affects telomeres and the ability to fend off illness. Furthermore, less oxytocin is released into the system that can help the body control blood pressure, respiration and heart rate. Sleep patterns can be disrupted, and digestive problems may emerge that include acid reflux and ulcers. It is important to be able to express emotions and not to take things personally. Cognitive control helps control emotions and place them in a social environment that is appropriate.

Exercise mind and body

In 1995, the World Health Organisation estimate that, worldwide, there are two hundred (200) million obese adults. In 2000, the estimate is three hundred (300) million (House of Commons Health Committee, 2004). In 2016, the World Health Organisation (2018b) estimate that six hundred and fifty (650) million adults are obese, accounting for 39% of the world's adult population. In the UK, obesity is reported to occur in 25% of the adult population (The National Health Service, UK, 2019). In the USA, obesity ranges from 22.6% in Colorado to 38.1% in West Virginia. Overall obesity exceeds 25% in forty-eight (48) states (State of obesity, 2018). It can lead to type two diabetes, cancer, stroke and heart disease. Studies have been undertaken on obesity, investigating if there is a relationship with genetic inheritance. Maes, Neale and Eaves, (1997) find that genetic factors account for 50% -90% of the variance in body mass index (BMI). Herrera and Lindgren (2010) find that it accounts for 40% - 70% variance. Franzini, Elliott, Cuccaro, Schuster et al. (2009) suggest that there may also be a link with physical and social neighbourhood environments on children's physical activity and obesity. Whereas studies suggest that obesity is genetically inherited, the percentage of those who are obese appears to be increasing and, genetics only answers part of the reason for such a dramatic increase. For example, we have a more sedentary style of life both at home and work. We do not burn up the calories as previous generations have done. We also have wider diets (including fast food) that are more economically accessible. As cultures, we seem to have fast food outlets embedded in almost every high street providing high processed meals at a low cost. This can have added influence in reducing telomeres aging people faster and reducing lifespan.

Stress is part of daily lives and takes many forms. However, chronic stress can cause physical and psychological illness reducing telomeres and increasing changes of premature aging. Furthermore, chronic ailments (for example: arthritis, cancer, celiac disease) can lead to inflammation and premature aging and death. Those with shorter telomeres appear to allow their minds to wander and to ruminate on things and are more inclined to experience anxiety and depression while suppressing emotions and feelings (Nolen-Hoeksema, 2000). In their study about introspection, Wilson and Schooler (1991) find that just thinking about depression can make a person more depressed. Blackburn and Epel (2017) comment that suppressing thought can lead to depression or chronic stress (hyperactive stress syndrome). This is supported by O'Donovan, Tillie, Dhabhar, Wolkowitz et al., (2009) who find that pessimism relates to shortening of telomeres. Placing the experience in context can be helpful; understanding the cause and what can be done to address the feelings and emotions. A positive mindset can have a significant influence on maintaining control of physical and psychological well-being. However, trying to analyse yourself in too much depth can be counterproductive as it may engage the mind in rumination of negative thoughts and emotions. It is important not to dwell on past events and not to worry about the future.

Reflection: 10-minute exercise
- Close your eyes and focus on your breathing.
- Breathe in and count one to three and then out through your mouth one to five. Do this a few times.
- While breathing in and out repeat quietly to yourself a word such as "content", "peaceful", "safe".
- Do this for ten minutes and then ask yourself how you are feeling. Continue to do this on a regular basis.

Having a positive view of the world around us can have beneficial outcomes. It is helpful to have a positive view of aging and to identify yourself with good health and to have a positive self-image and to see *"how trivial the things we want so passionately are"* (Marcus Aurelius, 2006). Exercising the mind and the body can refocus thinking away from negative thoughts. It helps to improve mood and benefits the body to become more resilient to stress and ill health. Exercising can be in the form of aerobics, swimming, walking and going to the gym. Exercising can also be in the form of meditation, mindfulness and yoga that can help attenuate telomere reduction. Indeed, exercising can help replenish the telomeres.

It is important to note that exercising is not necessarily an alternative to medicine. However, it can help the mind and the body maintain better health and control, reducing and hopefully, eliminating potential damage that may otherwise be caused. It can also help reduce stress and anxiety, improve sleep and have overall benefits to the feeling of well-being.

Reflection: The inner self
1. Have a look in the mirror and ask yourself how old you look and feel?
2. Consider your overall physical and psychological health? Ask yourself if you feel as healthy as others of a similar age?
3. Let negative thoughts go by. Do not ruminate on them.
4. Focus on what you enjoy. Focus on what brings you happiness.
5. Be kind and compassionate to yourself.
6. Become more aware and in tune with your inner self.
7. Consider what you can do to reduce wear on the telomeres. How about:
   a. Eating more healthy foods and limiting fast food intake?
   b. Regular health checks?
   c. Attending a weekly yoga or mindfulness class?
   d. Regular walks?
   e. Improving sleeping patterns?
   f. Swimming?
   g. Regular visits to the gym?
   h. Reviewing work/ life balance?

The above are a few examples. As mentioned elsewhere in this book, what is important is that **action** is taken.

Summing up

This chapter begins with a discussion around physical and psychological well-being explaining that it can be seen as a continuum with illness at one end and growth at the other. 28% of the world's population are reported as not being sufficiently active, with the UK at 35.9% and the USA at 40%. Studies show that exercising correlates with feelings of less stress and anxiety and improved well-being. Whereas, we do like to have our own space and time to be alone, whether a child or adult, building good interpersonal relationships and *"being socially connected"* are shown to correlate with feelings of positive well-being (Cacioppo and Patrick, 2009). It is important to address feelings of loneliness and isolation as they can lead to long-lasting damage to well-being (Cacioppo and Cacioppo, 2014; Cacioppo, Hughes, Waite, Hawkley et al., 2006).

Some people may be more predisposed feelings of stress and emotional imbalance that can lead to psychological and physical illness. Others may regard the experiences as just a slight irritation. Personality is shown to be a strong determinant as to how someone experiences emotion. For example, being an introvert and/ or negative thinking, they are likely to experience more illness such as catching a cold (Cohen, Doyle, Turner, Alper et al., 2003). Being susceptible to illness appears to be more than genetic inheritance. The environment in which we live, together with socio-economic factors, are acknowledged as likely causes of psychological and physical illness (Marmot, 2015).

Western society identifies with the "*macho*" style of "*I can take it*". Some thrive in this pugilistic *go getter* approach demonstrating "*strong*" and "*resilient*" personalities. Others may find it challenging to cope with the stresses and pressures that come with engaging in this environment. Eastern cultures are associated with more passive behaviour respecting the collective "*whole*" where people are interdependent on each other. It explains why cultural differences and personality types can be influential in being able to cope with Western culture and management style. The stresses experienced can impact upon the immune system increasing pressure on the body's immune system that can lead to psychological and physical illness.

The chapter then discusses the role that emotions have to play in the cognitive process: encoding, consolidation, and retrieval of information. Most memories are encoded with emotion that are made up of pixels that create "*fuzzy photographs*". However, there are exceptions where events standout above others creating *flashbulb memories* allowing the person to remember detail and emotions felt at the time. Once short-term memories are consolidated they are transferred to the long-term memory forming positive and negative experiences from which they are retrieved. It may be only part of the experience that is recalled, and this can be in the form of emotion. Misinterpretation may occur, or false memories created. As such new contexts can be formed helping to place the experience in a different context.

The chapter also discusses the role of creativity that is associated with the ability to broaden or narrow attention. Creative people have the ability to mix what appear to be incompatible states such as calmness and euphoria. They are more likely to show greater connections between areas of the brain associated with spontaneous thought and cognitive control. Creativity has an important role to play as organisations face increased globalised competition. Rather than trying to suppress emotions, organisations could nurture staff members to engage with emotions, encouraging them to be more creative.

Those who work in a more creative environment may feel less pressured and stressed. Staff members may feel more motivated and this could improve service delivery, performance and output.

Those with a negative outlook on life appear to age sooner. They are more likely to experience physical and/ or psychological illness earlier and find it more challenging to recover from illness. Some people appear to think, behave and look younger than they actually are, and are more likely to live longer than a person who has a negative outlook of life. Therefore, it is helpful to engage with positive thinking and attitude, reducing the effect of illness. Reframing the way our minds think can help reduce stress levels distancing negative experiences as an observer rather than a participant.

Telomeres are located at each end of the chromosome. As we get older, chromosomes divide and a little bit more of the telomere is lost. We get to the "*senescence*" age where chromosomes and telomeres are no longer functioning as well, and this can make us more susceptible to illness and disease such as cancer and diabetes. Stress caused by heavy workloads, long working hours and, financial problems also adds to the pressure on well-being, reducing the length of telomeres further. It is also important to have enough sleep each night, at least seven hours, especially as we get older. Maintaining good health and managing stress can help protect the telomeres. It reinforces the mantra to exercise, to have a balanced diet and to have a sensible work/ life balance.

The dark triad is discussed explaining the role of psychopathy, Machiavellian and narcissism. Those with this type of personality are likely to be in every organisation, throughout the world, and can be damaging to interpersonal relationships and the very foundation of the organisation. The damage caused can be irreparable. They appear to be convincing but underneath, there is no conscience.

The dualistic view of separating emotions and rational thought has been espoused for millennia. Keeping emotions hidden requires conjuring up strong cognitive willpower and strength. Suppressing emotions may suggest that we are keeping calm; however, to suppress them can have an adverse impact upon well-being. It can result in chronic stress. Sleep patterns can be disrupted, and digestive problems may emerge. Long term damage can be caused to physical and psychological well-being. It is, therefore, important to be able to express emotions and not to take things personally.

The chapter enters into discussion as to the importance of exercising the body and the mind. We appear to be visiting and eating from fast food outlets on a regular and frequent basis and levels of obesity have now risen to 35.9% in the UK and 40% in the USA. It can reduce the length of the telomeres and can lead to debilitating illnesses such as type 2 diabetes, cancer, stroke, and heart disease. People can age faster, and their lifespan reduced. We are facing challenges to work/ home life balance where stress appears to be experienced in many guises. Chronic stress can develop, reducing telomeres and increasing changes of premature aging. It is worth reflecting on how busy you may be and to find a little "*me time*". It is important not to dwell on past events and to worry about the future. Try and maintain a positive mindset and to place things in context. Improve your mind and body and find time to exercise and to take regular breaks. As Seneca (2004) comments *"the one who puts the finishing touches on their life each day is never short of time"*.

Chapter 8

Training and development

Developing skills and knowledge of emotional intelligence can be helpful in supporting staff members coping with challenging and stressful experiences. Effective examples of training and development include: communication, stress management techniques and, handling conflict.

Cherniss (2000) refers to strategies associated with workplace training and development, that can be grouped into three (3) phases of change: 1) Preparation for change; 2) Engaging in the work associated with change and; 3) Maintaining and monitoring change. Each of the phases can engage with developing skills in understanding your own emotions, understanding the emotions in others and managing them effectively. Change can be daunting and sometimes difficult to handle. New hardware or software may be introduced, restructuring may occur, new ways of working may be introduced. Being prepared means developing and gaining skills so that when change does occur you are able to cope. Doing the work puts into practice skills and knowledge gained in the preparation stage. It is also building on the skills and knowledge that the new way of working becomes the *"norm"*; encouraging, maintaining and evaluating change incorporates good management technique and style that helps understand personality types in the team, while engaging in positive reinforcement.

Evaluating the change means reflecting and building on experience creating a climate for learning and well-being (Cohen, 2006; Cooper, 1997). Training in emotional intelligence can be instrumental in the success to change. This is supported in a study from findings of a case study in healthcare by Clarke (2006). Developing skills in emotional intelligence can lead to greater career success, improvement in interpersonal relationships and improving effective leadership skills. In a study of sixty (60) managers, undertaken by Slaski and Cartwright (2003), findings show that training in emotional intelligence does improve health and well-being. In another study, training in emotional intelligence is shown to be an important component for effective leadership and is particularly helpful in supporting and guiding staff members (Palmer, Walls, Burgess and Stough, 2001).

It is also important that managers recognise personality types and that some people are much more able to *"take it"* than others. There is a continuum, as shown below.

Diagram 8.1. The *"I can take it"* continuum.

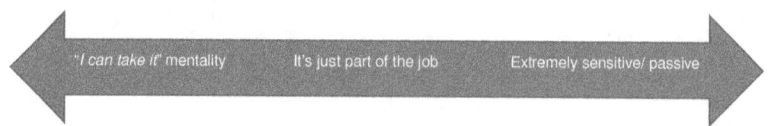

At one end are those who say that "*I can take it*" and can thrive on confrontation and stress. In the middle are those who accept it as being part of the job and do not necessarily absorb stress. At the other end of the spectrum are those who are sensitive and passive and are more inclined to feel stress and anxiety. Management style needs to be flexible, understanding the personality types and appreciating that personal and professional criticism can be damaging to those who are more inclined to be sensitive. Training and development in self-awareness and understanding emotions in others can help all staff members to build skills and knowledge that can help facilitate change taking all the people with them in a positive and constructive environment. It is developing skills in emotional intelligence.

This chapter reflects upon ways to develop and include emotional intelligence skills into the workplace and home. It begins by discussing the role inspiration has to play and the importance to reframe management style to encourage staff members. Different techniques are then introduced, commencing with mindfulness and how it can help reconnect the mind with body. The chapter then reflects on how walking, talking and smiling can be constructive in lifting emotions and goes on to discuss reframing of the mindset. This can be a helpful tool, identifying negative feelings and irrational judgement and replacing them with positive and constructive thoughts. Self-awareness is then discussed. We spend almost 50% of our time allowing our minds to wander (Killingsworth and Gilbert, 2010). We do not seem to spend enough time in the "*now*". Being more self-aware can help focus on the present moment and improve thinking processes while acknowledging and placing emotions and feelings within a sensible and reasonable context. This brings us to the "*white room*", a short exercise that can help refocus the mind and help you to relax.

Motivating and inspiring

How many times have you asked someone to do something and they do not do what you expected or wanted? How many times have you been asked to do something to be informed at the end that that was not what I wanted? It can lead to disagreement, conflict and in some instances hostile words and actions that may include anger and tears. As a child, your mother may say do not touch

Training and development 163

the hot stove. Don't eat sweets before your meal. Don't cross the road without holding my hand. It is understandable, as a child needs to know what is right and what is wrong. However, negative reinforcement can establish itself very early on in life and this can build into a weapon of mass emotional destruction as you get older. The teacher tells you that you are not capable, not to fiddle. It is constant negative reinforcement. If conforming is such a challenge, it may be easier to become rebellious. Rebelling may cause more frustration from the teacher. They report you to the head teacher and then back to your parents. Whatever you seem to do is not good enough. Negative reinforcement can go on throughout our formative years and lays the foundations for adulthood. This may gain momentum as the years pass. Emotions are experienced that engage with fear, dread, anger, frustration. It can lead to feelings of isolation and lack of confidence. Why do something if you are going to be criticised? You end up giving up before you start. Emotions are experienced that are triggered by life's earlier experiences. You then enter the workplace with emotions and personality formed. You receive the same negative comments. You are making errors. You are late. You need to be at your desk more. Emotions bubble to the surface reminding you of events, or emotions, from so many years ago in the classroom. It can be wearing for both managers and staff members. The manager asks, *"Why don't people do as they are asked?"* and they use the metaphorical stick to hit people harder It can leave staff members demoralised and demotivated. No matter how hard you try, it isn't good enough. It adds to demoralisation and can affect self-esteem. Any motivation that is left is driven more by fear than desire. It can only go on for so long before something boils over. It may lead to sullen behaviour where you close off colleagues and those close to you. It may lead to emotional outbursts that result in hostile emotions being felt by those present. It may be that you are referred to the Human Resource team to undertake a capability procedure. Alternatively, you can take out a grievance against your line manager. Whether it is a capability or grievance procedure, it can lead to a break down in relationship between manager and staff member. It can deplete energy and confidence to such an extent that the stress caused can lead to physical and psychological illness. It affects performance and output. Something has to give.

The constant attrition on competency and output can have wider implications. It doesn't just affect one or two people. Others in the team are observing and can be affected by simply observing the increasing conflict. Stress levels go up and good performing staff members may be less productive and start to find work elsewhere. You can take time off from work due to stress and anxiety but know that sooner or later you have to go back where you have to engage with the same line managers that caused you to go off sick in the first place. You are not the only one taking long term sick leave. Others are doing the same. Work that you would otherwise do is being covered by colleagues who are already overworked. Those who have left are not being replaced, adding further pressure on colleagues to cover even more work. Understandably performance and output are affected. Customers may complain about poor service delivery. Management may put more rules and directives in place to improve service delivery and performance. It is moving in ever decreasing circles that can have wide and damming implications to the organisational success while increasing the human and financial costs to the organisation.

Let's pull this back a little and use a little thought as to what could be done differently. Making or forcing someone do something can be challenging taking up time, effort and energy. It is more helpful to inspire and encourage staff members. The emotionally intelligent approach is to create an environment in which staff members can motivate themselves (Zijlmans, Embregts, Gerits, Bosman et al., 2014). It is looking at the short, medium and long term; building a working environment in which staff members feel happy, content and exited to be in the workplace while helping them to achieve their aspirations. However, *"things happen"* that can come out of the blue and surprise us. They detract our focus from what may have been a well-planned day. It may be that you have been called to attend an urgent meeting to discuss the latest performance figures. You may have been asked to produce a report or deliver a seminar/ workshop. Personal factors can also detract focus. The school has just rung to say that your child needs to be picked up as they are feeling unwell. A letter has arrived from the bank saying that you are overdrawn and have been charged. It can give rise to increased levels of fear, sadness, anxiety and reinforce neurotic rumination. As Holiday (nd) points out, emotions such as fear and anxiety are rooted in uncertainty and ignorance. It can affect the way we function, think and behave. No matter how much you plan, these *"problems"* intrude into daily life. They can redirect thought and preoccupy our mind. Problems can be perceived as difficult to overcome. It is a *"negative"* word, similar to *"can't, won't, and never"*, that can create negative feelings, emotions and mood. Rather than seeing them as *"problems"* it is better to recognise them as *challenges*. Whereas challenges need to be identified and acknowledged, feelings and emotions can remain positive. Negative words can be replaced by positive words. For example, *"calm, caring, amiable, happy, content, loving"*. As a member of a team, it is important to remain positive and optimistic and to support colleagues. As a line manager, it is important to share good news and to show staff members how valued their work is. The work that that person is doing should be placed in a wider context demonstrating how significant it is to organisational success. It is engaging with *"positive"* emotions, dispositions and outcomes, guiding staff members to succeed. It is giving them the <u>belief and confidence</u> so that they can achieve aspirations and goals.

> **Reflection: Positive thoughts**
> - From a personal point, reflect on the work that you do and use positive words to explain how the work fits with your own aspirations and the aims and objectives of the organisation.
> - Maintain positive thoughts and words to reinforce what you do.
> - Now think: What are your personal aspirations?
> - Where do you want to be in a year's time, three years' time and ten years' time? Now ask yourself how you will achieve your aspirations.
> - How do your personal aspirations fit with the organisations aims and objectives?
> - What training do you think would be helpful to achieve your aspirations?
> - It is not just you. Remember what you are adding to organisation.

Mindfulness

Our daily lives seem to be one big rush, from the moment we get up in the morning to the time we go to bed. We become caught up in our own thoughts while, losing contact with our emotions and, spending little or no time reflecting upon our own well-being. Feelings of stress can be self-destructive. As human beings, we seem to give a lot of our conscious and subconscious thinking to rumination and worry. Dwelling on events and being in a state of fear or anxiety can deepen moods that drive thoughts and emotions. It is not just the mind that is affected. It can affect the immune system as well. The body can become hypersensitive to stimuli that can result in allergic reactions. Stress becomes a social pollutant that disrupts the immune system resulting in illnesses such as asthma, eczema, and allergic rhinitis.

Glucocorticoids is a naturally occurring hormone and released into the body during a stressful event. They control levels of fat and sugar in the system and can cause inflammation where the body produces more chemicals and white cells that help the body heal. For example, asthma is the inflammation of the airways that affect the ability to breathe. Short term exposure may have little effect. However, if experienced over long periods, glucocorticoids can remain at high levels in the system for months or even years and lead to irreparable damage (Sapolsky, 1996, 2018; Stanford-News, 1996). It is possible to take medicines such as manmade glucocorticoids that can help to manage and control illnesses such as asthma and rhinitis. However, long term use can reduce their potency, leaving the body more susceptible to further attack. There are also long-term side effects such as weight gain, lowered immune system, glaucoma, cataracts and high blood sugar levels.

Rather than solely relying on medicines such as glucocorticoids, other approaches are offered. One of these is mindfulness that has become popular in the West over the last few decades but can be found in ancient Buddhist practice dating back millennia. It is a form of meditation and consists of focusing on "*the now*"; paying moment by moment awareness to feelings and emotions (Fulton, 2005; Germer, Siegel and Fulton, 2005). Studies show that mindfulness training can be effective in managing stress levels and academic success (Creswell, 2017; Kerrigan, Chau, King, Holman, Joffe and Sibinga, 2017; McConville, McAleer and Hahne, 2016). Rather than allowing stress and anxiety to take control, mindfulness can help us become aware of signs earlier on and to take appropriate action.

An eight-week programme in mindfulness-based cognitive therapy (MBCT) has been designed by Segal, Williams and Kabat-Zinn (2012). It provides a step by step guide to support those who experience repeated bouts of depression and has been shown to be an effective tool in clinical trials that have been undertaken. Davis and Hayes (2011) state that mindfulness can help psychotherapist to find ways in which to positively affect aspects of therapy. For example, it can help those who experience depression-relieving feelings of chronic unhappiness (Williams, Teasdale, Segal, and Kabat-Zinn, 2007). Williams and Penman (2013) add that is now recognised as a preferred treatment recommended by the National Institute for Health and Clinical Excellence (UK) and is as successful as antidepressants. This is supported by studies including one carried out by Davidson, Kabat-Zinn, Schumacher, Rosenkranz, Muller et al. (2003) in which findings suggest that alterations in immune and brain function are produced through mindfulness meditation. A further study shows that meditation can also help anxiety disorders (Kabat-Zin, Massion, Kristeller, Peterson Fletcher et al. 1992). With practice, it can lead to improved feelings of contentment, happiness and overall well-being. Mindfulness can also help increase sense of purpose, reduce feelings isolation and, reduced symptoms such as headaches and chest pain. Furthermore, the benefits of mindfulness include improved: mental clarity and concentration, emotional intelligence and, interpersonal relationships. It can prevent feelings of stress and anxiety descending into longer periods of exhaustion that include sleep disturbance, tiredness, irritability, and unexplained physical symptoms. Being emotionally aware and managing emotions is fundamental to mindfulness. Increasing emotional competencies can improve social relationships, employability as well as psychological and physical well-being (Nelis, Kotsou, Quoidbach, Hansenne, Weytens et al., 2011; Penedo and Dahn, 2005). Mindfulness can help train the mind to alter brain patterns managing emotions and place experiences in context.

There can be occasions where we may be taken off guard or where we face a really challenging and possibly confrontational meeting. Attention is given over to *fight or flight* and we engage with emotions such as anger or fear. "*Things*" can build up over time and we start to feel tired and burned out.

Stress and anxiety take control and we revert back to old ways of thinking. Kabat-Zinn (1990) recommends having a *"Three-minute breathing space"* to help take back control. This three-minute exercise can be done at any time of day and place. The reflection below provides a summary of the *"three-minute breathing space"*.

Reflection:
- In a quiet place, find a place to sit upright and close your eyes.
- Focus on what thoughts and feelings you are experiencing at that moment. Focus on your body's reaction (for example: tightness of chest, shortness of breath).
- Now focus your mind on your breathing. As the breath goes in your abdomen expands. As the breath goes out your abdomen contracts.
- Follow the breath in and out.
- Continuing to focus on your breathing, become more aware of your whole-body posture and facial expressions.
- Acknowledge the sensations and allow your mind to focus on your breathing and body posture.

Source: Kabat-Zinn (1990); Williams and Penman (2013).

This book provides a little information on mindfulness. John Kabat-Zinn, together with colleagues, has written extensively on this subject and they provide excellent and recommended sources of information to build and develop on skills associated with mindfulness.

It is worth noting that reports are received that there is a *"dark side"* to mindfulness, that can exacerbate existing problems such as anxiety and stress. Rather than helping, mindfulness could have negative implications. For example, feelings and emotions that have been held in the subconscious can be stirred up that can affect physical and psychological well-being. Emotions, that may have been buried for years, may be brought to the surface and focus is then given to them. Eve Simmons of the Daily Mail (Simmons, 2018) report on a lady who experienced crippling anxiety. Following her doctor's advice, she downloaded a smartphone app that provided a ten-minute daily audio session with the intention of helping her to feel less worried and calmer. Rather than helping to ameliorate symptoms she began to obsess about the food she had eaten. She also tried mindful walking where you focus on sounds, sights and smells around you. However, she felt the need to run. Anxiety appeared to be heightened rather than reduced and this went on for weeks. This is supported by academic studies where the person undertaking mindfulness training may be susceptible to false memories (Grant, 2007; Wilson, Mickes, Stolarz-Fantino, Evrard and Fantino, 2015). Luttrell, Brinol and Petty (2014) point out that it is important to recognise that techniques associated with mindfulness can backfire for some people.

Similar findings appear in other academic sources (for example: Brinol, Gasco, Petty and Horcajo, 2013) Mindfulness may, therefore, not suit all people and should not be seen as the panacea to every illness. Furthermore, there may be underlying biological, chemical or psychological reasons that cannot be solely addressed by mindfulness. It is why it is so important to obtain expert advice and counselling and that books such as this be used to provide a little information and guidance.

Walking/ talking and smiling

Lifestyle intervention, including exercise, is shown to have a beneficial effect on physical and psychological well-being. One good way of exercising is to take daily walks. Walking is an easy way of keeping fit and is an effective way of preserving motor skills and mobility as we get older. This is supported by studies suggesting that there is a relationship between feelings of well-being and walking. For example, participants who walked on a treadmill report increased satisfaction with life (Hicks, Adams, Martin Ginis, Giangregorio, Latimer et al., 2005). In a sample of one hundred and eighty (180) participants, Duranso (2018) finds that walking is beneficial in self-efficacy (self-image, self-worth). Whether we are at home or at work, walking is part of our daily lives. Unfortunately, the nature of work and home life has become much more sedentary in recent generations. Either we are sitting at home watching the TV or sitting at desks in the workspace. We have escalators and lifts to take us from one floor to the next. We have private and public transport to take us to and from our destinations. We seem to minimise walking and yet we have to use the mind to think through, what are often, complex and difficult tasks. It is no wonder that obesity is rising, stress levels are rising, and overall feeling of well-being challenged.

It is also helpful to talk with friends and colleagues that can be trusted. Sharing concerns and challenges can help reduce feelings of stress and anxiety. Maybe during discussion, constructive and positive ideas pop up into your mind. It may be that friends and colleagues make constructive suggestions. Rather than trying to make a decision while feeling stressed and anxious, wait for a day or two, possibly longer. Talk with family members or close friends. Allow the emotions and feelings to dissipate. Look at what needs to change. Then take action.

Smiling is often a great tonic when feeling low. For example, watching a comedy can help lift the mood. This is supported by studies where signs of well-being, such as smiling are associated with happiness and contentment (Kahneman and Krueger, 2006, Stevenson and Wolfers, 2008). However, it may not simply be that smiling increases happiness. It is that the person is already happy when they genuinely smile. The smile has to be genuine. It comes from neural pathways controlled by the unconscious limbic system rather than being controlled consciously. This then increases the feeling of well-being.

Reflection:
Share pleasant thoughts and memories with friends and colleagues.
Allow the mind to think of pleasant thoughts, thoughts that bring a smile to your face.

Reframing the mindset

Hebb's law refers to *"Neurons that fire together, wire together"* (Hebb, 1949). Therefore, when we think of experiences, neurons connect. It is what helps form the mindset, that is made up of assumptions and attitudes, forming a fixed mental attitude. It is reviewing and reframing the way we think by adopting a positive view of ourselves, that includes developing and improving positive ways of thinking. *"Reframing"* is the identification of negative and irrational thought and replacing them with a positive and constructive view. Reframing the way we think can help decrease the emotional impact. As we dwell on the experience, links are reinforced. It is therefore understandable that reframing can take effort and time. New connections are needed and wired together but as time passes the connections become stronger. Neuroplasticity takes place where memory can be amended. This *"transient plasticity"* can help modify memory (Doidge, 2007; Nader and Einarsson, 2010).

A good way to start is by changing words that are used. For example, rather than saying *"problem"*, use the word *"challenge"*. A challenge can be overcome whereas a problem can be an immovable obstruction. Rather than saying that you have *"failed"* an interview, say that you have gained new experience and *"learned"* from it. It is worth noting that those who often succeed are those who are tenacious. If they are unsuccessful on the first occasion, they keep trying and trying until they succeed. Many of us do not apply for another job if we are unsuccessful the first time. We seem to accept that there is no point applying for a similar job the next time round as we anticipate the same outcome. However, there are those who never seem to stop. They appear to go on from one success to the next. In an informal meeting with a very senior manager, I was informed that he kept applying for job after job until he was successful. As soon as he was in that role, he would start applying for the next level up. He became one of the youngest people to reach the level of Director.......and yet he still pressed on to become Chief Executive. He informed me that, at an early age, he reframed his mind to think positively and that all job applications were steps on the career ladder. He had normal academic success in school and had no particular aspiration to achieve greatness. It was while he was studying at university that he learned about reframing the way he thought. This changed his whole mindset. He set out focusing on what he wanted to achieve and then planned and organised the strategy to achieve his aims. We ended the conversation with him saying that it was not just work but also home life that he reframed.

It is worth placing things in context. You may experience a really stressful experience where people's voices are raised. You may have confrontational experiences with colleagues or line manager. You may face the *"teen from hell"* who has still not cleaned their room after so many times of asking. Your first reaction is to shout at them and to get in a temper engaging negative thoughts and emotions in the process. It is important to acknowledge feelings, thoughts and emotions. Count to five. Rather than reacting to the experience, maintain a firm voice but keep calm. Reframing the mindset can build confidence and lead to feelings of being happier and more content. It is taking back control.

Developing self-awareness

As human beings, we seem to engage with irrational thoughts and emotions, spending 46.9% of our time on *"automatic pilot"* thinking about the past and future while allowing our minds to wander (Killingsworth and Gilbert, 2010). We could spend more time thinking about the inner self and the present moment. Being here and now can have a beneficial effect upon well-being and we may not give ourselves the time. We are faced with the challenges and pressures of daily life and may not find the time to focus on our inner selves, becoming more in tune with what our body and mind is telling us. It is therefore helpful to understand and build upon self-awareness, a key foundation stone to emotional intelligence. Goleman (1998, 2012) defines self-awareness as the ability to monitor our inner selves while Duval and Wicklund (1973) describe it as a temporary state of self-consciousness. Dierdorff and Rubin (2015) suggest that it is understanding how similar or different we are to others. Notwithstanding the different viewpoints, self-awareness requires introspection. Becoming more self-aware is to monitor and recognise internal thoughts, feelings and emotions and is associated with empathy, self-esteem and, well-being. However, it is important to acknowledge that introspection can exacerbate existing illnesses such as depression and anxiety. This is a valid reason to seek professional support and guidance.

Listening is an important contributor to self-awareness. It is not just *"hearing"* but making a connection to the inner self, actively *"listening"* and, paying attention to what is going on in the body and mind (Haley, Heo, Wright, Barone, Rettiganti et al. 2017). It is also the ability to listen to others, a skill that can be difficult to master.

As human beings, we are influenced by beliefs and values that trigger feelings and emotions that can bias thoughts and reaction. Barriers such as background, religion, gender, race can shape the way we understand the world around us. We are all influenced by our own experiences, personality traits, background and culture. Findings from a study, containing over three hundred and fifty thousand (350,000) people, show a low correlation between self-evaluation and objective assessments (Zell and Krizan, 2014). In other words, people only have a low, and at best moderate, insight into their own abilities and performance. Furthermore, we may fabricate thoughts and emotions that give rise to introspection illusion; an illusion that we believe to be true but is a narrative that is concocted by fiction. We believe one thing when maybe the opposite is true. For example, 64% of Americans rate themselves as "*excellent*" or "*very good*" drivers. When they are asked to rate their friends, the figure drops to 29%. 89% of American drivers say they have driven faster than the speed limit. 34% have sent a text message or email while driving (Allstate, 2011). Another good example is where people go on talent competitions believing that they are brilliant singers when they are pretty awful. Estimating how competent we are, and the actual reality is referred to as the Dunning-Kruger effect (Kruger and Dunning, 1999). It is important that we acknowledge and recognise these limitations.

A further challenge that we all experience is cognitive bias where we draw incorrect conclusions from thoughts and behaviour. We can lie to ourselves. We seek to rationalise and maintain positive views about ourselves by simplifying what may otherwise be a highly complex experience. We are also unaware of external influences on our subconscious mind, which is in constant operation helping us to breathe, blink and swallow. To take in everything would be information overload and would likely frazzle the best of minds, so the unconscious part of the brain minimises information that subsequently reaches the conscious part of the mind. Information can also be mixed up and true experiences confused with a new narrative made up of fictional thoughts, and emotions. Blind spots occur in our thinking and we make up a story. It is having to rely on those relating a story to remember an event clearly and how they felt at the time. It is often cited as a limitation when studies are undertaken within social science. It does suggest that we are not very good at being self-aware. We can learn to understand our own feelings, emotions and thoughts, becoming much more self-aware. Paying attention and listening to the inner self can transform self-awareness, helping to build stronger relationships with others in a more meaningful and constructive manner.

> **Reflection: Self-awareness**
>
> Ask yourself the following questions:
> 1. Who and what are the most important things in your life?
> 2. What do you value most in your life?
> 3. How do you see yourself?
> 4. How do you relate with others?
> 5. What are your strengths and weaknesses?
> 6. What are your biggest achievements in life?
> 7. What are your aspirations/ goals in life?
> 8. What motivates you?
> 9. What makes you happy?
> 10. What can you change?
>
> Review the above questions on a regular basis and reflect on how your self-awareness has improved.

The white room

As commented elsewhere in this book, it is important that professional advice be sought and that the contents be regarded as a guide to those interested in the role of emotional intelligence, stress management and coping. This section provides an example of how concentrating the mind can help engage with positive thoughts, feelings and emotions. It is a short exercise in focusing the mind.

Find a place that is quiet where you can sit down and focus on the following.

Sit upright with your feet firmly placed on the floor.

Setting the scene

- Imagine yourself sitting near the front row at the cinema. Lights are dimmed and the last few people come in and sit down. The cinema screen is straight in front of you with curtains pulled across it. There is a light at the centre of the screen that shines dimly through the curtain.

- Focus on your breathing and the light on the screen. Breathe in counting from one to three. Breathe out counting one to five. Do this for a few minutes. If your mind wanders bring it back to focus on the breathing.

Now that you have set the scene, let's enter **the white room**.

Training and development

- As you count, breathing in and out, focus your mind on the cinema screen and the light in the centre of the screen. As you do so, the curtains that are pulled in front of the screen begin to part. The light that is in the centre of the screen shines more brightly and begins to expand across the screen. You can see that the light is coming from a white room- white ceiling, white walls and white floor. In the far-left hand corner, you can see a spiral staircase going down and on the right-hand side, you can see an open window with doves flying in and out.

- Now, in your mind walk into the white room counting from one to ten- *slowly*. As you do so, say to yourself that *"I feel calm, positive, and relaxed"*.

- You are now standing in the white room. Turn to the right and look out of the open window. You can see doves flying in and out of the open window. In the far distance, you can see a snow-capped mountain at the foot of which there is a blue meandering river. The other side of the river there is a pine forest. Red squirrels jump from tree to tree and deer come down to the river to drink. At the river, the water is crystal clear. You can see stones at the bottom and fish swimming. This side of the river, there are fields of yellow, rape; red poppy and; green, wheat barley and maize. Back at the window, you can see the doves flying in and out.

- Turn around and walk down the ten steps in the spiral staircase, counting as you go while saying to yourself that *"I feel calm, positive and relaxed"*.

- At the bottom of the staircase, there is a white sandy beach. You can feel the warm sand on your feet as you squeeze your toes. The sun is in the sky. There is the odd cloud in the sky. Palm trees lean over onto the beach and the sea gently laps onto the beach.

- Now walk ten (10) paces along the beach until you reach an upturned rowing boat. You stop and look at the vista and you note that you are the only person on the beach. You repeat that *"I feel calm, positive and relaxed"* and walk another ten paces counting each step slowly as you go. You are now facing a lift that takes you up five floors to the white room. Count, one, two, three, four, five. You are back in the white room.

- Opposite you is the open window with doves flying in an out. You turn to the right and see where you were sitting. You walk back to your seat, counting the ten paces it takes and sit back in your seat.

- Now, you are looking back at the white room. It is the most peaceful and calm place you can imagine.

- Focus back on your breathing. Breathe in counting from one to three. Breathe out counting one to five. Do this for a few minutes.

- Finally, count from five to one slowly while focusing on your breathing and then place yourself in the room where you are sitting.

- How do you feel?

When you have been through the above a few times, close your eyes and repeat the same exercise. Initially, try not to deviate from the story. However, in time, the above narrative can be changed, and you can build your own landscape to help refocus your thoughts on positive emotions.

Summing up

The chapter begins by identifying that training in emotional intelligence can be influential in change that includes greater career success, improved interpersonal relationships and more effective leadership skills (Clarke, 2006; Nelis, et al, 2011; Palmer, Walls, Burgess and Stough, 2001; Penedo and Dahn, 2005; Slaski and Cartwright, 2003). There appears to those a continuum where at one end are those who are much more able to cope with challenging experiences and thrive on stress and confrontation- the "*I can take it*" group. At the other end of the continuum are those who are much more sensitive and likely to experience greater levels of stress and anxiety.

The chapter then delves into differing approaches to managing and motivating staff members. Negative reinforcement (including uncertainty and ignorance) can severely affect how people feel that can lead to anxiety, stress and fear while, inspiring and motivating people can create belief and confidence, focusing on positive outcomes and emotions. The chapter then considers how helpful mindfulness can be in the day to day pressures placed on us all helping to copes with stressful experiences. It focuses on *"the now"* making us emotionally aware of how we feel. It can help improve feelings of happiness and overall well-being. *"Things"* can build up over time and we start to feel stressed. Kabat-Zinn (1990) recommends having a *"Three-minute breathing space"* to help take back control. Techniques associated with mindfulness can backfire (Luttrell, Brinol and Petty, 2014). Therefore, consideration needs to be given to the possible *"dark side"* of mindfulness that can exacerbate existing problems such as stress and anxiety. Furthermore, there may be physiological and psychological reasons that mindfulness cannot answer on its own. It is therefore important to obtain advice and guidance from professional experts. We seem to engage with irrational thoughts and emotions, thinking about the past and future, while allowing our minds to wander (Killingsworth and Gilbert, 2010) The chapter explains that walking, talking and smiling can be effective in improving physical and psychological well-being. Discussion is also given to the importance of becoming more self-aware, reframing the mindset so that neurons that fire together, *"wire together"* (Hebb, 1949). The final part of the chapter provides an example of the white room concentrating the mind on pleasant thoughts, feeling and emotions helping to build and improve on how we cope with challenging experiences.

Chapter 9

Emotional intelligence: Does it really matter?

This chapter reflects on how education and society focus on the importance of remembering things. It is embedded in student learning from an early age and reinforced throughout the school years. The intention is to provide students with information so as to pass their next exam. Games shows on television also encourage those with skills in remembering and retrieving information. It demonstrates how "*intelligent*" we are. Practical application of information is often lost in the process. Those in management are provided with decrees to meet statistical demands and expectations that place pressure and stress on members of staff. Students focus on gaining the certificate. All students and staff members are required to follow the same educational system. Those who remember and recall information and pass their exams are more likely to find places at University and subsequently, a good job. However, not all those participating in the system will meet with the demands and expectations and may leave school without the requisite qualifications. They may find it more challenging to find a suitable job. These students may decide to take on an apprenticeship where they can learn a trade. However, this is likely to occur later in their teenage years, after they leave school. In 2020, "T level" qualifications are being brought into the school education system engaging students in technical related qualifications However, these will be studied towards the end of the school education experience. They do go some way to help address in the imbalance between academic qualifications and practical experience. However, they may develop a further tiering of the education system where greater status may be given to those undertaking academic qualifications. Once school education is completed, students may then move into higher education, at Universities. By this time, they may be more focused on passing the module and the end certificate. Their interest in practical and work-related application is affected by their earlier educational experience. They then enter the work environment with the same imprinted approach to education. They may see education may be seen as finite. Once school and higher education are completed, no more exams and assignments. However, it is seeing education with a fixed minded approach rather than having a growth-minded attituded Education should not be short term. Life is a journey through which new skills and knowledge can be learned and applied helping to improve our own lives and those of others. It is important to build and develop a growth mindset that can be an asset to the daily challenges that we all have to face.

This chapter goes on to discuss skill development that is regarded as fundamental to strategic success (International Labour Organisation, 2011). However, organisations appear to focus on staff training and development that meets with the specific needs and demands of the job. Focus is on the short term. Focus is inward. Organisations seem to focus on the immediate without thinking long term. It is acknowledged that there is a cost to training and developing that may be seen by some as an unnecessary risk. The risk may be considered from an alternative point of view. The risk of not training and developing staff members could prejudice the success and possible existence of the organisation. Therefore, training and development could be seen as an important *asset* rather than a risk.

The chapter then talks about risk-taking that appears to be a part of decision making in many organisations. The risk takers are the ones that may impress other senior managers when they say that their ideas will revitalise the organisation and bring in more income. They are rewarded when the high decision risk pays off. However, there are occasions where risk-taking can affect the soul and heart of the organisation. Taleb (2019) refers to the term "*skin in the game*". It is where a person has a personal interest in the risks taken. They have something to lose when making high-risk decisions. This may have a moderating effect upon the decision taken. It is not a simple question as to whether something is right or wrong. It is balancing the risk and impact of the decision on the overall success/ failure of the organisation. It is placing the decision in context.

The chapter also considers that we are all likely to have a "*breaking point*" where we feel enough is enough. We are encouraged to work harder and longer, placing pressure on work/ life balance that can damage personal relationships both at home and at work. The individual can engage in ways of reducing stress and pressure. For example, undertaking sports activities, meditation, mindfulness training. However, there is a point where it may be no longer possible to say "*I can take it*". Some may meet that point earlier than others. It is recognising this both at a personal level and at an organisational level. Action is needed. As a society, we are encouraged to conform. We think as a group. At the same time, we are individuals. The challenge that we face is that our own way of thinking may conflict with the way other people may think that can manifest itself in stress and the inability to cope. Conforming may be to the detriment of creative thinking. Trying to cope and fend off stress can be at the expense of individual drive and motivation. Having a pessimistic view of life can affect the immune system. If we think "*negatively*" then this can impact upon well-being. In western society, the *"I can take it"* mentality appears to be built into organisations. Some may be more able to cope with the pressure and stress of daily life, others less so. It is, therefore, helpful to try and maintain a positive and optimistic view of life. It is finding the right balance. The final part of the chapter considers the question being asked in this book "*emotional intelligence: does it really matter*"?

Memory

It is very easy to pontificate, to tell people what they should and shouldn't do. Newspapers and online media "*tell*" us with so-called "news" explaining events and informing us as to what is going on around us. Friends and family give their advice whether it is wanted or not. The Government sets out legislation that we are encouraged to comply with and society sets out expected norms and demands. We rely on other people's thoughts and views to help us form an understanding of the world around us. It influences our decision making and behaviour. On the other hand, we like to see ourselves as individuals, making our own decisions based upon rational thought and decision-making processes. How can we rationalise on something that may or may not be reported accurately, honestly and unbiased? How do we make a decision when opinions, views and advice change? There is so much information to absorb we unable to remember all the information that we experience. There is so much information that we may not even be aware of it. We are full of contradictions that are often difficult to reconcile. Emotions influence our thoughts and behaviour. Our beliefs and emotions often override rational thinking.

Not all is lost though. We can train the mind to remember things. There are a few who are able to remember items by using memory techniques (mnemonics) such as an amusing image or rhyme. For example, 30 days has September, April, June and November, etc.). First associated with Simonides of Ceos (556BC-468BC), the ancient skill of memory training uses the memory palace, where items are placed in each room and, later, recalled. For those interested, Joshua Foer's (2012) book "*Moon walking with Einstein*" provides a fascinating read into the art of training the memory.

There is also a small number of people whose brains are wired a little differently. They may have brain disorders that provide them with the capacity to remember detail, for example, what the weather was like on a certain day in their life, what they wore, and what they ate. In her book "*Unthinkable*", Helen Thomson (2018) provides excellent examples of these amazing people. However, such examples are exceptional. It would overload the brain if we remembered everything, and, as such, we would find it difficult to function. For example, ask yourself what is on page twenty-eight (28) of this book. You may have an overall understanding of the content, but detail is often left out.

Remembering the content, word for word, is highly unlikely. To help us formulate decisions, we simply remove what we believe to be noise and detritus. Furthermore, to simplify the way we try to understand, we often place things in two (2) columns that are headed *"right"* and *"wrong"*. Yet it appears that school education is built around the memory game, remembering information that is often verbatim. You are required to remember as much information as possible that is then regurgitated back out in exam conditions. It is then on to the next topic. The student's focus is on gaining the certificate and applying the same memory tactics in the next topic. It focuses on how good one student is against another; comparing and contrasting our own self-worth against others. It creates a stratified system in which we are encouraged to feel superior or inferior. It reaffirms status that continues into adulthood, affecting self-esteem. It creates greater feelings of stress and anxiety that are amplified further as inequality between the very rich and poorest increases (Wilkinson and Pickett, 2019). Teachers are often embedded in paperwork, tight deadlines and heavy workload while they are expected to meet the demands placed upon them by senior managers. Understandably, they may have little time to engage in student learning and development outside the curriculum. When the student comes to university, they may have the ability to absorb and repeat information. However, application to the organisational context can often be a challenge. They need to learn new skills which can be applied to the working environment. It seems that management focus is often on a spreadsheet of statistical data, improving results on previous years. Application of the knowledge, for life's journey, can be lost in meeting the rigorous requirements for short term student *"learning"*.

Our social lives seem to be built around memory as well. Television delivers games shows, requiring people to remember obscure information. We also engage in pub quizzes in which teams compete in memory recall. People are rewarded for memory whether it is by qualification or prize. It continues to be regarded as a demonstration of greater intelligence

Application of knowledge is often overlooked in favour of the actual skill in remembering minutia. Whereas there are those who have skills in the application of knowledge it appears that many of us make use of a narrow, short term, memory. It may be helpful if education was more focused upon success through life's journey, looking at the long term, rather than focus on short term success. Students of all ages could be encouraged to engage in embedding knowledge and skills that they can apply to the personal and work life. It may help engage students to find a passion for learning that is presently regarded as a chore and necessity. At the time of writing this book, students are able to undertake an apprenticeship from the age of sixteen, (16). "T level" qualifications are being brought in to the latter end of the school education system that may help provide interest and motivation to student learning. However, it may be helpful to develop this idea further to encourage students to engage in skills associated with the trades and professions at an earlier age. For example, car mechanics, construction, healthcare, sport. It may be helpful to demonstrate to students the practical application of knowledge has on themselves, family and society.

Furthermore, training and development could be given to *all* students, from an early age, about the importance of developing skills associated with emotional intelligence helping them understand the role that emotions play in a social interaction. It could help build and develop a growth-minded approach that learning new skills and knowledge is not only interesting but enjoyable. It may also help students to feel more valued and to be more engaged with society.

Explaining personal application of a theory with practice may help students build a portfolio of knowledge and skills that can be called upon in later life. It can help place information in the long-term memory that can benefit both the student in later years and society as a whole. Rather than status stratification and sometimes exclusion, students may feel more valued and included into an education system fit for the twenty-first (21st) century. It may engage students' interest, and also help the teacher to be more inspired and motivated to meet the challenges that each day brings.

Life's a journey

Understanding different mindsets is helpful in focusing a little more on how we think as human beings. Carol Dweck (2017) talks about fixed and growth mindsets. Those with a fixed mindset would say that you either have it or you don't. The growth mindset says that you can learn and develop. Dweck adds that it is possible to change and develop from a fixed mindset to a growth mindset. She points out that those with a growth mindset embrace a challenge and are able to persist in the face of obstacles. They consider effort as the path to mastery and learn from criticism. Those with a growth mindset also find inspiration in the success of others. Developing and having a growth mindset can be an asset when faced with challenging experiences. Learning skills, in its application, together with emotional intelligence can help provide tools to cope with feelings of stress. Life is a journey through which new skills and knowledge can be learned and applied helping to improve our own lives and those of others.

The working environment

The World Economic Forum (2018) points out that the fourth (4th) industrial revolution, involving artificial intelligence, is leading to increasing challenges requiring organisations, staff members and Governments to be proactive in planning for the future. The window of opportunity is closing fast. The World Economic Forum identifies key factors that influence the global marketplace including artificial intelligence, cloud technology, high-speed mobile internet and big data analytics. Organisations, individuals and countries regard skill development as fundamental to strategic success (International Labour Organisation, 2011). However, the skills gap appears to be increasing. In the very near future, employers expect skills and knowledge required to perform most jobs will have significantly changed. This may lead to increased demands on existing staff members. They may need to learn new skills, adapt and adopt new ways of working. They may find that the job no longer exists due to changes in globalised demand. The World Economic Forum (2018) add that organisations plan to address the skills gap by appointing permanent new members of staff, automating the tasks associated with the job and retrain the existing workforce. However, staff training, and development, can be costly to an organisation and is often focused on covering the needs and demands of that expected within that job. Focus is on the short term. We may have organisational three (3) or five (5) year plans, but how does anyone know what is actually going to happen in a year or so, let alone five (5) to ten (10) years in the future. Training and development are therefore focused on the job and tasks at hand and what can be reasonably prophesied. What is the point of training and developing someone on a whim or idea that may never materialise? Therefore, knowledge and skills are often limited to that specific area of the job. Training for the future roles, responsibility and jobs appears limited. There is likely to be a limited expertise in those that the organisation train, limiting development to that needed to meet the demands of the existing job. Furthermore, there is likely to be a limited pool of expertise in the area that the organisation is recruiting. The skills gap continues to get wider. This places more strain on the organisation to compete in the global market. Wages and salaries for the majority of staff may be kept as low as possible to minimise costs. Staff motivation and aspirations may be limited due to low pay and lack of opportunities. Productivity and output are affected. Very senior managers, the 1%, are paid more to be "*incentivised*". More pressure is placed on members of staff to perform and to work "*harder*". More people become disenfranchised as inequality increases and the divide between the richest and poorest becomes wider. It has become a vicious circle that society in countries such as the UK and the USA has become acclimatised.

Those who are less skilled may find that they earn similar levels year after year. They may do what is needed. They may do as they are told and managed as such. Similarly, managers may be limited to in house training and development specific to that job and the organisation splutters on to face another day. It is focusing on the immediate, the now. The focus is inward. It is moving faster and faster in ever decreasing circles into a blackhole, when, at some point, the event horizon is crossed from which the organisation never returns.

From an individual point of view, developing new skills requires using the memory to absorb new information, going beyond existing parameters of knowledge and skills. It makes them saleable to the organisation seeking new blood, expertise and commitment. It is having a growth mindset (Dweck, 2017) However, if the member of staff is motivated to develop their skills and knowledge, and has aspirations that extend beyond the existing organisation, it can be seen as a potential risk and financial loss by the company they work for. Therefore, once the member of staff has gained the new skills and knowledge, they may simply leave the organisation for pastures new. If the person remains in the organisation, managers may see the newly skilled member of staff as a threat to their position. If the newly acquired skills are not used, the application may be lost. Limiting training and development to a specific job maintains an equilibrium, but in the medium and long term can limit the ability of the organisation to grow and succeed. It is inward thinking, naval gazing. It is having a fixed mindset (Dweck, 2017).

Alternatively, the member of staff may feel that they do not want to develop additional skills and knowledge. They may use memory for repetitive tasks and are happy with keeping information to the minimum. They don't want to spend those long hours absorbing new information that may or may not be used in the future. These people often stay in a similar role for years. They are comfortable with the role of working within known parameters of knowledge and skills. It may be a risky strategy to rely on existing skills and knowledge learned many years in the past. It may be that tasks associated with such jobs are at risk of automation, placing the member of staff at risk of future employment. Without new skills and knowledge, they may find it really challenging to find new employment. They may feel that they have become disenfranchised from society as a whole. Their focus may be less on personal drives and aspirations and more on feelings of external threats and fear from organisations and individuals from outside their own geographical area. Again, it is inward thinking and having a fixed mindset.

Being an individual with up to date skills and knowledge can place you in a good position to work effectively within the group. It may require a radical rethink of the education system where students are encouraged to remember content to pass exams. It may require a radical review of training and development in organisations, looking at the long term. A radical rethink of education, training, and development could facilitate ways in which to support individual and organisations in the competitive global marketplace. There is need to look outwards and have a growth-minded approach.

Losing someone with expert skills that can help the organisation face the challenges of the global marketplace can be costly. There is also the cost of recruitment to the role that also necessitates further in-house training and development. The incentive to train and develop for the medium- and long-term future is invariably down to the individual. They need to develop themselves if they are seeking a career; building a portfolio of experience, together with skills and knowledge, that are considered an asset by the recruiting organisation. It is personal drive and motivation. Relying on organisation training and development alone may not be sufficient. It requires personal commitment to develop oneself so as to be ready when change does occur. If people do not wish to train and develop themselves, their skills may come obsolete or difficult to place in the work environment. These people may become more disenfranchised from work and society. They may earn less or become unemployed increasing the level of inequality. Those with the newly acquired skills and knowledge may find that they are in demand and can achieve higher levels of income moving to a new organisation. However, the hierarchy of inequality increases, where those at the top are considered important and those at the lower end less so. We judge each other on our status and where we fit within the hierarchy of inequality. We compare and contrast ourselves with each other more and feelings of stress and anxiety continue to increase (Wilkinson and Pickett, 2019). Even those earning more money and engaging in productive employment are affected. It is no wonder that stress and anxiety continue to affect so many people. Engaging in personal action to help cope with challenging experiences is helpful. As a society, maybe a radical rethink is needed as to the way we live and work. Inequality in society needs to be addressed. It may go a long way to improve feelings of psychological and physiological well-being.

Right or wrong?

The rationalised aspect of how we think is only a small part. Emotions influence our decisions. Emotions can take us along a path that the rationalised part of the brain may not approve of. For example, we may know that there are insufficient funds in the bank account and that further expenditure may result in an overdraft and subsequent pressure on next month's budget, but we look at that a new pair of shoes or an electronic device and persuade ourselves that that item will bring pleasure, even if it is short lived. The rational side of the brain says to hold off and to wait until there are enough funds to purchase the item. The emotional side may say that you want the item now. The pleasure of owning the item outweighs the rational side. Consequences? Worry about it tomorrow. When tomorrow comes, the bills still arrive and need paying, but we reassure ourselves that the decision was correct. This is one example. However, it could be expanded to wider issues such as organisational strategy, product design, investment in new services and products. There could be many influential factors that it may not be possible to provide a simple rationalised argument. To rationalise the decision may require a spreadsheet showing costs and potential income. Then the question can be asked as to whether or not it is worth taking the risk. For example, spend one (1) million now and get a return of three (3) million over the next five (5) years. Alternatively, spend five (5) million now and possibly get a return on investment (ROI) that could exceed one hundred (100) million. Being rational, cautious and sensible, spending the one (1) million now will bring a reasonable return of three (3) million over the next five (5) years. However, taking the risk of a three (3) million investment could lead to a substantial return of one hundred (100) million. Many people will take the cautious route and less likely to risk the investment in case it has a negative impact upon organisational success. However, the emotions may kick in and override the rationalistic thinking. There are those who will take a gamble and hope that it pays off. Sometimes it will, and the decision maker is rewarded accordingly. If the gamble doesn't pay off, there is the possibility that the organisation may fail. The risk taker may simply move on to another organisation and continue with similar thinking.

Analysis and evaluation of data may be undertaken and presented. The rationalised viewpoint may be not to invest. However, if there are potentially high returns and profits risks may be taken; emotions may engage. Those who take risks may do so based upon intuition, using their gut feeling, using emotions. It does seem that being a risk taker is often considered as an essential attribute to good leadership. They may also demonstrate behaviour, associated with the "*dark triad*", that is mistaken for strong leadership skills and decision making. It may be helpful if those who are making these high-risk decisions had personal and financial investment in the outcome. This is exemplified by Taleb (2019) who refers to the company man as someone who has "*skin in the game*". They feel they have something to lose if they don't behave as a company man. Taleb adds that the longer the person stays at the company the more emotional investment they will have. However, overcompensation of feelings of job security can lead to complacency. In the example of IBM, given by Taleb, the rise of personal computers and Microsoft result in a number of employees being made redundant. They lack the capacity to find work elsewhere as they become embedded in IBM's corporate culture. The company man is, therefore, replaced by companies' persons, those who fear upsetting their own employer and potential employers. Once more the question can be raised, who is "*right*" and who is "*wrong*"? It is not such a simple question when competition in the globalised marketplace becomes more and more competitive and decisions may be accompanied by emotions.

Context is so important. Risk taking in the globalised market place can bring rewards but also raise challenges as Governments also intervene to support organisations. They place tariffs and barriers to imports and exports from one country to another. They provide tax breaks and handouts to support industry.

Each decision has to be considered on its own merits and judgements made accordingly. It may not be so clear and defined as to whether a decision is right or wrong, until it is considered in hindsight.

Being emotionally intelligent acknowledges that emotions have a role to play in decision making and people management. Those who are cautious may be regarded by senior managers as less inclined to succeed. They may be seen as an irritant, with no drive, no motivation, and no forward thinking. However, risk-taking appears to be a part of modern management and leadership practices. Risk takers are the ones that impress other senior managers when they say that their ideas will revitalise the organisation and bring in more income. It is why behaviour, associated with the "*dark triad*" is often rewarded by organisations.….until it is too late.

It is clear we are a complex species and very difficult to understand. We see and hear a lot about the term *"well-being"*. We smoke, we misuse substances and, we eat food that is not good for us. We say to ourselves that we are enjoying ourselves and continue to indulge. We may think that substance use may not be having a negative impact upon well-being, indeed we feel that it has a positive effect on well-being. We internalise and live a hedonistic lifestyle that others may frown upon. However, others pontificate and tell us what is good or bad for us to eat and drink. For example, smoking and alcohol. This eudaimonic view may be seen as interference to our own internal urges and regarded as paternalistic and protective. That question again, who is "*right*" and who is "*wrong*"? The rational side may recognise the impact that substance misuse has on the body and the mind; however, the emotional side reinforces the pleasure that is gained. It adds to the complexity of trying to understand the way we think and behave and gives rise to challenges as to assessing, evaluating and measuring well-being. Notwithstanding, decisions that are made often incorporate emotions. Developing and understanding skills associated with emotional intelligence can be helpful in navigating through the travails and challenges faced within organisational change. It is recognising that there may not be a binary decision of what and who is right and wrong, but a continuum where *"right"* is at one end and *"wrong"* is at the other.

Breaking point

The modern working environment appears to reward the "*macho*" approach to work; the *"I can take it"* syndrome. We are encouraged to work harder and longer, placing pressure on work/ life balance that can damage personal relationships both at home and at work. It can affect well-being. Stress can materialise and affect how we think and behave. There is a breaking point for each person. However, senior management in organisations continue to press on the good will of staff members. We may regard ourselves as resilient and able to stand up to the demands and pressures of modern. However, we can be fragile and break when faced with stressful experiences. In his book *"Antifragile: things that gain from disaster"*, Nassim Taleb (2012) provides an example of a boxer, someone who is in peak physical condition, and able to face up to fight after fight but can be fragile if they are dropped by their girlfriend. It is, therefore, important to acknowledge that in life, there may be experiences that you can cope with that have little or no impact upon stress. However, there may be other experiences that, even with the slightest of nudges can cause immeasurable distress, that can lead to lifelong physical and psychological harm. As income inequality increases, so do the challenges of living and working in modern society. It reinforces the need to develop and build skills to cope with the demands, pressure and stress that come from working in the globalised market place.

IQ and multiple intelligences

The view is often put forward that you are born with a level of IQ that is fixed over the human lifespan and cannot be changed. Whereas there remain proponents of the idea that IQ is fixed, it is now becoming more acceptant that we can develop and improve IQ levels. We can continue to build on life's experience. We can continue to learn new skills and knowledge. Furthermore, there may be more than just IQ. There may be multiple intelligences that include those put forward by Gardner (1983,1999). It is only recently that it has been possible to look into the brain to see how it works. However, there still appears to be insufficient findings to provide a definitive answer as to whether or not multiple intelligences actually exist, and this includes emotional intelligence. Questionnaires have been devised to measure emotional intelligence and academic studies that have been undertaken in recent decades suggest that it does exist. However, to complicate the matter further, there does not appear to be a consensus as to the definition of what emotional intelligence is and how it can be measured (For example: mixed (Bar-On, 1997; Goleman, 1995, 1998); ability (Salovey and Mayer, 1990; Mayer and Salovey, 1997); trait (Petrides, 2009a, 2009b, 2011; Petrides and Furnham, 2001, 2003).

Further knowledge is being gained that allow scanning to look inside the brain (For example, Craig, 2002, 2004; Davidson and Begley, 2012; Kim and Whalen, 2009); LeDoux, 1999, 2003, 2019). This may provide scientists to find out which parts of the brain relate to particular functions. Studies are regularly being added to the existing literature to help provide greater understanding. Studies undertaken rely on the person participating in the study as being honest and reliable, while remembering events clearly. The problem is that each person has their own perspective on how they see the world. This can be really challenging to identify and measure as it relies on each person having the same bench level of assessment and evaluation. For example, one person may see a stressful experience as a clear threat and identify it on a Likert chart as "5" (*"I do this a lot"*). Another person may see the stressful experience as a passing experience and place it on the Likert chart as "1" (*"I don't this at all"*). The studies that have been undertaken do suggest that there is more than one intelligence. As further research is undertaken, evidence may emerge that supports this finding, adding pixels to the screen to provide a clearer picture.

Conforming

Sloman and Fernbach (2017) point out that as individuals, we are limited on what we can learn and conceive. However, as a group or community, we can expand learning and development and achieve greater things. Group working, and groupthink are part of the human make up. We think as a group. At the same time, we are individuals. We have our own way of thinking that may conflict with the way other people may think that can in turn affect working practices and working relationships. As a society, we are encouraged to conform. Similarly, as part of an organisation, we are required to conform. We are expected to conform to the expectations and demands of the group. For example, we are required to meet with a particular dress code, behave in a civil manner, work within expected norms, and to interact with others in a cooperative manner. However, conforming may be to the detriment of creative thinking that is essential for organisations to succeed in the global marketplace (Kaufman, 2015). Creativity leads to improved output, motivation and performance. It is allowing people to live life with intensity and passion in an environment where there is less control, criticism and restraint. The conflict between self and conforming with group demands and expectations can manifest itself in stress and the inability to cope. Trying to cope and fend off stress can be at the expense of individual drive and motivation. It can deplete the strengths that make up the individual to such an extent that it can lead to psychological and physical illness. It is, therefore, important to recognise that suppression of creativity and individual thinking can be to the detriment of the organisation and staff members.

Pessimism, optimism and hormones

As studies are carried out on the way we behave and think, it is becoming clearer that it is not a simple switch that we can turn on and off, moving us from being a pessimist or an optimist. Sigman (2018) explains there are physiological factors that can influence how we see the world. For example, when there is more activity in the frontal gyrus in the right hemisphere of the brain the person may experience greater activity and, therefore, maybe more likely to be a pessimist. Someone who is inclined to be more optimistic is likely to experience less activity in this area of the brain (Sigman, 2018).

Hormones are chemicals that circulate through the body that influence the way we cope with stressful experiences and react to the world around us. For example, glucocorticoids control levels of fat and sugar in the system and can cause inflammation where the body produces more chemicals and white cells that help the body heal. Short term exposure may have little effect. However, if experienced over long periods, glucocorticoids can remain at high levels in the system for a very long time and lead to irreparable damage (Sapolsky, 1996, 2018; Stanford-News Service, 1996).

Noradrenalin is sometimes referred to as a stress hormone and when released into the body as it communicates with the body and brain to fight or take flight. It can lead to increased heart rate, constriction of air passages and narrowing of blood vessels (Eysenck, 2004; Ghosh and Collier, 2012; Peterson, 2007).

Cortisol is associated with distress and levels may increase to such an extent that the body becomes overwhelmed, reducing proteins in the body. It is likely to stay in the system for several hours (Burnett, 2016). The distress experienced can lead to the immune system breaking down having a damaging effect upon well-being.

Having a pessimistic view of life can create an ever-decreasing circle, that is influenced by biological and physiological factors, and can be difficult to break out of. The more we ruminate and worry and the more we try and suppress negative experiences, the more likely cortisol levels, blood pressure and heart rate will go up. It can lead to increased levels of glucose and cortisol released into the body that in turn can encourage increased intake of high-calorie foods.

Compared with cortisol, oxytocin is associated with eustress and stays in the system for just a few minutes (Burnett, 2016). Oxytocin is associated with social interaction/ bonding and is often referred to as the "*love drug*" (Helm, 2016; Kazim, 2011). It reduces the *fight or flight* response (Kirsch, Esslinger, Chen, Mier, et al., 2005). It may help explain why too much cortisol and too little oxytocin result in people experiencing negative thinking, anxiety and depression (Lubuschagne, Phan, Wood, Angstadt et al., 2010; Sabihi, 2017). It also demonstrates that biological and physiological factors can influence how we think and behave, whether we regard life's glass as half full or half empty. Acknowledgement needs to be given to influences that hormones may have on the way we think and behave and the way we interact with others. It is not a simple equation where developing skills in emotional intelligence, meditation and mindfulness can address wider issues. They are another tool in life's box of skills.

Dissent in the ranks

Throughout this book, discussion has reflected on definitions and explanation of stress, coping, intelligence and emotional intelligence. However, there appears to be dissent and disagreement to the definition of terms and means of measurement. The desire is to have a common agreement to each term and to be able to measure the term using a common approach. It may be that minds may never meet and that there has to be an acceptance that there will be no agreement. However, the studies add to the information that help provide greater pixilation in gaining further knowledge and a clearer picture.

"I can take it"

The *"I can take it"* mentality appears to be built into organisations in the west. Whereas, some people are more able to cope with the pressure and stress of daily life, others may feel that they are less able to cope. It seems that the daily onslaught of life metres out challenges and when these challenges become overpowering, they can lead to feelings of psychological and physical stress that, to some, can be debilitating. This not only has a devastating impact upon the person and close family, it can also have an impact upon the organisation. Those who experience stress may take long term absence. Their work needs to be covered by others, adding additional stress on those who may already feel overworked. There may be increased attrition rates where staff members seek alternative work. This all adds up to human and financial costs to the organisation. It would be helpful to be more inclusive and recognise that not all people are built with the *"I can take it"* attituded. Reducing the control, criticism and restraint and encouraging passion and commitment, amongst staff members, may reduce stress levels while increasing levels of motivation and personal drive. There may be less attrition, and lower levels of absence, and the organisation may see financial cost benefits. The advantage to the organisation is that staff members may be more productive. This could enrich the standing and productivity of the organisation, enhancing the learning experience for stakeholders. It may help reduce the human and financial burden that organisations and society are having to pay. Furthermore, voluntary training and support could be given by the organisation that is made part of continued professional development (CPD) helping staff members to become more aware of his/ her own emotions, understanding and evaluating emotions in others, and managing intra/ inter personal relationship- keeping calm in stressful situations. In other words, developing skills associated with emotional intelligence. The training and development could provide staff members a greater understanding of terms such as: stress, managing emotions, emotional demands, well-being and work/home life balance.

It could have been worse

As described by Pinker (2019) we don't live in a perfect world. Each generation faces challenges and our present generation is no different to that experienced by our ancestors. Pinker acknowledges that there are challenges such as inequality, climate change, the threat from a nuclear weapon, and the implications of the next information technology revolution of artificial intelligence. However, worldwide, the present generation is living longer, is more prosperous, and is healthier and happier. It is living in a new age of enlightenment. Pinker comments that it is an illusion to think of past generations having idyllic existence. People often had hard and difficult working conditions, lived shorter lives and education was limited to the very few. People died from diseases and illness. However, one critic describes Pinker (2019) as being *"blinded by the light"* when it comes to his description of enlightenment of the modern age; an age when we have advances in technology, medicine and science. As with previous generations, the twenty-first (21st) century experiences conflict, poverty, and inequality. We have the ability to wipe out large swathes of the world's population by pressing the nuclear button. People die from malnutrition and disease. Prejudice and bias continue. It may not be *"blinded by the light"*. It may be that areas of our lives are still shrouded in darkness and a little more light on these dark corners may help in alleviating the challenges faced by the less fortunate. We still have a long way to go but we have the ability to make the world a better place in which to live. Pinker explains that rather than live in an illusion of historical amnesia, we can embrace change and the challenges that it brings. Things could be a lot worse than they are.

As human beings, we have a tendency to ruminate over experiences and dwell on negative emotions. Marcus Aurelius (2006) states that *"The impediment to action advances action. What stands in the way becomes the way"*. The stoics, discussed at the beginning of this book, seem to understand that things experienced may actually be less serious than we really think. Irvine (2015) states a simple technique is to think how our day went and then to think how much worse it could have gone.......but *not* to dwell on it.

Emotional intelligence: does it really matter?

Neurath (1935/1983) points out that philosophers, who assume that there can be a completely rational system to explain the world about us, make a fundamental error. Our understanding of the world around is incomplete. Our knowledge is limited. We have *"bounded rationality"* that influences the way we think and the decisions we make (Simon, 1997). We are not machines. However, there are those who demonstrate a pseudo rationalistic belief in their own intelligence and have an inability to recognise the limitations of rationality (Popper, 1962). These people may not only influence their own thinking and decisions making, they may also influence others. It does appear that pseudo-rationalism can gain traction developing from a small number of believers into beliefs shared by a mass movement. As discussed earlier in this book, this is exemplified by cults, and cult leaders, such as Heaven's Gate, Jim Jones, and Charles Mason.

To help us make decisions, we often rely on emotions that are sometimes described as *"gut feelings"* that influence beliefs. Emotions are part of us. They show others how we are feeling. It is not a simple dualist approach where rationalistic thinking can be separated from emotions. Our understanding of emotions and their role in decision making is acknowledged as part of us that makes us human. To help communicate information, emotions are used and can be manipulated in others with the purpose of gaining acceptance of an idea or a viewpoint that may lack scientific rigour. Understanding emotions in oneself and in others is, therefore, helpful. Developing skill in managing these emotions is also helpful. There does need to be an acknowledgement as to our own limitations and knowledge and to recognise that we are unable to grasp wide and complex arguments without undertakinga detailed investigation. Even then, we may not have full information to arrive at a reasonable conclusion. Discussion in this book demonstrates this gap, reflecting upon differences of opinion and theory. The question in the title of the book asks *"emotional intelligence: does it really matter"*? Considering the research, studies and academic journal articles that have been published, the answer to the aforementioned question is a firm *"yes"*. However, like much of the discussion in this book, consideration has to be given to context and individual differences. Emotional intelligence helps place emotions in context. For example, when in discussion with a colleague or manager, rather than getting angry or upset over a personal disagreement, ask yourself how and why the other person is acting the way they are. Does it really help, showing anger? It may help reduce stress levels and release of cortisol into the system. It may help with coping with difficult situations that could otherwise escalate out of control. However, it is necessary to acknowledge that emotional intelligence may not be the panacea that can help and address *all* the challenges faced in life. There may be other factors that influence how we feel and think.

Like mindfulness and meditation, emotional intelligence should be considered as a beneficial tool and regarded as an instrument in the *"skills"* box of life, helping to build and develop a wider portfolio of personal competencies.

Consideration also has to be given to individual differences, including physiological and biological factors that can influence how we cope with challenging experiences. For example, there may be chemical and hormone balance/ imbalance that influence our decision making. Further, there may be more deep-seated psychological factors that may include characteristics associated with the *"dark triad"*. In such circumstances, it is difficult to try and understand and manage emotions when there may be personality flaws in the person.

Whereas we have travelled a long way over the last few decades, the journey continues. As further studies are carried out in emotional intelligence, the findings can help add pixilation to the photograph providing more detail and explanation together with a greater understanding of the topic.

This book has been written to help add a little more information to understand the way we think and how we relate to the world around us. If only a small part of this book helps and guides you, it is a book that has been well worth writing. I trust that you have found it interesting and wish you every success in the future.

A final quote from Marcus Aurelius (2006) *"Choose not to be harmed- and you won't feel harmed. Don't feel harmed- and you haven't been"*.

Bibliography

Introduction

Aldwin, C. M. and Park, C. L. (2004) Coping and physical health outcomes: an overview. *Psychology and Health,* **19**, pp.277-281.

Aristotle (1992) A theory of civic discourse on Rhetoric. Translated by G. A. Kennedy. OUP USA.

Aristotle (350BC) Translated by J.A. Smith (n.d.) [Online] Available from: http://classics.mit.edu/Aristotle/soul.1.i.html.

Ashforth, B.E. and Humphrey, R. H. (1995) Emotion in the workplace: A reappraisal. *Human Relations,* **48**(2), pp.97-125.

Ashkanasay, N. M., Zerbe, W. J. and Hartel, C. E. J. (2002) *Managing Emotions in the Workplace.* New York. M.E. Sharpe.

Bar-On, R. (1997) *The Emotional Inventory (EQ-i): Technical manual.* Toronto: Multi-Health Systems.

Bar-On, R. (2000) *The handbook of emotional intelligence: Theory, development, assessment, and application at home, school and in the workplace.* Jossey-Bass.

Bowen, P., Pilkington, A. and Rose, R. (2016) The relationship between emotional intelligence and well-being in academic employees. *International Journal of Social Science Studies,* **4**(5).

Bowery, A-M. (2007) Know thyself: Socrates as storyteller. In G. A. Scott, Philosophy in dialogue: Plato's many devices. Northwestern University Press.

Brickhouse, T. C. and Smith, N. D. (2015) Socrates on the emotions. Plato Journal. *The Journal of the International Plato Society,* **15**, pp. 9-28.

Briner, R.B (1999) The neglect and importance of emotion at work. *European Journal of work and organisational psychology,* **8**(3), pp. 323-346.

Briner, R. B. (2005) What can research into emotion at work tell us about researching well-being at work? *International Journal of Work Organisation and Emotion,* **1**(1), pp. 67-73.

Brody, N. (2004) *What Cognitive Intelligence Is and What Emotional Intelligence Is Not* [online]. Available from: http://psychometriclab.com/Brody.pdf. Department of Psychology Wesleyan University.

Carter, R. (2012) *Mapping the mind.* W & N.

Carver, C. S. (1997) You want to measure coping but your protocol's too long: consider the brief COPE. *International Journal of Behavioural Medicine,* **4**, pp. 92-100.

Cian, L., Krishna, A. and Schwarz, N. (2015) Positioning rationality and emotion: rationality is up and emotion is down. *Journal of Consumer Research,* **42**(4) pp. 632-651.

Costa, P. T. Jr. and McCrae, R. R. (1992) *Revised NEO Personality Inventory (NEO-PI-R) and NEO Five-Factor Inventory (NEO-FFI) professional manual.* Odessa, FL: Psychological Assessment Resources.

Crivellato, E. and Ribatti, D. (2007) Soul, mind, brain: Greek philosophy and the birth of neuroscience. *Brain Research Bulletin,* **71**(4), pp. 327-336.

Dalgleish, T. and Bramham, J. (1999) Cognitive perspective. In D. Levinson, J. J. Ponzetti Jr. and, P. F. Jorgensen (Eds). *Encyclopaedia of Human Emotions,* New York: Macmillan, pp. 118-121.

Damasio, A. (1994). *Descartes' Error: Emotion, Reason, and the Human Brain.* New York: Grosset/ Putnam.

Davidson, R. J. and Begley, S. (2012) *The emotional life of your brain: How to change the way you think, feel and live.* Hodder and Stoughton.

Dembroski, T. M., MacDougall, J. M., Williams, R. B., Haney, T. L. and Blumenthal, J. A. (1985) Components of type A hostility and anger-in: Relationship to angiographic findings. *Psychosomatic Medicine,* **47**, pp. 219-233.

Descartes, R. (2017) *Treatise on the passion of the soul.* Translated by J. Bennett. [Online] Available from: https://www.earlymoderntexts.com/assets/pdfs/descartes1649part2.pdf.

De Sousa, R. (1990) *The rationality of emotion.* MIT Press.

Diogenes Laertius (7.1) (2018) *Lives of the eminent philosophers.* (Ed J. Miller) Translated by P. Mensch. OUP USA.

Dufour, R. (2004) *Chrysippe. Oeuvre philosophique,* two volumes, Paris: Les Belles Lettres. [Online] Available from: https://www.lesbelleslettres.com/livre/1927-oeuvre-philosophique-t-i-et-ii.

Ekman, P. (1973) Cross cultural studies of facial expression. In P. Ekman (Ed) *Darwin and facial expressions: A century of research in review.* New York: Academic Press, pp. 169-222.

Fawzey, F., Fawzey, N., Hyun, C., Elashoff, R., Gulthries, D., Fahey, J. and Morton D. (1993) Malignant melanoma: Effects of an early structured psychiatric intervention, coping and affective state on recurrence and survival 6 years later. *Archives of General Psychiatry,* **50**, pp. 681-689.

Fineman, S. (2003) *Understanding emotion at work.* Sage Publications Ltd.

Fortenbaugh, W. W. (2014) Aristotle and Theophrastus on the emotions. In J. T. Fitzgerald, (Ed). *Passions and moral progress in Greco-Roman thought.* Routledge. Taylor and Francis Group.

Friedman, H. S. (1990) *Personality and disease.* New York: Wiley.

Goleman, D. (1995) *Emotional Intelligence: Why It Can Matter More than IQ.* Bantam Books, New York. NY.

Goleman, D. (1998) What makes a leader? *Harvard Business Review,* **76**, pp. 93-102.

Gross, J. J. (1998) The Emerging Field of Emotion Regulation: An Integrative Review. *Review of General Psychology,* **2**(3), pp. 271-299.

Gross, D.M. (2006) *The secret history of emotion: From Aristotle's rhetoric to modern brain science.* The University of Chicago Press Ltd, London.

Hammen, C. (2005) Stress and depression. *Annual Review of Clinical Psychology,* **1**, pp. 293-319.

Hergenhahn, B. R. (2009) *An introduction to the history of psychology*, (6th ed) Wadsworth Cengage Learning.

Holiday, R. (nd) *Daily stoic: what is stoicism? A definition and 9 stoic exercises to get you started.* [Online] Available from: https://dailystoic.com/what-is-stoicism-a-definition-3-stoic-exercises-to-get-you-started/.

Irvine, W. B. (2009) *A guide to the good life: The ancient art of stoic joy*. Oxford University Press.

Irvine, W.B. (2015) *Putting the Greek back into stoicism*. BBC News [Online] Available from https://www.bbc.co.uk/news/magazine-33346743.

Izard, C. E. (1977) *Human Emotions*. New York: Plenum Press.

James, W. (1884) *What is emotion?* Mind, 9, pp.188-205.

James, W. (1902) *The varieties of religious experiences*. London, Longmans Green.

Jorgensen, R. S., Johnson, B. T., Kolodziej, M. E. and Schreer, G. E. (1996) Elevated blood pressure and personality: A meat analytic review. *Psychological Bulletin*, **120**, pp. 293-320.

Julkunen, J., Salonen, R., Kaplan, G. A., Chesney, M. A. and Salonen, J. T. (1994) Hostility and the progression of carotid atherosclerosis. *Psychosomatic Medicine*, **56**, pp. 519-525.

Kinman, G. (2001) Pressure Points: A review of research on stressors and strains in UK academics. *Educational Psychology*, **21**(4), pp. 473-492.

Kinman, G., Jones, F. and Kinman, R. (2006) The well-being of the UK academy, 1998-2004. *Quality in higher education*, **12**(1), pp. 15-27.

Kraut, R. E. (2010) *Aristotle's ethics* [Online] Available from: http://plato.stanford.edu/entries/aristotle-ethics/.

Kringelbach, M. L. and Phillips, H. (2014) *Emotion: pleasure and pain in the brain*. Oxford.

Kumar, S. and Rooprai, K. Y. (2009) Role of emotional intelligence in managing stress and anxiety at the workplace. *Proceedings of annual conference of the American Society of Business and Behavioural Sciences (ASBBS)*, Annual conference: Las Vegas. **16**(1).

Lewis, D. (2004) Bullying at work: The impact of shame among university and college academics. *British Journal of Guidance and Counseling*, **32**(3), pp. 281-299.

Lyons, W. (1999) The philosophy of cognition and emotion. In: T. Dalgleish and M.J. Power (Eds) *Handbook of cognition and emotion*, John Wiley and Sons.

Magai, C. and McFadden, S. H. (1995) *The role of emotions in social and personality development: history, theory and research*. Plenum Press. New York.

Mayer, J. D. (2012) What is Emotional Intelligence, [online]. Available from: www.unh.edu/emotional_intelligence/ei.

Mayer, J. D. and Salovey, P. (1997) What is emotional intelligence? In: P. Salovey, and D. Sluyter, (Eds). *Emotional Development and Emotional Intelligence: Educational Implications*, (2nd ed). Basic: New York, pp. 3-31.

Meinwald, C. (2008) The *Philebus*. In G. Fine (Ed) *The Oxford handbook of Plato*. Oxford: Oxford University Press, pp. 484-503.

Mortiboys, A. (2012) *Teaching with emotional intelligence: A step by step guide for higher and further education professionals.* (2nd ed). Routledge.

Nelson, D. B., Low, G. R. and Nelson, K. (2006) *The emotionally intelligent teacher: A transformative.* Institute for Emotional Intelligence [online]. Available from: http://www.tamuk.edu/edu/kwei000/Research/Articles/Article_files/Emotionally_Intelligent_Teacher.pdf.

O'Boyle, E.J. (2001) Salary compression and inversion in the University workplace. *International Journal of Social Economics*, **28**(10-12) pp. 959-979.

Papez, J. W. (1995) A proposed mechanism of emotion. 1937. The Journal of Neuropsychiatry and Clinical Neuroscience, Winter, 7(1), pp. 103-112.

Pennebaker, J. W. (1990) *Opening up: The healing powers of confiding in others.* New York: Morrow.

Pennebaker, J. W., Kiecolt-Glaser, J. K. and Glaser, R. (1988) Disclosure of traumas and immune function: Health implications for psychotherapy. *Journal of Consulting and Clinical Psychology*, **56**(2), pp. 239-245.

Petrides, K. V. (2009) *Technical manual for the trait emotional intelligence questionnaire (TEIQue).* London, England: London Psychometric Laboratory.

Petrides, K. V. (2011). Ability and trait emotional intelligence. In: T. Chamorro-Premuzic, A. Furnham, and S. von Stumm (Eds). *The Blackwell-Wiley handbook of individual differences*, New York: Wiley.

Petrides, K. V. and Furnham, A. (2001) Trait emotional intelligence: Psychometric investigation with reference to established trait taxonomies. *European Journal of Personality*, 15, pp. 425-448.

Plato (380BC) *The Republic.* [Online] Available from: http://www.idph.net.

Plutchik, R. (1980) *Emotion: Theory, research, and experience: Theories of emotion.* New York: Academic.

Salovey, P. and Mayer, J. D. (1990) Emotional Intelligence. Imagination. *Cognition and Personality*, **9**, pp. 185-211.

Scherer, K. R. (2005) What are emotions? And how can they be measured. Social Science Information, Sage Publications, London, Thousand Oaks, CA and New Delhi. [Online] Available from: http://citeseerx.ist.psu.edu/viewdoc/download?doi=10.1.1.818.2716&rep=rep1&type=pdf.

Schirmer, A. (2015) *Emotion.* Sage Publications, Inc.

Schwabe, L. and Wolfe, O. T. (2010) Learning under stress impairs memory formation. *Neurobiology of Learning and Memory*, **93**(3), pp. 183 -188.

Schultz, A-M. (2013) *Plato's Socrates as narrator: A philosophical muse.* Lexington Books.

Seneca (4BC to 65AD) (1963) *On anger.* In J. W. Basore (Trans), Moral Essays. Cambridge, MA: Harvard University Press.

Simpson, R. and Cohen, C. (2004) Dangerous work: The gendered nature of bullying in the context of higher education. *Gender Work and Organisation*, 11(2), pp.163-186.

Simon, H. A. (1997) Models of bounded rationality. *Empirically grounded economic reason.* The MIT Press, **3**.

Solomon, R.C. (2010) The Philosophy of emotion. In M. D. Lewis, J. M. Haviland Jones and L. Feldman Barrett (Eds) *Handbook of emotions* (3rd ed). Guildford Press.

Sparrow, T. and Knight, A. (2006) *Emotional intelligence: The importance of attitudes inn developing emotional intelligence.* Jossey- Bass

Spiegel, D., Bloom, J. R., Kraemer, H. C. and Gottheil, E. (1989) Effect of psychosocial treatment on survival of patients with metastatic breast cancer. *The Lancet*, **2**, pp. 888-891.

Suls, J., Wan, C. K. and Costa, P.T. Jr. (1995) Relationship of trait anger to resting blood pressure: A meta-analysis. *Health Psychology*, **14**, pp. 444-456.

Taleb, N. N. (2012) *Antifragile: Things that gain from disorder.* Penguin Books.

Taleb, N. N. (2019) *Skin in the game: hidden asymmetries in daily life.* Penguin Books.

Van Sertima, I. (1992) *The Golden Age of the Moor.* Transaction Publisher.

Vogt, K. M. (2006) Anger, present injustice and future revenge in Seneca's De Ira. In k. m. Volt and G. Williams (Eds). *Seeing Seneca whole: Perspective on philosophy, poetry and politics.* Leiden: Brill, pp. 57-74.

Wang, J. (2005) Work stress as a risk factor for major depressive episode(s). *Psychological Medicine*, **35**, pp. 865-871.

Watson, R. I. and Evans, R. B. (1991) The great psychologists: A history of psychological thought. *The History of Behavioural Sciences*, **27**(4), pp. 382-384.

Woods, C. (2010) Employee well-being in the higher education workplace: a role for emotion scholarship. *High Education*, **60**, pp. 171-185.

Wundt, W. (1904) Principles of physiological psychology. (Translated by E. B. Titchener). [Online] Available from: https://psychclassics.yorku.ca/Wundt/Physio/.

Zeidner, M., Matthews, G. and Roberts, R. D. (2001) Slow down, you move too fast: Emotional intelligence remains an "elusive" intelligence. *Emotion*, **1**, pp. 265-275.

Chapter 1: Emotional Intelligence

Ali, F., Amorim, I. S. and Chamorro-Preuzic, T. (2009) Empathy deficits and trait emotional intelligence in psychopathy and Machiavellianism. *Personality and Individual Differences*, **47**, pp. 758-762.

Barchard, K. A. and Russell, J. A. (2006). Bias in consensus scoring, with examples from ability emotional intelligence tests. *Psicothema*, **18**, pp. 49-54.

Bar-On, R. (1997) *The Emotional Inventory (EQ-i): Technical manual.* Toronto: Multi-Health Systems.

Bar-On, R. (2000) *The handbook of emotional intelligence: Theory, development, assessment, and application at home, school and in the workplace.* Jossey-Bass.

Bar-On, R. (2005) The Bar-On model of emotional-social intelligence. In P. Fernández-Berrocal and N. Extremera (Eds), *Special Issue on Emotional Intelligence. Psicothema*, **17**, pp. 1-26.

Beyer, S. (1998) Gender differences in self-perception and negative recall biases. *Sex roles*, **38**, pp. 103-133.

Beyer, S. and Bowden, E. M. (1997) Gender differences in self-perceptions: convergent evidence from three measures of accuracy and bias. *Personality and Social Psychology Bulletin*, **23**, pp. 57-172.

Bharwaney, G. (2007) *Emotionally intelligent living*. Carmarthen: Crown House.

Boyatzis, R. E. (2006) Using tipping points of emotional intelligence and cognitive competencies to predict financial performance of leaders, *Psicothema*, **18** supplement, pp. 124-131.

Brannick, M. T., Wahi, M. M., Arce, M., Johnson, H. A., Nazian, S. and Goldin, S. B. (2009) Comparison of trait and ability measures of emotional intelligence in medical students. *Medical education*, **43**, pp. 1062-1068.

Briner, R. B (1999) The neglect and importance of emotion at work. *European Journal of Work and Organisational Psychology*, **8**(3), pp. 323-346.

Coco, C. M. (2011) Emotional Intelligence in Higher Education: Strategic Implications for Academic Leaders, *Journal of Higher Education Theory and Practice*, **11**(2).

Cooper, A. and Petrides, K. V. (2009) A psychometric analysis of the trait emotional intelligence questionnaire short form (TEIQue-SF) using item response theory. *Journal of Personality Assessment*, **92**(5), 449-457.

Costa, P. T. Jr. and McCrae, R. R. (1992) *Revised NEO Personality Inventory (NEO-PI-R) and NEO Five-Factor Inventory (NEO-FFI) professional manual*. Odessa, FL: Psychological Assessment Resources.

Craig, L., Fisk, J. E., Montgomery, C., Murphy, P. N. and Wareing, M. (2010) Is emotional intelligence impaired in ecstasy polydrug users? *Journal of Psychopharmacology*, **24**, pp. 221-231.

Damasio, A. (1994). *Descartes' Error: Emotion, Reason, and the Human Brain*. New York: Grosset/Putnam.

Damasio, A. R. (1996). The somatic marker hypothesis and the possible functions of the prefrontal cortex. *Proceedings of the Royal Society*, **351**, pp. 1413-1420.

Darwin, C. (1872) *The expression of emotions in man and animals*. New York: D. Appleton and Co.

Davies, M., Stankov, L. and Roberts, R. D. (1998) Emotional intelligence: In search of an elusive construct. *Journal of Personality and Social Psychology*, **75**(4), pp. 989-1015.

Dawda, D. and Hart, S. D. (2000) Assessing emotional intelligence: reliability and validity of the Bar-On Emotional Quotient-Inventory (EQ-i) in university students. *Personality and Individual Differences*, **28**, pp. 797-812.

Diener, E. (2009) Subjective well-being. In E. Diener (Ed), *The science of well-being: The collected works of Ed Diener*. New York: Springer, **37:** pp. 11-58.

Epstein, S. (1998) *Constructive thinking: The key to emotional intelligence*, Westport, CT: Praeger Publishers.

Eysenck, H. J. (1947) *Dimensions of personality*. London: Routledge and Kegan Paul.

Eysenck, H. J. (1958) *Sense and nonsense in psychology*. Middlesex: Penguin.

Eysenck, H.J. (1973) *Eysenck on extroversion*. Crosby, Lockwood Staples.

Eysenck, H. J. (1991) Dimensions of personality: 16, 5, or 3? Criteria for a taxonomic paradigm. *Personality and Individual Difference*, **12**, pp. 773-790.

Fredrickson, B. L. (2001) The role of positive emotions in positive psychology- The broaden and build theory of positive emotions. *American Journal of Psychology*, **56**(3), pp. 218-226.

Freudenthaler, H. H. and Neubauer, A. C. (2007) Measuring emotional management abilities: Further evidence of the importance to distinguish between typical and maximum performance. *Personality and Individual Differences*, **29**, pp. 105-115.

Freudenthaler, H. H., Neubauer, A. C., Gabler, P. and Scherl, W. G. (2008) Testing the Trait Emotional Intelligence Questionnaire (TEIQue) in a German speaking sample. *Personality and Individual Differences*, **45**, pp. 673-678.

Gardner, H. (1983) *Frames of mind: The theory of multiple intelligences*. New York: Basic Books.

Gardner, H. (1999) *Intelligence reframed. Multiple intelligences for the 21st century*. New York. Basic Books.

Gardner, K. and Qualter, P. (2009) Emotional Intelligence and Borderline personality disorder. *Personality and Individual Differences*, **47**, pp. 94-98.

Goleman. D. (1995) *Emotional Intelligence: Why It Can Matter More than IQ*. Bantam Books, New York. NY.

Goleman, D. (1998a) What makes a leader? *Harvard Business Review*, **76**, pp. 93-102.

Goleman, D. (1998b) *Working with emotional intelligence*. Bantam Books: New York.

Goleman, D. (2000). Leadership that gets results. *Harvard Business Review*, **78**(2), pp. 78-90.

Harma, A. M., Katiala-Heino, R., Rimpela, M. and Rantanen, P. (2002) Are adolescents with frequent pain symptoms more depressed? *Scandinavian Journal of Primary Health Care*, **20**, pp. 92-96.

Henderson, L. W. and Knight, T. (2012) Integrating the hedonic and eudaimonic perspectives to more comprehensively understand well-being and pathways to well-being. *International Journal of Well-being*, **2**(3), pp. 196-221).

Kahneman, D. (2011) *Thinking fast and slow*. Penguin: Random House, UK.

Katz, I. M. and Campbell, J. D. (1994) Ambivalence over emotional expression and well-being: nomothetic and idiographic tests of the stress buffering hypothesis. *Journal of Personality and Social Psychology*, **67**, pp. 513-524.

Keltner, D. and Haidt, J. (2001) Social functions of emotions. In: T. Mayne and G. Bonanno (Eds). *Emotions: Current issues and future directions*. New York: Guilford Press, pp. 192-213.

King, L. A. and Emmons, R. A. (1990). Conflict over emotional expression: psychological and physical correlates. *Journal of Personality and Social Psychology*, Vol. **58**, pp. 864-877.

King, L. A. and Emmons, R. A. (1991) Psychological, physical and interpersonal correlates of emotional expressiveness, conflict and control. *European Journal of Personality*, **5**, pp. 131-150.

Leuner, B. (1966) Emotionale Intelligenz und Emanzipation [Emotional intelligence and emancipation]. *Praxis der Kinderpsychologie und Kinderpsychiatry*, **15**, pp. 196–203.

Martinez-Pons, M. (1997) The relation of emotional intelligence with selected areas of personal functioning. *Imagination, Cognition and Personality*, **17**, pp. 3-13.

Martins, A., Ramalho, N. and Morin, E. (2010) A comprehensive Meta-analysis of the relationship between emotional intelligence and health. *Personality and Individual Differences*, **49**, pp. 554-564.

Matthews, G., Zeidner, M. and Roberts, R. D. (2004) *Emotional Intelligence*, MIT Press.

Matthews, G., Zeidner, M. and Roberts, R. D. (2007) Emotional intelligence: consensus, controversies, and questions. In G. Matthews, M. Zeidner and R. D. Roberts (Eds) Series in affective science. The science of emotional intelligence: knowns and unknowns. New York, US: Oxford University Press, pp. 3-46.

Mavroveli, S., Petrides, K. V., Rieffe, C. and Bakker, F. (2007) Trait emotional intelligence, psychological well-being and peer rated social competence in adolescence, *British Journal of Development Psychology*, **25**, pp. 263-275.

Mavroveli, S., Petrides, K. V., Sangareau, Y. and Furnham, A. (2009) Relating trait emotional intelligence to objective socioemotional outcomes in childhood. *British Journal of Educational Psychology*, **79**, pp. 259-272.

Mavroveli, S. and Sanchez-Ruiz, M.J. (2011) Trait emotional intelligence influences on academic achievement and school behaviour. *British Journal of Educational Psychology*, **81**(1) pp. 112-134.

Mayer, J. D., Caruso, D. and Salovey (1999) Emotional Intelligence meets traditional standards for intelligence. Intelligence. 27. (267-298). In: M. A. Brackett, and S. E. Rivers, (2006). Relating Emotional Abilities to social functioning: A comparison of self-report and performance measure of emotional intelligence, *Journal of Personality and Social Psychology*, (2006), **91**(4).

Mayer, J. D. and Ciarrochi, J. (2006) Clarifying concepts related to emotional intelligence: A proposed glossary, In J. Ciarrochi, J. J. Forgas and J. D. Mayer (Eds). *Emotional Intelligence in Everyday life* (2nd ed) Psychology Press, Inc, pp. 261-267.

Mayer, J. D. and Salovey, P. (1997) What is emotional intelligence? In: P. Salovey, and D. Sluyter, (Eds). *Emotional Development and Emotional Intelligence: Educational Implications*, (2nd ed). Basic: New York, pp. 3-31.

Mayer, J. D., Salovey, P. and Caruso, D. (2000) Emotional intelligence. In: R. Sternberg. *Handbook of intelligence*, Cambridge, UK. Cambridge University Press, pp. 528-549.

Mayer, J. D., Salovey, P., Caruso, D. and Sitarenios, G. (2003) *Measuring emotional intelligence with the MSCEIT V2*. The American Psychological Association Inc.

Mikolajczak, M., Bodarwe, K., Laloyaux, O., Hansenne, M. and Nelis, D. (2010) Association between frontal EEG asymmetric and emotional intelligence among adults. *Personality and Individual differences*, **48**, pp. 177-181.

O'Boyle, E. H., Humphrey, R. H., Pollack, J. M., Hawver, H. and Story, P. A. (2011) The relation between emotional intelligence and job performance. A meta-analysis. *Journal of Organisational Behaviour*, **32**(5), pp. 788-818.

Orbach, S. (1994) *What's really going on here?* Virago Press, St Ives.

(The) *Oxford Dictionaries* (2016). [Online] Available from: https://en.oxforddictionaries.com/word-of-the-year/word-of-the-year-2016.

Parker, J. D. A., Taylor, R. N., Eastabrook, J. M., Schell, S. L. and Wood, L. M. (2008) Problem gambling in adolescence: Relationships with internet misuse and emotional intelligence. *Personality and Individual differences*, **45**, pp. 174-180.

Payne, W. L. (1986) A study of emotion: Developing Emotional Intelligence; Self-Integration; Relating to fear, Pain and Desire. *Dissertation Abstracts International*, **47**, pp. 203.

Perez, J. C., Petrides, K. V. and Furnham, A. (2005) Measuring trait emotional intelligence. In: R. Schulze and R. D. Roberts, (Eds). *Emotional intelligence: An International handbook*. Cambridge, MA: Hogrefe and Huber. (181-201).

Petrides, K. V. (2009a) Psychometric properties of the Trait Emotional Intelligence Questionnaire. In: C. Stough, D. H. Saklofske, and J. D. Parker, *Advances in the assessment of emotional intelligence*. New York: Springer.

Petrides, K. V. (2009b) *Technical manual for the trait emotional intelligence questionnaire (TEIQue)*. London, England: London Psychometric Laboratory.

Petrides, K. V. (2011) Ability and trait emotional intelligence. In: T. Chamorro-Premuzic, S. von Stumms, A. Furnham. *The Wiley Blackwell Handbook of individual differences*. John Wiley and Sons Ltd. (656-678).

Petrides, K. V. and Furnham, A. (2001) Trait emotional intelligence: Psychometric investigation with reference to established trait taxonomies. *European Journal of Personality*, **15**, pp. 425-448.

Petrides, K. V. and Furnham, A. (2003). Trait emotional intelligence: Behavioural validation in two studies of emotion recognition and reactivity to mood induction. *European Journal of Personality*, **17**(6), pp. 39–57.

Petrides, K. V., Pita, R. and Kokkinaki, F. (2007) The location of trait emotional intelligence in personality factor space. *British Journal of Psychology*, **98**(2), pp. 273-289.

Petrides, K. V., Vernon, P. A., Schermer, J. A., Lighart, L. Boomsma, D. I. and Veselka, L. (2010) Relationships between trait emotional intelligence and the big five in the Netherlands. *Personality and Individual Differences*, **48**(8), pp. 906-910.

Redman, T. and Wilkinson, A. (2002) *The informed student guide to human resource Management*. London Thomson Learning.

Robbins, S. P. and Judge, T. A. (2013) *Organisational Behaviour*, (15th ed). Pearson.

Robinson, M. D. and Clore, G. L. (2002) Belief and feeling: evidence for an accessibility model of emotional self-report. *Psychological Bulleting*, **128**(6), pp. 934-960.

Russell, J. A. and Barrett, L. F. (1999) Core affect, Prototypical emotional episodes, and other things called emotion: Dissecting the elephant". *Journal of Personality and Social Psychology*, **76**(5), pp. 805-819.

Russo, P. M., Mancini, G., Trombini, E., Baldaro, B., Mavroveli, S. and Petrides, K. V. (2012) Trait Emotional Intelligence and the Big Five: A study on Italian Children and Preadolescents. *Journal of Psychoeducational Assessment.* Sage. **30**, pp. 274-283.

Salovey, P., Brackett, M. A. and Mayer, J. D. (2004) *Emotional Intelligence: Key Readings on the Mayer and Salovey Model*, Dude Publishing.

Salovey, P. and Mayer, J. D. (1990) Emotional Intelligence. Imagination. *Cognition and Personality*, **9**, pp. 185-211.

Salovey, P., Mayer, J. D., Goldman, S., Turvey, C. and Palfai, T. (1995) Emotional attention, clarity and repair: exploring emotional intelligence using the Trait Meta Mood scale. In: J.W. Pennebaker (ed.) *Emotion, Disclosure and Health.* American Psychological Association: Washington, DC, pp. 125-154.

Seligman, M. (2006) *Learned optimism.* USA. Vintage Books.

Taylor, S. E. and Armor, D. A. (1996) Positive illusions and coping with adversity. *Journal of Personality*, **64**(4), pp. 873-898.

Taylor, S. E. and Brown, J. D. (1988) Illusions and well-being: A social psychological perspective on mental health. *Psychological Bulletin*, **103**, pp. 193-210.

Uva, M. C. D., de Timary, P., Cortesi, M., Mikolajczak, M., de Blicquy, P. D. and Luminet, O. (2010) Moderating effect of emotional intelligence on the role of negative affect in the motivation to drink in alcohol dependent subjects undergoing protracted withdrawal. *Personality and individual differences*, **48**, pp. 16-21.

Vernon, P. A., Villani, V. C., Schermer, J. A., Kirilovic, S., Martin, R. A., Petrides, K. V., Spector, T. D. and Cherkas, L. F. (2009) Genetic and environmental correlations between trait emotional intelligence and humour styles. *Journal of individual differences*, **30**(3), pp. 130-137.

Vernon, P. A., Villani, V. C., Schermer, J. A. and Petrides, K. V. (2008) Phenotypic and genetic associations between the big five and trait emotional intelligence. *Twin Research and Human Genetics*, **11**, pp. 524-530.

Williams, C., Daley, D., Burnside, E. and Hammond-Rowley, S. (2010) Does item overlap account for the relationship between trait emotional intelligence and psychopathology in preadolescents? *Personality and Individual Differences*, **48**, pp. 867-871.

Zeidner, M., Matthews, G. and Roberts, R. D. (2012*) What we know about emotional intelligence: How it affects learning, work, relationships, and our mental health.* MIT Press.

Chapter 2: Stress

Abraham, R. (1998a) Emotional dissonance in organisations: conceptualising the roles of self-esteem and job induced tension, Leadership and Organisation Development Journal, **20**(1), pp. 18-25.

Abraham, R. (1998b) Emotional dissonance in organisations: Antecedents, consequences and moderators. *Genetic, Social and General Psychology Monographs*, **124**(2), pp. 229-246.

Abraham, R. (1999) The impact of emotional dissonance on organisational commitment and intention to turnover. *Journal of Psychology*, **133**(4), pp. 441-455.

Akbari, A. and Khormaiee, F. (2015) The predication of mediating role of resilience between psychological well-being and emotional intelligence in students. *International Journal of School Health*, **2**(3).

Alpert, R. and Haber, R. N. (1960) Anxiety in academic achievement situations. *The Journal of Abnormal Social Psychology*, **61**(2), pp. 207-215.

Anisman, H. (2015) *Stress and your health: From vulnerability to resilience*. John Wiley and Sons Ltd.

Atkinson, W. (2004) Stress: Risk management's most serious challenge? *Risk Management*, **51**, pp. 20-26.

Austin, A. and Pilat, M. (2000) Tension, stress, and the tapestry of faculty lives. *Academe*. January/ February, pp. 38-42.

Ball, J. (2014) Explained: how is it possible to triple tuition fees and raise no extra cash? *The Guardian*. 21st March [online]. Available from: http://www.theguardian.com/news/datablog/2014/mar/21/explained-triple-tuition-fees-no-extra-cash.

Barrett, L. F. and Gross, J. J. (2001) Emotion representation and regulation: A process model of emotional intelligence. In: T. Mayne and G. Bonnano (Eds), *Emotion: Current Issues and Future Directions*. New York: Guilford, pp. 286-310.

Bartlett, D. (1998) *Stress: Perspectives and processes*. London: Open University Press.

Becher, T. and Trowler, P. R. (2001) *Academic tribes and territories* (2nd ed). SRHE and Open University Press.

Benson, T. (2012) Ten things I never knew about being an academic chair: lessons learned from year one in administration. *Academic Leader*, **28**(9), pp. 3–6.

Blix, A. G., Cruise, R. J., Mitchell, B. M and Blix G. G. (1994) Occupational stress among university teachers. *Educational Research*, **36**, pp. 157-169.

Bodenmann, G., Meuwly, N., Bradbury, T. N., Gmelch, S. and Ledermann, T. (2010) Stress, anger, and verbal aggression in intimate relationships: Moderating effects of individual and dyadic coping. *Journal of Social and Personal Relationships*, **27**, pp. 408-424.

Bolton, P. (2012) *Social and General Statistics. Education: Historical statistics*. Standard note: SN/SG/4252. House of Commons Library.

Bosma, H., Peter, R., Siegrist, J. and Marmot, M.G. (1998) Two alternative stress models and the risk of coronary heart disease. *American Journal of Public Health*, **88**(1), pp. 68-74.

Bowen, P., Pilkington, A. and Rose, R. (2016) The relationship between emotional intelligence and well-being in academic employees. *International Journal of Social Science Studies*, **4**(5).

Boyd, S. and Wylie, C. (1994) *Workload and stress in New Zealand Universities.* Wellington: New Zealand Council for Educational Research / Association of University staff of New Zealand.

Brackett, M. (2013) Creating emotionally intelligent schools. Keynote speaker. *Book of Abstracts, 4th International Congress on emotional intelligence. International Society for Emotional Intelligence Inc.* New York City. 8th to 10th September.

Brackett, M. A., Mayer, J. D. and Warner, R. M. (2004) Emotional intelligence and its relation to everyday behaviour. *Personality and individual differences*, **36**, pp. 1387-1402.

Bradley, J. and Eachus, P. (1995) Occupational stress within a UK higher education institution. *International Journal of Stress Management*, **2**(3), pp. 145-158.

Briner, R. B. (1999) The neglect and importance of emotion at work. *European Journal of work and organisational psychology*, **8**(3), pp. 323-346.

Burnett, D. (2016). *The Idiot Brain.* Guardian Books, London

Cahill, L., Gorski, L. and Le, K. (2003) Enhanced human memory consolidation with post learning stress: Interaction with the degree of arousal at encoding. *Learning and Memory*, **10**, pp. 270.

Cameron, K. and Tschirhart, M. (1992) Post-industrial environments and organizational effectiveness in colleges and universities. *Journal of Higher Education*, **63**(1), pp. 87-108.

Carter, R. (2010) *Mapping the mind.* W & N.

Cartwright, S. and Cooper, C. L. (1997) *Managing workplace stress.* Sage. London.

Chandola, T., Britton, A., Brunner, E., Hemmingway, H., Malik, M., Kumari, M., Badrick, E., Kivimaki, M. and Marmot, M. (2008) Work stress and coronary heart disease: what are the mechanisms. *European Hearth Journal*, **29**(5), pp. 640-648.

Chandola, T., Brunner, E. and Marmot, M. (2006) Chronic stress and the metabolic syndrome: prospective study. *British Medical Journal*, **4**(7540), pp. 521-525.

Chang, C. and Tseng, Y. (2009) An exploration of job stress among academic heads in Taiwanese Universities. *Social Behaviour and Personality*, **37**(5), pp. 583-590.

(The) Chartered Institute of Personnel and Development (CIPD) (2019) *Health and Well-being at work survey, 2019.* [Online] Available from: https://www.cipd.co.uk/Images/infographic-health-and-well-being-2019_tcm18-56171.pdf.

Cilliers, F. and Pienaar, J. W. (2014) The career psychological experiences of academic department chairpersons at a South African university. *South African Business Review*, **18**(3), pp. 22-45.

Clarkson, G. P. and Hodgkinson G. (2007) What can occupational stress diaries achieve that questionnaires can't? *Personnel Review*, **36**(5), pp. 684-700.

Cohen, J., Cohen, P., West, S. G., and Aiken, L. S. (2003). *Applied multiple regression/correlation analysis for the behavioural sciences (3rd ed).* Mahwah, NJ: Lawrence Erlbaum Associates.

Cohen, S., Janicki-Deverts, D. and Miller, G. E. (2007). Psychological stress and disease. *Journal of the American Medical Association*, **298**(14), pp. 1684-1687.

Cross, G. and Carroll, D. (1990) *Goodwill under stress: Morale in UK universities*. London: Association of University Teachers.

Crum, A. J., Salovey, P. and Anchor, S. (2013) Rethinking Stress: The role of mindsets in determining the stress response. *Journal of Personality and Social Psychology*, **104**(4), pp. 716-733.

Court, S. (1996) The use of time by academic and related staff, *Higher Education Quarterly*, **50**, pp. 237-260.

Daniels, K. and Guppy, A. (1994a) An exploratory study of stress in British University. *Higher Education Quarterly*, **48**, pp. 135-144.

Daniels, K. and Guppy, A. (1994b) Occupational stress, social support, job control and psychological well-being. *Human Relations*, **47**, pp. 1523-1544.

Davidson, R. J. and Begley, S. (2012) *The emotional life of the brain: How to change the way you think, feel and live*. Hodder and Stoughton.

Dienstbier, R. A. (1989) Arousal and physiological toughness: Implications for mental and physical health. *Psychological Review*, **96**, pp. 84-100.

Doyle, C. (1998) The work experience of senior academic women: stress, coping, career progression. *Paper presented at 1st international work psychology conference, Institute of work psychology*, University of Sheffield, UK, July.

Doyle, C. and Hind, P. (1998). Occupational stress, burnout and job status in female academics. *Gender, work and organisations*, **5**, pp. 67-68.

Early, P. (1994) *Lecturers' workload and factors affecting stress levels*. Slough: NFER.

Eysenck, M. W. (2004) *Psychology: an international perspective*. Psychology Press Ltd

Fay, D. and Sonnentag, S. (2002) Rethinking the effects of stressors: A longitudinal study on personal initiative. *Journal of Occupational Health Psychology*, **7**, pp. 221-234.

Ferrie, J. E., Shipley, M. J., Marmot, M. G., Stansfeld, S. and Smith, G. D. (1998) The health effects of major organizational change and job insecurity. *Social Science and Medicine*, **6**(2), pp. 243-254.

Fisher, S. (1994) *Stress in academic life: The mental assembly line*. Buckingham: Open University Press.

Fleming, P. (2018) Do you work more than 39 hours a week? Your job could be killing you. *The Guardian*. Monday, 15th January. [Online] Available from: https://www.theguardian.com/lifeandstyle/2018/jan/15/is-28-hours-ideal-working-week-for-healthy-life.

Fredrickson, B. L. (2001) The role of positive emotions in positive psychology: The broaden and build theory of positive emotions. *American Psychologist*, **56**(3), pp. 218-226.

Freudenberger, H. J. (1974) Staff burnout. *Journal of Social Issues*, **30**(1), pp.159-165.

Ghosh, S. and Collier, A. (2012) *Churchill's pocketbook of diabetes*. Elsevier Ltd.

Gillespie, N. A., Walsh, M., Winefield, A. H., Dua, J. and Stough, C. (2001) Occupational stress in universities: Staff perceptions of the causes, consequences and moderators of stress. *Work and Stress*, **15**(1), pp. 53-72.

Gleaves, A. and Walker, C. (2006) How does digital caring differ from physical caring? In: J. Fanghanel and D. Warren (Eds). *International Conference on the Scholarship of Teaching and Learning: proceedings 2005 and 2006*. London, Centre for Educational and Academic Practices. City University, pp. 250-259.

Hammen, C. (2005) Stress and depression. *Annual Review of Clinical Psychology*, **1**, pp. 293-319.

(The) Health and Safety Executive (HSE) (2013) *Stress and Psychological disorders in Great Britain 2013. National Statistics*. [online]. Available from: http://www.hse.gov.uk/statistics/causdis/stress/stress.pdf.

(The) Health and Safety Executive (HSE) (2018a) Work-related ill health and occupational disease in Great Britain. [Online] Available from: http://www.hse.gov.uk/statistics/causdis/.

(The) Health and Safety Executive (HSE) (2018b) *Causes of stress at work*. [Online] Available at: http://www.hse.gov.uk/stress/causes.htm.

Hancock, P. A. and Weaver, J. L. (2005) On time distortion under stress. *Theoretical Issues in Ergonomics Science*, **6**, pp. 193-211.

Helm, K. M. (2016) Hooking up: *The psychology of sex and dating*. ABC-CLIO, LLC.

(The) Higher Education Statistics Agency (HESA) (2015). *Staff in higher education* [online]. Available from: https://www.hesa.ac.uk/pr/2694-press-release-187.

(The) Higher Education Statistics Agency (HESA) (2019). *Staff in higher education* [online]. Available from: https://www.hesa.ac.uk/news/24-01-2019/sb253-higher-education-staff-statistics

Hobfoll, S. E. (1989) Conservation of resources: a new attempt of conceptualising stress. *The American Psychologist*, **44**(3), pp. 513-524.

Hobfoll, S. E. (1998) *Stress, culture and community*. New York: Plenum.

Hochschild, A. (1983) *The managed heart: Commercialisation of human feeling*. Berkeley: University of California Press.

Holmes, T. H. and Rahe, R. H. (1967) The social readjustment rating scale. *Journal of Psychosomatic Research*, **11**, pp. 213-218.

Iqbal, F. and Abbasi, F. (2013) Relationship between emotional intelligence and job burnout among universities professors. *Asian Journal Social Sciences and Humanities (AJSSH)*, **2**(2), pp. 219-229.

Jackson, C. and Hayday, S. (1997) *Staff attitudes at the University of Central Lancashire*. Brighton: Institution for Employment Studies.

Johnson, S. B., Perry, N. W. and Rosensky, R. H. (2002) *Handbook of clinical health psychology: Medical disorder and behavioural applications*. Washington. DC. American Psychological Association.

Jones, J. R. and Hodgson, J. T. (1998) *Self-reported work-related illness in 1995: Results from a household survey*. London: HSE books.

Journal of Occupational and Environmental Medicine (2015) Job strain linked to increased sick leave due to mental disorders. *ScienceDaily*, (16th July).

[Online] Available from: https://www.sciencedaily.com/releases/2015/07/150716124744.htm

Kanoy, K., Book, H.E. and Stein, S.J. (2013) *The student EQ edge: Emotional intelligence and your academic and personal success: student workbook.* Jossey-Bass.

Kazim, E. (2011) *Scientific commentary of Suratul Faatehah* (3rd ed). Nice Printing Press, Delhi.

Kelly, S., Charlton, J. and Jenkins, R. (1995) Suicide deaths in England and Wales (1982-92). The contribution of occupation and geography. *Population trends,* **80**, pp. 16-25.

Kinman, G. (1996) *Occupational stress and health among lecturers working in further and higher education.* London: National Association for Teachers in Further and Higher Education.

Kinman, G. (1998) *Pressure points: A survey into the causes and consequences of occupational stress in UK academic and related staff.* London: Association of University Teachers.

Kinman, G. (2001) Pressure Points: A review of research on stressors and strains in UK academics. *Educational Psychology,* **21**(4), pp. 473-492.

Kinman, G. (2008) Work stressors, health and sense of cohesion in UK academic employees. *Educational Psychology,* **28**(7), pp. 823-835.

Kinman, G. (2010) Psychosocial hazards in UK universities: Adopting a risk assessment approach. *Higher Education Quarterly,* **64**(4), pp. 413-428.

Kinman, G. (2014) Doing more with less? Work and well-being in academics. *Somatechnics,* **4**(2), pp. 219-235.

Kinman, G. and Jones, F. (2003). Running up and down escalator: stressors and strains in UK academics. *Quality in Higher Education,* **9**(1) pp. 21-39.

Kinman, G. and Jones, F. (2008) Effort-reward imbalance, over-commitment and work-life conflict: testing an expanded model. *Journal of Managerial Psychology,* **23**(3), pp. 236-251.

Kinman, G. and Wray, S. (2013) *Higher Stress: A Survey of Stress and Well-being among Staff in Higher Education.* University and College Union (UCU), [online]. Available from: http://www.ucu.org.uk/media/pdf/4/5/HE_stress_report_July_2013.pdf

Kirsch, P., Esslinger, C., Chen, Q., Mier, D., Lis, S., Siddhanti, S., Gruppe, H., Mattay, V. S., Gallhofer, B. and Meyer-Lindenberg, A. (2005) Oxytocin modulates neural circuitry for social cognition and fear in humans. *The Journal of Neuroscience,* **25**(49), pp. 11489-11493.

Klenke-Hamel, K. E. and Mathieu, J. E. (1990) Role strains, tension, and job satisfaction influences on employee's propensity to leave: A multi-sample replication and extension. *Human Relations,* **43**, pp. 791-807.

Labar, K. S. (2010) Emotion-cognition interactions. In G. Koob, M. Le Moal and R. Thompson (eds), *Encyclopaedia of Behavioural Neuroscience.* Elsevier, (Vol. 1).

Lambert, R. and McCarthy, C. (2007) *Understanding Teacher Stress in an Age of Accountability.* Information Age Publishing: Charlotte.

Lazarus, R. S. (1966). *Psychological stress and the coping process.* New York: McGraw-Hill.

Lazarus, R. S. (1982) The psychology of stress and coping. In: N. A. Milgram (ed). *Stress and anxiety,* **8.** New York: Hemisphere Publishing.

Lazarus, R. S. (1990) Theory based stress measurement. *Psychological Inquiry,* **1,** pp. 3-13.

Lazarus R. S. (1991) *Emotion and adaption.* Oxford: Oxford University Press.

Lazarus, R. S. (1993) Coping theory and research: Past, present and future. *Psychosomatic medicine,* **55,** pp. 234-247.

Lazarus, R. S. (1999). *Stress and Emotion: A new Synthesis.* Springer Publishing Company, Inc.

Lazarus, R. S. (2007) Stress and emotion: A new synthesis. In: A. Mondat, R. S. Lazarus, and G. Reevy (Eds). *The Praeger handbook on stress and coping.* Westport, CT. Praeger/ Greenwood. **1,** pp. 33-51.

Lazarus, R. S. and Folkman, S. (1984) *Stress, Appraisal and coping.* New York: Springer.

Lazarus, R. S. and Folkman, S. (1986) Cognitive theories of stress and the issue of circularity. In: M. H. Appley and R. Trumbull (Eds) *Perspectives in interactional psychology.* New York: Plenum, pp. 287-327.

Lazarus, R. S. and Launier, R. (1978) Stress related transactions between person and environment. In: L.A. Pervin and M. Lewis (Eds). *Perspectives in interactional psychology.* New York: Plenum, pp. 287-327.

Li, J., Atasoy, S., Fang, X., Angerer, P. and Ladwig, K. H. (2019) Combined effect of work stress and impaired sleep on coronary and cardiovascular mortality in hypertensive workers: The MONICA/ KORA cohort study. European Journal of Preventative Cardiology. [Online] Available from: https://journals.sagepub.com/doi/10.1177/2047487319839183

Lubuschagne, I., Phan, K. L., Wood, A., Angstadt, M., Chua, P., Heinrichs, M., Stout, J. C. and Nathan, P. J. (2010) Oxytocin attenuates amygdala to fear in generalised social anxiety disorder. *Neuropsychopharmacology.* **35**(12), pp. 2403-2413.

Marmot, M. (2015) *The health gap.* Bloomsbury.

Maslach, C. and Jackson, S.E. (1981) The measurement of experienced burnout. *Journal of Occupational Behaviour,* **2,** pp. (99-113).

Masters, R. (2004) *Counselling criminal justice offenders.* Sage publications.

Masuda, M. and Holmes, T. H. (1967) Magnitude estimations of social readjustments. *Journal of Psychosomatic Research,* **11,** pp. 219-225.

McInnis, C. (1999) Change and diversity in work patterns of Australian academics. *Higher education management,* **8**(2), pp. 105-117.

(The) Mental Health Foundation (2018a) *Mental Health Statistics.* [Online] Available from: https://www.mentalhealth.org.uk/statistics/mental-health-statistics-stress.

(The) Mental Health Foundation (2018b). Mental Health Statistics: UK and worldwide. [Online] Available from:
https://www.mentalhealth.org.uk/statistics/mental-health-statistics-uk-and-worldwide.

Mitra, P. (2015) Determinants of organisational stress and work-life balance: A review of literature. *International Journal of Innovative Research and Development*, **4**(4), pp. 391-396.

Myers, D. G. and Diener, E. (1995) Who is happy? *Psychological Science*, **6**, pp. 10-19.

The National Education Union (2018) *NEU survey shows workload causing 80% of teachers to consider leaving the profession*. [Online] Available from: https://neu.org.uk/press-releases/neu-survey-shows-workload-causing-80-teachers-consider-leaving-profession

Nelson, D. B., Low, G. R. and Nelson, K. (2006) *The emotionally intelligent teacher: A transformative.* Institute for Emotional Intelligence [online]. Available from: http://www.tamuk.edu/edu/kwei000/Research/Articles/Article_files/Emotionally_Intelligent_Teacher.pdf.

(The) National Health Service (England NHS (2018) *Mental Health.* [Online] Available from: https://www.england.nhs.uk/mental-health/.

Noriah, M. I., Iskandar, I.P. and Ridzauddin, R. (2010) Emotional intelligence of Malaysian teachers: Implications of workplace productivity. International Journal of Vocational Education and Training, **14**(2), pp. 7-24.

The Organisation for Economic Co-operation and Development (2019) OECD stats. [Online] Availablefrom:.https://stats.oecd.org/Index.aspx?DataSet Code=PDB_LV

Ostir, G. V., Markides, K. S., Peek, M. K. and Goodwin, J. S. (2001) The association between emotional well-being and the incidence of stroke in older adults. *Psychometric medicine*, **63**, pp. 210-215.

Perreau-Linck, E., Beauregard, M., Gravel, P., Paquette, V., Soucy, J. P., Diksic, M. and Benkelfat, C. (2007) In vivo measurements of brain tapping of C labelled alpha-methyl- L- tryptophan during acute changes in mood states. *Journal of Psychiatry and Neuroscience*, **32**(6), pp. 430-434.

Peterson, R. L. (2007) *Inside the investor's brain: the power of mind over money.* John Wiley and Sons.

Raiden, A. B. and Raisanen, C. (2013) Striving to achieve it all: men and work-family life balance in Sweden and the UK. Special Issue: Equality, diversity and inclusion in the construction industry. *Construction Management and Economics*, **31**(8).

Reddy, G. L. and Poornima, R. (2012) Occupational stress and professional burnout of university teachers in south India. International *Journal of Educational Planning and Administration*, **2**(2), pp. 109-124.

Repetti, R. L. (1993) The effects of workload and Social Environment on Health. In L. Goldberger and S. Breznitz (Eds). *Handbook of Stress: Theoretical and Clinical Aspects.* New York: Free Press.

Rhodes, C. and Nevill, A. (2004) Academic and social integration in higher education: a survey of satisfaction and dissatisfaction within a first-year education studies cohort at a new university. *Journal of Further and Higher Education*, **28**(2), pp. 179-193.

Ryff, C. D. and Singer, B. H. (2000) Interpersonal flourishing: A positive health agenda for the new millennium. *Personality and Social Psychology Review.* **4**

(1 Special Issue: Personality and Social Psychology at the Interface: New Directions for Interdisciplinary Research), pp. 30-44.

Sabihi, S. (2017) *Role of oxytocin and GABA in the prefrontal cortex in mediating anxiety behaviour*. Ohio State University.

Sagaya, M. T., Vasumathi, A. and Subashini, R. (2015) The influence of emotional intelligence on work-life balance of faculty members' performance and satisfaction in the educational institutions using multivariate analysis, India- an empirical study. International *Journal of Services and Operations Management*, **22**(2), pp. 189-209.

Salovey, P., Bedell, B. T., Detweiler, J. B. and Mayer, J. D. (1999) Coping intelligently: Emotional intelligence and the coping process. In C.R. Snyder (ed). *Coping: The psychology of what works*. New York: Oxford University Press, pp. 141-164.

Sarros, J. C., Gmelch, W. H. and Tanewski, G. A. (1998) The academic dean: a position in need of a compass and clock. *Higher Education Research and Development*, **17**(1), pp. 65-88.

Saul, H. (2014) Universities receive 20,000 complaints from students demanding more for £9,000 fee. *The Independent*. 3rd June [online]. Available from: http://www.independent.co.uk/student/universities-receive-20000-complaints-from-students-demanding-more-for-9000-fee-9476384.html.

Schneiderman, N., Ironson, G. and Siegel, S. D. (2005) Stress and health: Psychological, behavioural and biological determinants. *Annual Review of Clinical Psychology*, **1**, pp. 607-628.

Schwabe, L. and Wolfe, O. T. (2010) Learning under stress impairs memory formation. *Neurobiology of learning and Memory*, **93**(3), pp. 183 -188.

Selye, H. (1956) *The Stress of Life*. London, Longmans, Green and Co.

Selye, H. (1976) Forty years of stress research: principal remaining problems and misconceptions. *Canadian Medical Journal*, **15**, pp. 53-56.

Shin, J. C. and Jung, J. (2013) Academics job satisfaction and job stress across countries in the changing academic environments. *Higher Education*, **67**(5), pp. 603-620.

Sparks, K., Cooper, C., Fried, Y. and Shirom, A. (1997) The effects of hours of work on health: A meta-analytic review. *Journal of Occupational and Organisational Psychology*, **70**(4), pp. 391-409.

Steptoe, A. and Kivimaki, M. (2013) Stress and cardiovascular disease: an update on current knowledge. *Annual Review of Public Health*, **34**, pp.337-354.

Sundquist, J. and Johansson, S-V. (2000) High demand, low control, and impaired general health: working conditions in a sample of Swedish general practitioners. *Scandinavian Journal of Public Health*, **28**(2), pp. 123-131.

Taleb, N. N. (2012) *Antifragile: Things that gain from disorder*. Penguin Books.

Tapper, T. (1998) Continuity and change in the collegial tradition. *Higher Education Quarterly*, **52**, pp. 142-161.

Taris, T. W., van Beek, I. and Schaufeli, W. B. (2010) Why do perfectionists have a higher burnout risk than others? The mediational effect of workaholism. *Romanian Journal of Applied Psychology*, **12**(1), pp. 1-7.

Thomas, L. (2002) Student retention in higher education: The role of institutional habitus. *Journal of Education Policy*, **17**(4), pp. 423-442.

Trow, M. (1993) Managerialism and the Academic Profession: the case of England. *Higher Education Policy*, **7**, pp. 11-18.

Tsaousis, I. and Nikolaou, I. (2005) Exploring the relationship of emotional intelligence with physical and psychological health functioning. *Stress and Health*, **21**, pp. 77-86.

Tytherleigh, M. Y., Webb, C., Cooper, C. L. and Ricketts C. (2005) Occupational stress in UK higher education institutions: a comparative study of all staff categories. *Higher Education Research and Development*, **24**(1), pp. 41-61.

University and College Union report (2012). *An analysis of student: staff ratios and academics' use of time, and potential links with student satisfaction.* [online]. Available from: http://www.ucu.org.uk/media/pdf/p/p/ucu_ssranalysis_dec12.pdf.

Wang, J. (2005) Work stress as a risk factor for major depressive episode(s). *Psychological Medicine*, **35**, pp. 865-871.

Weinberg, A. and Cooper, C. (2007) *Surviving the workplace: A guide to emotional well-being.* Thomson Learning.

Wilke, P. K., Gmelch, W. H. and Lovrich, N. P. (1984) Stress and productivity: Evidence of the inverted U function in a national study of university faculty. *Public Productivity Review*, **9**(4) pp. 342-356.

Winefield, A. H., Gillespie, N. A., Stough, C., Dua, J., Hapuarachchi, J. and Boyd, C. (2003) Occupational stress in Australian university staff: Results from a national survey. *International Journal of Stress Management*, **10**, pp. 51-63.

(The) World Economic Forum (2018) This country works the longest hours in Europe. [Online] Available from: https://www.weforum.org/agenda/2018/02/greeks-work-longest-hours-in-europe/

Wortman, C., Biernat, M. and Lang, E. (1991) Coping with role overload. In: M. Frankenhaeuser, U. Lundberg, and M. Chesney (Eds). *Women, work, and health: Stress and Opportunities.* London: Plenum, pp. 85-110.

Young, S. N. (2007) How to increase serotonin in the human brain without drugs. *Journal of Psychiatry and Neuroscience*, **32**(6), pp. 394-399

Zang, J., Liu, Y. and Sun, L. (2017) Psychological strain and suicidal ideation: A comparison between Chinese and US college students. Psychiatry Research, Sep, pp. 255-262.

Chapter 3: Understanding and processing emotions

Abraham, R. (1998a) Emotional dissonance in organisations: conceptualising the roles of self-esteem and job-induced tension, Leadership and Organisation Development Journal, **20**(1), pp. 18-25.

Abraham, R. (1998b) Emotional dissonance in organisations: Antecedents, consequences and moderators. *Genetic, Social and General Psychology Monographs*, **124**(2), pp. 229-246.

Abraham, R. (1999) The impact of emotional dissonance on organisational commitment and intention to turnover. *Journal of Psychology*, **133**(4), pp. 441-455.

(The) Advisory, conciliation and arbitration service (ACAS) (2018). *Bullying, harassment, victimisation: What's the difference?* [Online] Available from: http://www.acas.org.uk/index.aspx?articleid=5535.

(The) American Academy of Professional Coders (AAPC) (2013) *Coding for major depressive disorder.* [Online] Available from: http://www.sccma-mcms.org/portals/19/assets/docs/depressive-disorder-icd-10-bh.pdf

(The) Annual report of the Chief Medical officer (2013) *Public Metal Health Priorities: Investing in the evidence* [online]. Available from: https://www.gov.uk/government/uploads/system/uploads/attachment_data/file/413196/CMO_web_doc.pdf.

Armstrong, A. R., Galligan, R. F. and Critchley, C.R. (2011) Emotional intelligence and psychological resilience to negative life events. *Personality and Individual differences*, **51**, pp. 331-336.

Arnold, M. B. (1960) *Emotion and personality, Psychological aspects, Vol. 1*, New York, NY, Columbia University Press. [Online] Available from: http://darwin-online.org.uk/content/frameset?pageseq=1&itemID=F1142&viewtype=text.

Ashforth, B. E. and Humphrey, R. H. (1993) Emotional labour in service roles: The influence of identity. *Academy of Management Review*, **18**(1), pp. 88-115.

Austin, E. J., Saklofske, D. H. and Egan, V. (2005) Personality, well-being and health correlates of trait emotional intelligence. *Personality and Individual Differences*, **38**, pp. 547-558.

Bain, A. (1859) *The emotions and the will.* London, UK: Parker

Barrett, L. F. (2006) Are emotions natural kinds? *Perspectives on Psychological Science*, **1**(1), pp.28-58.

Barrett, L. F. (2017). *How Emotions are Made: The Secret Life of the Brain.* Houghton Mifflin Harcourt.

Brackett, M. A., Mayer, J. D. and Warner, R. M. (2004) Emotional intelligence and its relation to everyday behaviour. *Personality and individual differences*, **36**, pp. 1387-1402.

Brennan, K. (2006) The managed teacher: Emotional labour, education, and technology. *Educational Insights*, **10**(2), pp. 55–65.

(The) *British Association for Behavioural and Cognitive Psychotherapies* [Online] Available from: https://www.babcp.com/Default.aspx.

Carver, C. S. (1998) Resilience and thriving: Issues, models and link-ages. *Journal of Social Issues*, **54**, pp. 245-266.

Chida, Y. and Steptoe, A. (2008) Positive Psychological well-being and mortality: A quantitative review of prospective observational studies. *Psychosomatic Medicine*, **70**(7), pp. 741-756.

Christensen, K. G., Doblhammer, R., Rau, R. and Vuupel, J. W. (2009) Aging populations: The challenge ahead. *The Lancet*, **374**(9696), pp. 1196-1208.

Cohen, J. (1999). *Educating minds and hearts: Social emotional learning and the passage into adolescence.* New York: Teachers College Press.

Cohen, J., Cohen, P., West, S. G., and Aiken, L. S. (2003). *Applied multiple regression/correlation analysis for the behavioural sciences (3rd ed).* Mahwah, NJ: Lawrence Erlbaum Associates.

"The Conversation" (2018) *Sexual abuse, harassment and discrimination "rife" among Australian academics.* 1st July. [Online] Available from: http://theconversation.com/sexual-abuse-harassment-and-discrimination-rife-among-australian-academics-97856.

Cooke, W. (1838*) Mind and the emotions, considered in relation to health and disease.* London, UK: Longman.

Craig, A. D. (2002) How do you feel? Introception: The sense of the physiological condition of the body. *Nature Reviews Neuroscience,* 3(8), pp. 655-666.

Craig, A. D. (2004) Human feelings: why are some more aware than others? *Trends in Cognitive Sciences,* **8**(6), pp. 239-241.

Darwin, C. (1872) *The expression of the emotions in man and animals,* (1st ed), London: John Murray,

Day, A. L., Therrien, D. L. and Carroll, S. A. (2005). Predicting psychological health: assessing the incremental validity of emotional intelligence beyond personality. Type A behaviour and daily hassles. *European Journal of Personality,* **19**, pp. 519-536.

Davidson, R. J. and Begley, S. (2012) *The emotional life of the brain: How to change the way you think, feel and live.* Hodder and Stoughton.

Diefendorff, J. M., Croyle, M. H. and Gosserand, R. H. (2005) The dimensionality and antecedents of emotional labour strategies. *Journal of Vocational Behaviour,* **66**(2), pp. 339-357.

Dixon, T. (2012) "Emotion": The history of a keyword in crisis. *Emotion Review.* 4(4), pp. 338-344.

(The) Diagnostic and Statistical Manual of Mental Disorders, DSM-5 (2013) (5th ed) fifth edition, *American Psychiatric Association* [Online] Available from: https://doi.org/10.1176/appi.books.9780890425596.

Dweck, C. (2017) *Mindset: changing the way you think to fulfil your potential.* Robinson.

Dworkin, A. G. (1987) Teacher burnout in the public schools: structural causes and consequences for children. Albany. NY: State University of New York (SUNY) Press.

Ekman, P. (1992) An argument for basic emotions. *Cognition and Emotion,*6, pp. 169–200.

Ekman, P. (1999) Basic emotions. In T. Dalgleish and M. Power (Eds), Handbook of cognition and emotion, Sussex, UK. John Wiley and Sons Ltd, pp.45-60.

Ekman P. (2003) *Emotions revealed,* New York, New York: Times Books.

Ekman, P. and Friesen, W. V. (1971) Constants across culture in the face and emotion. *Journal of Personality and Social Psychology,* **17**(2), pp. 124-129.

Ekman, P., Friesen, W. V., O'Sullivan, M., Chan, A., Diacoyanni-Tarlatzia, I., Heider, K., Krause, R., LeCompte, W. A., Pitcairn, T., Ricci-Bitti, P. E., Scherer,

K., Tomita, M. and Tzavaras, A. (1987) Universal and cultural differences in the judgements of facial expression of emotion. *Journal of Personality and Social Psychology,* **53**(4), pp.712-717. [Online] Available from: https://pdfs.semanticscholar.org/6d75/df4360a3d56514dcb775c832fdc572bab64b.pdf.

The Equality Act (2010) [Online] Available from: http://www.legislation.gov.uk/ukpga/2010/15/contents

Erickson, R. J. and Ritter, C. (2001) Emotional labour, burnout and inauthenticity: Does gender matter? *Social Psychology Quarterly,* **64**(2), pp. 146-163.

Erickson, R. J. and Wharton, A. S. (1997) Inauthenticity and depression: Assessing the consequences and interactive service work. *Work and Occupations,* **24**(2), pp.188-213.

Extremera, N. and Fernandez-Berrocal, P. (2002) Relation of perceived emotional intelligence and health-related quality of life of middle-aged women. *Psychological Report,* **91**(1), pp. 47-59.

Foa, E. B. and Kozak, M. J. (1986) Emotional processing of fear: exposure to corrective information. *Psychological Bulletin,* **99**(1), pp.20-35.

Fredrickson, B. L. (2000) Cultivating positive emotions to optimise health and well-being. *Prevention and Treatment,* **3**(1).

Furnham, A. and Petrides, K. V. (2003) Trait emotional intelligence and happiness. *Social behaviour and personality,* **31**(8), pp. 815-823.

Glome, T. M. and Tews, M. J. (2004) Emotional labour. A conceptualisation and scale development. *Journal of vocational behaviour,* **64**, pp. 1-23.

Giorgi, G. (2012) Workplace bullying in academia creates a negative work environment. An Italian study. *Employee Responsibilities and Rights Journal,* **24**(2)

Goleman, D. (1998) *Working with emotional intelligence.* Bantam Books: New York.

Greene, C. A., Grasso, D. J. and Ford, J. D (2014) Emotion regulation in the wake of complex childhood trauma In R. Pat-Horenczyk, D., Brom and J. M. Vogel (eds), Helping children cope with trauma: Individual, family and community perspectives. Routledge, pp.19-40.

Greenberg, L. S. (2004) Emotion-focused therapy. *Special issue, Emotion,* **11**(1), pp. 3-6.

The Guardian (2018) *Hundreds of academics at top UK universities accused of bullying".* 28th September. [Online] Available from: https://www.theguardian.com/education/2018/sep/28/academics-uk-universities-accused-bullying-students-colleagues.

Hawkins, J. D., Von Cleave, E. and Catalano, R. F. (1991) Reducing early childhood aggression: Results of a primary prevention program. *Journal of the American Academy of Child and Adolescent Psychiatry,* **30**, pp. 208-217.

Hebson, G., Earnshaw, J. and Marchington, L. (2007) Too emotional to be capable? The changing nature of emotion work in definitions of capable teaching. *Journal of Education Policy,* **22**(6), pp. 675-694.

Hwang, F. F. (2006) The relationship between emotional intelligence and teaching effectiveness. *Paper presented at the 2" International conference on youth and education for the 21st century.* Texas A and M University Corpus Christ. (May 30 - June 2).

Izard, C. E. (1977) *Human emotions*, New York, New York: Plenum.

Izard, C. E. (1992) Basic emotions, relations amongst emotions and emotion-cognition relations. *Psychological Review*, **99**, pp. 561–565.

James, W. (1890) *The principles of psychology*, New York, NY: Holt.

Kahneman, D. (2011) *Thinking fast and slow.* Penguin: Random House, UK.

Kim, M. J. and Whalen, P. J. (2009) The structural integrity of an amygdala-prefrontal pathway predicts trait anxiety. *Journal of Neuroscience*, **29**(37), pp. 11614-11618.

Kokkinos, C. M. (2007) Job stressors, personality and burnout in primary school teachers. *British Journal of Educational Psychology*, **77**, pp. 229–243.

Lazarus, R. S. (1991a) Progress on a cognitive-motivational-relational theory of Emotion. *American Psychologist*, **46**(8), pp. 819-834.

Lazarus, R. S (1991b) *Emotion and adaption.* New York: Oxford University Press.

Lazarus, R. S. (1999). *Stress and Emotion: A new Synthesis.* Springer Publishing Company, Inc.

LeDoux, J. (1999) *The emotional brain: The mysterious underpinnings of emotional life.* W. and N.

LeDoux, J. (2003) *Synaptic self: How our brains become who we are.* Penguin Books.

LeDoux, J. (2019) *The deep history of ourselves: How ancient microbes became conscious brains.* Viking.

Little, B. R. (2014). *Me, myself and us- The science of personality and the art of well-being.* New York. Public Affairs.

Lim, N. (2016) Cultural differences in emotion: differences in emotion arousal level between the East and the West. *Integrated Medicine Research*, **5**(2), pp. 105-109.

Maier, S. F. and Seligman, M. E. (2016) Learned helplessness at fifty: Insights from neuroscience. *Psychological Review*, **123**(4), pp. 349-367.

Mayer, J. D. and Ciarrochi, J. (2006) Clarifying concepts related to emotional intelligence: A proposed glossary, In J. Ciarrochi, J. J. Forgas and J. D. Mayer (Eds). *Emotional Intelligence in Everyday life* (2nd ed) Psychology Press, Inc, pp. 261-267.

Moors, A., Ellsworth, P. C., Scherer, K. R. and Frijda, N. H. (2013) Appraisal theories of emotion: state of the art future development. *Emotion Review*, **5**(2), pp. 119-124. [Online] Available from: https://biblio.ugent.be/publication/2958617/file/6776022

Morrison, T. (2007) Emotional intelligence, emotion and social work: context, characteristics complications and contribution. *British Journal of Social work*, **37**, pp. 245-263.

Mortiboys, A. (2012) *Teaching with emotional intelligence: A step by step guide for higher and further education professionals.* (2nd ed). Routledge.

Nieto, S. (2005) Schools for a new majority: The role of teacher education in hard times. *The New Educator*, **1**(1), pp. 27-43.

Ogbonna, E. and Harris, L. C. (2004) Work intensification and emotional labour among UK university lecturers: An exploratory study. *Organisation Studies*, **25**(7), pp. 1185-1203.

Oldham, J. M., Skodal, A. E. and Bender, D. S. (2014) The American psychiatric textbook of personality disorders (DSM-5 edition) (2nd ed) American Psychiatric Association.

Ostir, G.V., Markides, K. S., Black, S.A. and Goodwin, J. S. (2000) Emotional well-being predicts subsequent functional independence and survival. *Journal of the American Geriatrics Society*, **48**(5), pp. 473-478.

Ostir, G. V., Markides, K. S., Peek, M. K. and Goodwin, J. S. (2001) The association between emotional well-being and the incidence of stroke in older adults. *Psychometric medicine*, **63**, pp. 210-215.

Paulle, B. (2005) *Anxiety and intimidation in the Bronx and the Bijlmer: An ethnographic comparison of two schools*. Amsterdam: Dutch University Press.

Philipp, A. and Schupbach, H. (2010) Longitudinal effects of emotional labour on emotional exhaustion and dedication of teachers. *Journal of Occupational Health Psychology*, **15**(4), pp. 494-504.

Plutchik, R. (2002) *Emotions and life, perspectives from psychology, Biology and evolution (1st ed)*, American Psychological Association.

Ramana, T. V. (2013) Emotional intelligence and teacher effectiveness- an analysis. *Voice of Research*, **2**(2), pp. 18-22.

Ramsay, G. (1848) Analysis and theory of the emotions. London, UK: Longman, Brown, Green and Longmans.

Sadler, M. E., Miller, C. J., Christensen, K. and McGue, M. (2011) Subjective well-being and longevity: a co-twin control study. *Twin Research and Human Genetics*, **14**(3), pp. 249-256.

Schachter, S. and Singer J. E. (1962) Cognitive, social, and physiological determinants of emotional state. *Psychological Review*, **69**, pp. 379–399.

Scherer, K. R. (1984) On the nature and function of emotion: a component process approach. In: K. R. Scherer, and P. Ekman (eds) *Approaches to emotion*, Hillsdale, New Jersey: Erlbaum, pp. 293–317

Scherer K. R. (1994) Toward a concept of "modal emotions." In D. Ekman and J. Davidson (Eds). *The nature of emotion: fundamental questions*, New York, NY: Oxford University Press, pp.25-31.

Scherer, K. R. (2001) Appraisal considered as a process of multilevel sequential checking. In: K. R. Scherer, A. Schorr, and T. Johnstone, *Appraisal processes in emotion: theory, methods, research*, New York, NY: Oxford University Press, pp. 92–120.

Scherer K. R. (2009) Emotion theories and concepts (psychological perspectives). In D. Sander and K. R. Scherer (Eds) *Oxford companion to emotion and the affective sciences*, Oxford, UK: Oxford University Press, pp. 145–149.

Seligman, M. E. P. (1974) Depression and learned helplessness. In: R. J. Friedman and M. M. Katz (Eds). *The psychology of depression: contemporary theory and research*. New York: Willey.

Seligman, M. E. P. (1991) *Learned optimism: How to change your mind and your life.* Vintage Books

Seligman, M. E. and Maier, S. T. (1967) Failure to escape traumatic shock. *Journal of Experimental Psychology*, **74**(1), pp. 1-9.

Smith, P. T. and Kemp-Wheeler, S. M. (1996) Why do we need emotions. In V. Bruce (ed) *Unsolved mysteries of the mind: Tutorial essays in cognition*. Psychology Press

Sutton, R. and Wheatley, K. (2003) Teacher's emotions and teaching A review of the literature and directions for future research. *Educational Psychology Review*, **15**(4), pp. 327-358.

Tomaka, J., Blascovich, J., Kibler, J. and Ernst, J. M. (1997) Cognitive and psychological antecedents of threat and challenge appraisal. *Journal of Personality and Social Psychology*, **73**(1), pp. 63-72.

Wharton, A. S. (1993) The affective consequences of service work: Managing emotions on the job. *Work and Occupations*, **20**, pp. 205-232.

Whiteford, H.A., Degenhardt, L., Rehm, J., Baxter, A. J., Ferrari, A. J. Erskine, H.E., Charlson, F. J. Norman, R. E., Flaxman, A. D., Johns, N. Burstein, R. Murray, C. J. L. and Vos, T. (2013) Global burden of disease attributable to mental and substance use disorders: findings from the Global Burden of Disease Study. *The Lancet*, 382(9904), pp. 9-15.

(The) World Health Organisation (WHO) (2018) *Depression: Key facts* [Online] Available from: http://www.who.int/news-room/fact-sheets/detail/depression.

Yin, H-b. (2015) The effect of teachers' emotional labour on teaching satisfaction: moderation of emotional intelligence. *Teacher and Teaching: theory and practice*, **21**(7), pp. 789-810.

Yin, H-b., Lee, J. C. K., Zhang, Z-h. and Jin, Y-l. (2013) Exploring the relationship among teachers' emotional intelligence, emotional labour strategies and teaching satisfaction. *Teaching and Teacher Education*, **35**, pp. 137-145.

Zeidner, M., Matthews, G. and Roberts, R. D. (2012*) What we know about emotional intelligence: How it affects learning, work, relationships, and our mental health*. MIT Press.

Zembylas, M. (2002). Structures of feeling in curriculum and teaching: Theorising the emotional rules. *Educational Theory*, 52, pp. 187-208.

Zembylas, M. (2005). Discursive practices, genealogies, and emotional rules; A poststructuralist view on emotion and identity in teaching *Teaching and Teacher Education*, **21**(8), pp. 935-948.

Chapter 4: Coping

Albert, N. M., Trochelman, K., Meyer, K. H. and Nutter, B. (2009) Characteristics associated with racial disparities in illness beliefs of patients with heart failure. Racial Disparities in Illness Beliefs, **35**, pp. 112-125.

Aldwin, C., Folkman, S., Schaefer, C., Coyne, J. C. and Lazarus, R. S. (1980) Ways of Coping: A process measure. *Presented at the 88th annual meeting of the American Psychological Association*. Montreal. Quebec. Canada.

Aldwin, C. M. and Park, C. L. (2004) Coping and physical health outcomes: an overview. *Psychology and Health*. **19**, pp.277-281.

Alter, L. D. (2015) *Tomorrow is today. A behaviour modification methodology guide and workbook to manage the job search process: The complete guide for getting and keeping your next job and advancing your career.* The Employment Clinic.

Argyris, C. (1957) *Personality and Organisation.* Harper and Row, New York, NY.

Bartholomew, T. T. and Brown, J. R. (2012) Mixed methods, culture and psychology: A review of mixed methods research. In D. K. Nagata, L. Kohn-Wood and L. A. Suzuki (Eds), Qualitative strategies of ethnocultural research. International Perspectives in Psychology: Research, Practice, Consultation, 1, PP. 177-190.

Bazeley, P. (2002) Computerised data analysis for mixed methods research. In A. Tashakkori and C. Teddlie (Eds). Handbook of mixed methods for the social and behavioural sciences. Thousand Oaks, CA. Sage, pp. 385-422.

Bishop, G. D. (1994) *Health Psychology.* Boston: Allyn and Bacon.

Bolger, N. and Zuckerman, A. (1995). A framework for studying personality in the stress process. *Journal of Personality and Social Psychology,* **69**, pp. 890-902.

Bowen, P., Rose, R. and Pilkington, A. (2018) Coping with Interpersonal Relationships within Higher Education (Universities). *International Journal of Academic Multidisciplinary Research,* **2**(4) pp.1-11.

Brocki, J. M. and Wearden, A. J. (2005) A critical evaluation of the use of interpretative phenomenological analysis (IPA) in health psychology. *Psychology and Health,* **21**(1), pp. 87-108.

Caruth, G. D. (2013) Demystifying mixed methods research design: A review of the literature. Melvana International Journal of Education, 3(2), pp. 112-122.

Carver, C. S. Scheier, M. F. Weintraub, J. K. (1989) Assessing coping strategies: A theoretical based approach. *Journal of Personality and Social Psychology,* **56**(2), pp. 267-283.

Clare, L. (2002) We'll fight it as long as we can: Coping with the onset of Alzheimer's disease. *Aging and mental health,* **6**, pp. 139-148.

Clare, L. (2003) Managing threats to self: Awareness in early-stage Alzheimer's disease. Social Science and Medicine, 57, 1017-1029.

Collins, K. and Nicolson, P. (2002) The meaning of "satisfaction" for people with dermatological problems: Reassessing approaches to qualitative health psychology research. *Journal of Health Psychology,* 7, pp. 615-629.

Compas, B. E., Connor-Smith, J. K., Saltzman, H., Thomsen, A. H. and Wadsworth, M. E. (2001) Coping with stress during childhood and adolescence: Progress, problems and potential in theory and research. *Psychological Bulletin,* **127**, pp. 87-127.

Connor-Smith, J. V. and Calvete, E. (2004) Cross-cultural equivalence of coping and involuntary responses to stress in Spain and the United States. *Anxiety, Stress and Coping,* **17**, pp.163-185.

Creswell, J. W. and Plano Clark, V. L. (2011) *Designing and conducting mixed methods research* (2nd ed). Sage.

Denzin, N. K. (1978) *The research act: A theoretical introduction to sociological methods.* New York: McGraw-Hill.

Dweck, C. (2017) *Mindset: changing the way you think to fulfil your potential.* Robinson

Folkman, S. and Lazarus, R. S. (1980) An analysis of coping in a middle age community sample. *Journal of health and Social behaviour*, Vol. **21**, pp. 219-239.

Folkman, S. and Lazarus, R. S. (1985) If it changes it must be a process: A study of emotion and coping during three stages of a college examination. *Journal of Personality and Social Psychology*, **48**, pp. 150-170.

Gillespie, N. A., Walsh, M., Winefield, A. H., Dua, J. and Stough, C. (2001) Occupational stress in universities: Staff perceptions of the causes, consequences and moderators of stress. *Work and Stress*, **15**(1), pp. 53-72.

Gladding, S. T. (1984) Training effective family therapists: Data and Hope. Journal of Counselling and Development, 63, pp.103-104.

Goldberger, L. and Breznitz, S. (1993) *Handbook of stress: Theoretical and clinical aspects.* The Free Press.

Gomez, R., Holmberg, K., Bounds, J., Fullarton, C. and Gomez, A. (1999) Neuroticism and Extraversion as Predictors of Coping Styles during Early Adolescence. *Personality and Individual Differences*, **27**, pp. 3-17.

Greene, J. C. (2007). *Mixed methods in social inquiry.* San Francisco: Jossey-Bass.

Holmes, T. H. and Rahe, R. H. (1967) The social readjustment rating scale. *Journal of Psychosomatic Research*, **11**, pp. 213-218.

Hoover, A. and Krishnamurti, S. (2010) Survey of college students. MP3 listening: Habits, safety issues, attitudes, and education. American Journal of Audiology, 19, pp. 73-83.

Johnson, R. B. and Onwuegbuzie, A. J. (2004) Mixed methods research: A research paradigm whose time has come. *Educational Researcher*, **33**(7), pp. 14-26.

Kahn, R. and Cannell, C. (1957) *The dynamics of interviewing.* New York and Chichester: Wiley.

Karoly, P. (1999) A goal systems self-regulatory perspective on personality, psychopathology and change. *Review of General Psychology*, 3, pp. 264-291.

King, N. and Horrocks, C. (2010) *Interviews in qualitative research.* Sage.

Krohne, H. W. (2002) *Stress and Coping Theories.* Johannes Gutenberg-Universitat Mainz Germany.

Kvale, S. (1996) *Interviews: An introduction to qualitative research interviewing.* Sage. Thousand Oaks, CA.

Lazarus, R. S. (1966). *Psychological stress and the coping process.* New York: McGraw-Hill.

Lazarus, R. S. (1982) The psychology of stress and coping. In: N. A. Milgram (Ed). *Stress and anxiety*, **8**. New York: Hemisphere Publishing.

Lazarus, R. S. (1990) Theory-based stress measurement. *Psychological Inquiry*, **1**, pp. 3-13.

Lazarus R. S. (1991) *Emotion and adaption.* Oxford: Oxford University Press.

Lazarus, R. S. (1993) Coping theory and research: Past, present and future. *Psychosomatic medicine,* **55,** pp. 234-247.

Lazarus, R. S. (2006) Emotions and interpersonal relationships towards a person-centred conceptualisation of emotions and coping. *Journal of Personality,* **74,** pp. 9-46.

Lazarus, R. S. and Folkman, S. (1984) *Stress, Appraisal and coping.* New York: Springer.

Lazarus, R. S. and Folkman, S. (1986) Cognitive theories of stress and the issue of circularity. In: M. H. Appley and R. Trumbull (Eds) *Perspectives in interactional psychology.* New York: Plenum, pp. 287-327.

Lazarus, R. S. and Launier, R. (1978) Stress-related transactions between person and environment. In: L.A. Pervin and M. Lewis (Eds). *Perspectives in interactional psychology.* New York: Plenum, pp. 287-327.

Litman, J. A. and Lunsford, G. D. (2009) Frequency of use and impact of coping strategies assessed by the COPE inventory and their relationships to post-event health and well-being. *Journal of Health Psychology,* **14**(7), pp. 982-991.

Mackenzie, C. S., Wiprzycka, U. I., Hasher, L. and Goldstein, D. (2008) Seeing the glass half full: Optimistic expressive writing improves mental health among chronically stressed caregivers. *British Journal of Health Psychology,* **13,** pp. 73-76.

Marks, D. F. Murray, M. Evans, B. Estacio, E. V. (2015) *Health Psychology: Theory, research and practice.* Sage Publications Ltd.

Masuda, M. and Holmes, T. H. (1967) Magnitude estimations of social readjustments. *Journal of Psychosomatic Research,* **11,** pp. 219-225.

Moos, R. H. and Holahan, C. J. (2003) Dispositional and contextual perspectives on coping: Toward an integrative framework. *Journal of Clinical Psychology,* **59,** pp. 1387-1403.

Perez, S. M., Gavin, J. K. and Diaz, V. A. (2015) Stressors and coping mechanisms associated with perceived stress in Latinos. U.S National library of medicine. National Institute of Health. Europe PubMed Central [online]. Available from: http://europepmc.org/abstract/med/25812256.

Quayhagen, M. P. and Quayhagen, M. (1982) Coping with conflict: Measurement of age-related patterns. Research on aging, **4,** pp. 364-377.

Reid, K., Flowers, P. and Larkin, M. (2005). Exploring lived experience: An introduction to interpretative phenomenological analysis. *The Psychologist,* **18,** pp. 20-23.

Robson, C. (2002) *Real World Research.* London: Blackwell.

Seligman, M. E. P. (1974) Depression and learned helplessness. In: R. J. Friedman and M. M. Katz (Eds). *The psychology of depression: contemporary theory and research.* New York: Willey.

Selye, H. (1956) *The Stress of Life.* London, Longmans, Green and Co.

Selye, H. (1976) Forty years of stress research: principal remaining problems and misconceptions. *Canadian Medical Journal,* **15,** pp. 53-56.

Sica, C., Novara, C., Dorz, S. and Sanavio, E. (1997) Coping Strategies: Evidence for cross-cultural differences? A preliminary study with the Italian version of coping orientations to problems experienced (COPE). *Personality and Individual Differences*, **23**, pp. 10325-10329.

Smith, J. (1996) Beyond the divide between cognition and discourse. *Psychology and Health*, **11**, pp. 261-271.

Smith, J. A. (2004) Reflecting on the development of interpretative phenomenological analysis and its contribution to qualitative research. *Qualitative Research in Psychology*, **1**, pp. 39-54.

Smith, J. A., Flowers, P. and Larkin, M. (2013) *Interpretative phenomenological analysis: Theory, method, research.* Sage publications, London.

Smith, J. A. and Osborn, M. (2003). Interpretative phenomenological analysis. In J. A. Smith (ed.). *Qualitative psychology: A practical guide to research methods.* London. Sage, pp. 53-80.

Snyder, C. R. (1999) Coping: Where are you going? In: C. R. Snyder (ed) *Coping: The psychology of what works.* New York: Oxford University Press, pp. 324-333.

Sontag, L. M. and Graber, J. A. (2010) Coping with perceived peer stress: Gender-specific and common pathways to symptoms of psychopathology. *Development psychology*, **46**(6), pp. 1605-1620.

Stange, K. C. (2006) Publishing multimethod research. Annals of Family Medicine, 4(4), pp. 292-294.

Tashakkori A. and Creswell, J. (2008) Mixed methodology across disciplines. Journal of Mixed Methods Research, **2**, pp. 2-3.

Teddlie, C. and Tashakkori (2009) Foundations of mixed methods research. Thousand Oaks, CA. Sage, pp.1.

Wadsworth, M. E., Rieckmann, T., Benson, M. A. and Compas, B. E. (2004) Coping and responses to stress in Navajo adolescents: Psychometric properties of the Responses to Stress Questionnaire. *Journal of Community Psychology*, **32**, pp. 391–411.

Weiten, W. and Lloyd, M. A. (2003) *Psychology Applied to modern life. Adjustment in the 21st century.* U.S.A: Wadsworth/Thomson Learning.

Willig, C. (2008) *Introducing qualitative research in psychology* (2nd ed.). Open University Press.

Yin, R. (2003) *Case study research: design and methods* (3rd ed). Sage. Thousand Oaks, CA.

Zeidner, M., Matthews, G. and Roberts, R. D. (2012) *What we know about emotional intelligence: How it affects learning, work, relationships, and our mental health.* MIT Press.

Chapter 5: Personality and individual differences

Allport, G. W. (1937) *Personality: A psychological interpretation.* New York, Henry Holt and Company.

Allport, G. W. and Odbert, H. S. (1936) Trait names: A psycho lexical study. *Psychological Monographs*, **47**(211).

Attar, M., Ather, M. and Bano, M. (2013) Emotional intelligence and personality traits among university teachers: Relationship and gender differences. *International Journal of Business and Social Science*, **4**(17), pp. 253-259.

Bar-On, R. (1997) *The Emotional Inventory (EQ-i): Technical manual*. Toronto: Multi-Health Systems.

Barrick, M. R., Mount, M. K. and Judge, T. A. (2001) Personality and performance at the beginning of the new millennium: What do we know and where do we go next? *International Journal of Selection and Assessment*, **9**, pp. 9-30.

Bolger, N. and Zuckerman, A. (1995). A framework for studying personality in the stress process. *Journal of Personality and Social Psychology*, **69**, pp. 890-902.

Bouchard, T. J. and Loehlin, J. C. (2001) Genes, evolution and personality. *Behaviour Genetics*, **31**(3), pp. 243-273.

Carver, C. S. (1997) COPE Inventory- Complete version. [Online] Available from: http://www.psy.miami.edu/faculty/ccarver/sclCOPEF.html

Carver, C. S. and Connor-Smith, J. (2010) Personality and Coping. *Annual Review Psychology*, **61**, pp. 679-704.

Cattell, R. B. (1947) Confirmation and clarification of primary personality factors. *Psychometrika*, **12**(3), pp. 197-220.

Chida, Y. and Hamer, M. (2008) Chronic psychological factors and acute physiological responses to laboratory-induced stress in healthy populations: a quantitative review of 30 years of investigations. *Psychological Bulletin*, **134**(6), pp. 829-885.

Connor-Smith, J. K. and Flachsbart, C. (2007) Relations between personality and coping: A meta-analysis. *Journal of Personality and Social Psychology*, **93**(6), pp. 1080-1107.

Costa, P. T. Jr. and McCrae, R. R. (1992) *Revised NEO Personality Inventory (NEO-PI-R) and NEO Five-Factor Inventory (NEO-FFI) professional manual*. Odessa, FL: Psychological Assessment Resources.

Deary, I. J., Egan, V., Gibson, G. J., Austin, E. J., Brand, C. R. and Kellaghan, T. (1996) Intelligence and the differentiation hypothesis. *Intelligence*, **23**, pp. 105–132.

De Longis, A. and Holtzman, S. (2005) Coping in context: The role of stress, social support and personality in coping. *Journal of Personality*, **73**, pp.1633-1656.

DeNeve, K. M. and Cooper, H. (1998) The happy personality: A meta-analysis of 137 personality traits and subjective well-being. *Psychological Bulleting*, **124**, pp. 197-229.

DeYoung, C. G. (2006) Higher-order factors of the big five in a multi-informant sample. *Journal of Personality and Social Psychology*, **91**(6), pp. 1138-1151.

Digman, J. M. (1990) Personality structure: emergence of the five-factor model. *Annual Review of Psychology*, **41**, pp. 417-440.

Digman, J. M. (1997) Higher-order factors of the big five. *Journal of Personality and Social Psychology*, **93**, pp. 880-896.

Eisenberg, N., Fabes, R. A. and Guthrie, I. (1997) Coping with stress: The roles of regulation and development. In: J.N. Sandler and S.A. Wolchik. (Eds). *Handbook of children's coping with common stressors: Linking theory, research, and intervention*. New York: Plenum, pp. 41-70.

Eysenck, H. J. (1947) *Dimensions of personality.* London: Methuen.
Eysenck, H. J. (1965) *Smoking, health and personality.* New York: Basic Books.
Eysenck, H. J. (1990) Genetic and environmental contributions to individual differences. The three major dimensions of personality. *Journal of Personality*, **58**, pp. 245-261.
Eysenck, H. J. (1991) *Smoking, personality and stress.* New York: Springer-Verlag.
Fickova, E. (2001). Personality regulators of coping behaviour in adolescents. *Studia Psychologica*, **43**, pp. 321-329.
Fisher, S. (1994) *Stress in academic life: The mental assembly line.* Buckingham: Open University Press.
Freud, S. (1923) *The ego and id.* Standard Edition, XIX. London: Hogarth.
Freud, S. (1933) *New introductory lectures on psycho-analysis.* Standard Edition, XXII. London: Hogarth.
Goldberg, L. R (1990) An alternative "description of personality". The big five-factor structure. *Journal of Personality and Social Psychology*, **59**(6), pp. 1216-1229.
Goldberg, L. R. (1992) The development markers for the big five structure. *Psychological Assessment*, **4**(1), pp. 26-42.
Goleman, D. (1995) *Emotional Intelligence: Why It Can Matter More than IQ.* Bantam Books, New York. NY.
Hogan, J. and Holland, B. (2003) Using theory to evaluate personality and job performance relations: a socioanalytic perspective. *Journal of Applied psychology*, **88**(1), pp.100-112.
James, W. (1907) *Pragmatism: A new name for some old ways of thinking.* Longman, Green and Co.
Kato, K. and Pederson, N. N. (2005) Personality and coping: a study of twins reared apart, and twins reared together. *Behaviour Genetics*, **35**(2), pp. 147-158.
Khan, A., Siraj, S. and Li, L. P. (2011) Role of positive psychological strengths and the big five personality traits in coping mechanism of university students. International Conference on Humanities, Society and Culture. *International proceedings of economics development and research* (IPEDR), **20**.
Lazarus, R. S. and Folkman, S. (1984) *Stress, Appraisal and coping.* New York: Springer.
Lord, W. and Rust, J. (2003) The big five revisited: where are we now? A brief review of the relevance of the big five for occupational assessment. *Selection and Development Review*, **19**(4).
Malouff, J. M. Thorsteinsson, E. B. and Schutte, N. S. (2006) The five-factor model of personality and smoking: A meta-analysis. *Journal of Drug Education*, **36**, pp. 47–58.
McWilliams, L. A., Cox, B. J. and Enns, M. W. (2003) Use of coping inventory for stressful situations in a clinically depressed sample: Factor structure, personality correlates and prediction of distress. *Journal of Clinical Psychology*, **59**, pp. 423-437.

Millward-Brown. (1996) *Powerful people: A survey of Britain's professional workforce.* London: Guardian Publishing.

Moos, R. H. and Holahan, C. J. (2003) Dispositional and contextual perspectives on coping: Toward an integrative framework. *Journal of Clinical Psychology,* **59**, pp. 1387-1403.

Musek, J. (2007) A general factor of personality: Evidence for the big one in the five-factor model. *Journal of Research in Personality,* **41**(6), pp.1213–1233.

Norman, W. T. (1963) Toward an adequate taxonomy of personality attributes: replicated factor structure in peer nomination personality ratings. *The Journal of Abnormal Psychology,* **66**(6), pp. 574-583.

Ozer, D. J. and Benet-Martinez, V. (2005) Personality and the prediction of consequential outcomes. *Annual Review of Psychology,* **57**, pp.401-421.

Penley, J. A. and Tomaka, J. (2002) Associations among the big five, emotional responses and coping with acute stress. *Personality and Individual Differences,* **32**, pp. 1215-1228.

Petrides, K. V. (2009) Psychometric properties of the Trait Emotional Intelligence Questionnaire. In: C. Stough, D. H. Saklofske, and J. D. Parker, *Advances in the assessment of emotional intelligence.* New York: Springer.

Petrides, K. V. and Furnham, A. (2001) Trait emotional intelligence: Psychometric investigation with reference to established trait taxonomies. *European Journal of Personality,* **15**, pp. 425-448.

Petrides, K. V., Vernon, P. A., Schermer, J. A., Ligthart, L., Boomsma, D. I. and Veselka, L. (2010) Relationships between trait emotional intelligence and the big five in the Netherlands. *Personality and Individual Differences,* **48**(8), pp. 906-910.

Pinker, S. (2003) *The blank slate: The modern denial of human nature.* Penguin Press Science.

Raby, K. L., Roisman, G. I., Fraley, R. C. and Simpson, J. A. (2014) The enduring predictive significance of early maternal sensitivity: social and academic competence through age 32 years. *Child Development,* **86**(3) May June 2015, pp. 695-708.

Revelle, W. and Wilt, J. (2013) The general factor of personality: a general critique. *Journal of Research in personality,* **47**(5), pp. 493-504.

Russo, P. M., Mancini, G., Trombini, E., Baldaro, B., Mavroveli, S. and Petrides, K. V. (2012) Trait emotional intelligence and the big five: a study on Italian Children and Preadolescents.

Samms, C. and Friedel, C. R. (2013) Cognitive style differences and student coping behaviour. *Academy of Educational Leadership Journal,* **17**(1).

Salovey, P. and Mayer, J. D. (1990) Emotional Intelligence. Imagination. *Cognition and Personality,* **9**, pp. 185-211.

Skinner, E. A. (1995) *Perceived control, motivation and coping.* Thousand Oaks. CA: Sage.

Steel, P., Schmidt, J. and Shultz, J. (2008) Refining the relationship between personality and subjective well-being. *Psychological Bulletin,* **134**, pp. 138-161.

Strelau, J. (2001) The concept and status of trait in research on temperament. *European Journal of Personality*, **15**, pp. 311-325.

Terracciano, A., McCrae, R. R., Brant, L. and Costa, P.T. (Jr). (2005) Hierarchical linear modeling analysis of the NEO-PI-R scales in the Baltimore Longitudinal study of aging. *Psychology and aging*, **20**, pp. 493-506.

Terry, D. J. (1994) Determinants of coping: The role of stable and situational factors. *Journal of Personality and Social Psychology*, **66**, pp. 895–910.

Tupes, E. C. and Christal, R. C. (1961) Recurrent personality factors based on trait ratings. *Technical Report*, USAF, Lackland Air Force Base, Texas.

Tytherleigh, M. Y., Webb, C., Cooper, C. L. and Ricketts C. (2005) Occupational stress in UK higher education institutions: a comparative study of all staff categories. *Higher Education Research and Development*, **24**(1), pp. 41-61.

Van der Linden, D., Schermer, J. A., de Zeeuw, E., Dunkel, C. S., Pekaar, K. A., Bakker, A. B., Vernon, P. A. and Petrides, K. V. (2018) Overlap between the general factor of personality and trait emotional intelligence: a genetic correlation study. *Behaviour Genetics*, **48**(2), pp. 147-154.

Van der Linden, D., te Nijenhuis, J. and Bakker, A. B. (2010) The general factor of personality: A meta analysis of the big five intercorrelations and a criterion-related validity study. *Journal of Research in Personality*, **44**(3), pp.315-327.

Vandervoort, D. J. (2006) The importance of emotional intelligence in higher education. *Current Psychology*, **25**(1), pp. 4-7.

Vollrath, M. (2001) Personality and stress. *Scandinavian Journal of Psychology*, **42**, pp. 335-347.

Vollrath, M. and Torgersen, S. (2000) Personality types and coping. *Personality and individual differences*, **29**(2), pp. 367-378.

Chapter 6: Intelligence and Groups

Bates, T. C. and Gupta, S. (2017) Smart groups of smart people: evidence for IQ as the origin of collective intelligence in the performance of human groups. *Intelligence*, **60**, pp. 45-56.

Binet, A. (1916) New methods for the diagnosis of the intellectual level of subnormals. In E. S. Kite (Trans.), *The development of intelligence in children*. Vineland, NJ: Publications of the Training School at Vineland. (Originally published 1905 in *L'Année Psychologique*, **12**, pp.191-244. [Online] Available from: https://bir.brandeis.edu/bitstream/handle/10192/28935/413%20p-5.pdf?sequence=1.

Binet, A. and Simon, T. (1911) *La mesure du développement de l'intelligence chez les jeunes enfants*. Paris: A. Coneslant.

Binet. A. and Simon, T. (1916) *The development of intelligence in children*. Baltimore, Williams and Wilkins. (Reprinted 1973, New York: Arno Press; 1983, Salem, NH: Ayer Company).

Boyce, W. T. (2019) *The orchid and the dandelion: why some children struggle and how all can thrive*. Knopf.

(The) Campaign to end loneliness. *Loneliness and physical health. Loneliness and mental health.* [Online] Available from: https://www.campaigntoendloneliness.org/threat-to-health/

Carroll, J. B. (1982) The measurement of intelligence. In R. J. Sternberg (ed) *Handbook of human intelligence*. Cambridge: Cambridge University Press, pp. 29-120.

Carroll, J. B. (1993) Human cognitive abilities: The state of the art. *Psychological Science*, **3**, pp. 266-270.

Carver, C. S. Scheier, M. F. Weintraub, J. K. (1989) Assessing coping strategies: A theoretical based approach. *Journal of Personality and Social Psychology*, **56**(2), pp. 267-283.

Cattell, R. B. (1963). Theory of fluid and crystallized intelligence: A critical experiment. *Journal of Educational Psychology*, **54**(1), pp. 1-22.

Davidson, R., Gardner, H., Goleman, D., Siegel, D., Lucas, G., Shirky, C. and Wolfe, N. (2012) *Wired to connect: Dialogues on social intelligence*. More than Sound.

Dawkins, R. (1976) *The selfish gene*. Oxford University Press.

Druskat, V. U. and Wolff, S. B. (2001) Emotional Intelligence: Building the emotional intelligence of groups, *Harvard Business Review*, (March).

Gladwell, M. (2001) *The Tipping point: How little things can make a big difference*. Abacus

Goleman, D. (1995) E*motional intelligence: why it can matter more than IQ*. Bloomsbury Publishing Plc.

Goleman, D. (2006) *Social Intelligence: The new science of human relations*. Random House Publishing Group.

Guilford, J. P. (1977) *Way beyond the IQ: Guide to improving intelligence and creativity*. Buffalo, NY: Creative Education Foundation.

Hamme, C. (2003) *Group Emotional Intelligence, The Research and Development of an Assessment Instrument*. (PhD Dissertation) Rutgers, New Brunswick.

Harris Interactive (2011) Seventy-one percent of employers say they value emotional intelligence over IQ, according to Careerbuilder survey. [Online] Available from: http://www.careerbuilder.com/share/aboutus/pressreleasesdetail.aspx?id=pr652&sd=8/18/2011&ed=08/18/2011.

Horn, J. L. and Cattell, R. B. (1967) Age difference in fluid and crystalised intelligence. *Acta Psychologica*, **26**, pp. 107-129.

Irving, J. (1973) *Victims of group think* (2nd ed). Houghton Mifflin.

Johnson, C. Y. (2010) *Group IQ: What makes one team smarter than another? A new field of research finds surprising answers*. Boston.com. [Online] Available from: http://archive.boston.com/bostonglobe/ideas/articles/2010/12/19/group_iq/

Lazarus, R. S. (1966). *Psychological stress and the coping process*. New York: McGraw-Hill.

Popper, K. (1962) Open Society and its enemies (4th ed). Routledge.

Rapisarda, B. A. (2002) The impact of emotional intelligence on work team cohesiveness and performance. *The International Journal of Organisational Analysis,* **10**(4), pp. 363-379.

Raven, J. S. (1938) *Progressive matrices.* London: Lewis.

Raven, R. C. (1962) Standard progressive matrices. London: Lewis.

Rozenblit, L. and Keil, F. (2002) The misunderstood limits of folk science: an illusion of explanatory depth. *Cognitive Science,* **26**, pp. 521-562.

Selimi, T. J. (2016) Loneliness: The virus of the modern age. Balboa Press.

Sloman, S. and Fernbach, P. (2017) *The knowledge illusion: The myth of individual thought and the power of collective wisdom.* Pan.

Spearman, C. (1904) General Intelligence, objectively determined and measured. *American Journal of Psychology,* **15**, pp. 201-293.

Spearman, C. (1927) *The abilities of man: Their nature and measurement.* New York: Macmillan.

Statista (2018) *Number of social network users worldwide from 2010 to 2021 (in billions).* [Online] Available from: https://www.statista.com/statistics/278414/number-of-worldwide-social-network-users/.

Suifan, T. Abdallah, A. and Sweis, R. (2015) The Effect of a Manager's Emotional Intelligence on Employees' Work Outcomes in the Insurance Industry in Jordan. *International Business Research.* **8**, pp. 67-82.

Sunstein, C. (2019) *How change happens.* MIT Press.

Sternberg, R. J. (1996) *Successful intelligence: How practical and creative intelligence determine success in life.* New York, NY: Simon and Schuster.

Sternberg, R. J. (2012) The triarchic theory of successful intelligence. In D. P. Flanagan and P. L. Harrison (Eds). *Contemporary intellectual assessment: Theories, tests and issues (3rd ed).* New York, NY: Guilford Press, pp. 156-177.

Stern, W. (1914) Die psychologischen Methoden der Intelligenzprüfung: und deren Anwendung an Schulkindern (The Psychological Methods of Testing Intelligence). *Educational psychology monographs,* **no. 13**. Guy Montrose Whipple (English translation). Baltimore: Warwick & York.

Terman, L. M. (1916) *The measurement of intelligence.* Boston: Houghton Mifflin.

Thaler, R. H. and Sunstein, C. R. (2009) Nudge: improving decisions about health, wealth and happiness. Penguin.

Thurstone, L. L. (1927). A law of comparative judgement. *Psychological Review,* **34**(4), pp. 278–286.

Thurstone, L. L. (1938). *Primary mental abilities.* Chicago: University of Chicago Press.

Thurstone, L. L. (1953) *Examiner manual for Thurstone's Temperament schedule.* Chicago: Science Research Associates.

Vernon, P. E. (1950) *The structure of human abilities.* London: Methuen.

Wechsler, D. (1939) The measurement of adult intelligence. Baltimore: Williams and Wilkins.

Williams, W. M. and Sternberg, R. J. (1988) Group intelligence: why some groups are better than others. *Intelligence,* **12**(4), pp. 351-377.

Wolff, S. B. (2006) Group emotional intelligence (GEI) survey: Technical Manual. [Online]. Available from:
http://www.eiconsortium.org/pdf/GEI_Technical_Manual.pdf.

Woolley, A. W., Chabris, C. F., Pentland, A., Hashmi, N. and Malone, T. W. (2010) Evidence for a collective intelligence factor in the performance of human groups. *Science*, **330**(6004), pp. 686-688.

Yerkes, R. M. (1921) *Psychological examining in the United States army: memoirs of the National Academy of Sciences, XV.* Washington, DC: US Government Printing Office.

Chapter 7: Emotional intelligence and well-being

Abraham, R. (1998) Emotional dissonance in organisations: conceptualising the roles of self-esteem and job-induced tension. *Leadership and Organisation Development Journal*, **20**(1), pp. 18-25.

Adler, N. E., Boyce, T., Chesney, M. A., Cohen, S., Folkman, S., Kahn, R. L. and Syme, S. L. (1994) Socioeconomic status and health: The challenge of the gradient. *The American Psychologist*, **49**(1), pp.15-24.

(The) Anxiety and Depression Association of America (2018) *Physical activity reduces stress.* [Online] Available from: https://adaa.org/understanding-anxiety/related-illnesses/other-related-conditions/stress/physical-activity-reduces-st.

Arthritis Research UK (2017) *Too many Brits are putting off exercise.* [Online] Available from: https://www.arthritisresearchuk.org/news/press-releases/2017/march/too-many-brits-are-putting-off-exercise.aspx.

Austin, E. J., Farrelly, D., Black, C. and Moore, H. (2007) Emotional intelligence, Machiavellianism and emotional manipulation: Does EI have a dark side? *Personality and individual differences*, **43**, pp.179-189.

Babiak, P. and Hare, D. (2006) *Snakes in Suites: When Psychopaths go to work.* Harper Collins.

Babiak, P. and Hare, D. (2016) *Business scan (B-Scan)* [Online] Available from: http://www.b-scan.com/.

Barrett, L. F. (2017) *How emotions are made: The secret life of the brain.* McMillan, UK.

Basu, N., Skinner, H. G., Litzelman, K., Vanderboom, R. Baichoo, E. and Boardman, L. A. (2014) Telomeres and telomere dynamics: relevance to cancers of the GI tract. *Expert Review of Gastroenterology and Hepatology*, **7**(8), pp. 733-748.

BBC (2018), *Who feels lonely? The result of the world's largest loneliness study* [Online] Available from:
http://www.bbc.co.uk/programmes/articles/2yzhfv4DvqVp5nZyxBD8G23/who-feels-lonely-the-results-of-the-world-s-largest-loneliness-study

Beaty, R. E., Benedek, M., Kaufman, S. C and Silvia, P. J. (2015) Default and executive network coupling supports creative idea production. *Scientific Reports*, **5**(10964).

Birkas, B and Csatho, A. (2015) Size the day: the time perspectives of the dark triad. *Personality and Individual Differences*, **86**, pp. 318-320.

Blackburn, E. and Epel, E. (2017) *The telomere effect*, Orion Spring.
Brown, R. and Kulik, J. (1977) Flashbulb memories. *Cognition*, **5**(1), pp. 73-99.
Cacioppo, J. T. and Cacioppo, S. (2014). Social relationships and health: The toxic effects of perceived social isolation. *Social and Personality Compass*, **8**, pp. 58-72.
Cacioppo, J. T., Hughes, M. E., Waite, L. J., Hawkley, L. C. and Thisted, R. A. (2006) Loneliness as a specific risk factor for depressive symptoms: cross-sectional and longitudinal analyses. *Psychology and Aging*, **21**, pp. 140-151.
Cacioppo, J. T and Patrick, W. (2009) *Loneliness: human nature and the need for social connection.* W. W. Norton and Company
Carver, C. S. Scheier, M. F. Weintraub, J. K. (1989) Assessing coping strategies: A theoretical based approach. *Journal of Personality and Social Psychology*, **56**(2), pp. 267-283.
Ceci, M. W. and Kumar, V. K. (2015) A correlational study of creativity, happiness, motivation and stress from creative pursuits. *Journal of Happiness*, **17**(2), pp. 609-626.
(The) Chartered Institute of Personnel and Development (CIPD) (2007) *What's happening with well-being at work?* Change agenda. London. CIPD, pp. 4.
Cherkas, L. F., Valdes, A. A., Hunkin, J. L., Gardner, J. P., Surdulescue, G. L. Kimura, M. and Spector, T.D. (2006) The effects of social status on biological aging as measured by white blood cells telomere length. *Ageing Cell*, **5**(5), pp. 361-365.
Christie, R. and Geis, F. L. (1970) *Studies in Machiavellianism.* New York: Academic Press.
Cohen, S., Doyle, W. J., Turner, R. Alper, C. M. and Skoner, D. P. (2003) Sociability and susceptibility to the common cold. *Psychological Science*, **14**(5), pp. 389-295.
Cohen, S., Janicki-Deverts, D., Turner, R. B., Casselbrant, M. L., Li-Korotky, H. S., Epel, E. S. and Doyle, W. J. (2013) Association between telomere length and experimentally induced upper respiratory viral infection in healthy adults. *The Journal of the American Medical Association*, **309**(7), pp. 699-705.
Cohen, S. and Williamson, G. M. (1991) Stress and infectious disease in humans. *Psychological Bulletin*, **109**(1), pp. 5-24.
Copeland, W. E., Wolfe, D., Angold, A. and Costello, J. (2013) Adult psychiatric outcomes of bullying and being bullied by peers in childhood and adolescence. *JAMA Psychiatry*, **70**(4), pp. 419-426.
Copeland, W.E., Wolfe, D., Lereya, S. T., Shanahan, L., Worthman, C. and Costello, E. J. (2014) Childhood bullying involvement predicts low-grade systematic inflammation into adulthood. *Proceedings of the National Academy of Science*, **111**(21), pp. 7570-7575.
Credit Suisse Research Institute (2018) *Global Wealth Databook 2018.* [Online] Available at: https://www.credit-suisse.com/corporate/en/research/research-institute/global-wealth-report.html
Cribbet, M. R., Carlisle, M., Cawthon, R. M., Uchino, B. N., Williams, P. G., Smith, T. W., Gunn, H. E. and Light, K. C. (2014) Cellular aging and restorative processes: subjective sleep quality and duration moderate the associa-

tion between age and telomere length in a sample of middle-aged and older adults. *Sleep*, **37**(1), pp. 65-70.

Crum, A. J., Salovey, P. and Anchor, S. (2013) Rethinking Stress: The role of mindsets in determining the stress response. *Journal of Personality and Social Psychology*, **104**(4), pp. 716-733.

Damasio, A. (1994) *Descartes' error.* Picador Vintage.

Denavas-Walt, C. and Proctor, B. D. (2015) *Income and poverty in the United States: current population reports.* [Online] Available from: https://www.census.gov/content/dam/Census/library/publications/2015/demo/p60-252.pdf

(The) Department of Health (2011) *Start active, stay active: A report on physical activity for health from the four home countries'* Chief Medical Officers. [Online] Available from: http://www.ssehsactive.org.uk/userfiles/Documents/startactivestayactive.pdf

Dutton, K. (2012) *The wisdom and psychopaths: Lessons in life from saints, spies and serial killers.* Arrow Books.

Epel, E. E., Puterman, J., Lin, E., Blackburn, A. Lazaro, A. and Mendes, W. (2013) Wandering minds and aging cells, *Clinical Psychological Science*, **XX**(X), PP. 1-9.

The Equality Act (2010) [Online] Available from: http://www.legislation.gov.uk/ukpga/2010/15/contents

(The) Equality Trust (2019) *The scale of economic inequality in the UK.* [Online] Available from: https://www.equalitytrust.org.uk/scale-economic-inequality-uk

Folkman, S. and Lazarus, R. S. (1980) An analysis of coping in a middle age community sample. *Journal of health and Social behaviour*, Vol. **21**, pp. 219-239.

Franzini, L., Elliott, M. N., Cuccaro, P., Schuster, M., Gilliland, J., Grunbaum, J. A. and Tortolero, S. R. (2009) Influences of physical and social neighbourhood environments on children's physical activity and obesity. *American Journal of Public Health*, **99**(2), pp.271- 278.

Fredrickson, B. L. (2001) The role of positive emotions in positive psychology: The broaden and build theory of positive emotions. *American Psychologist*, **56**(3), pp. 218-226.

Goldberger, L. and Breznitz, S. (1993) *Handbook of stress: Theoretical and clinical aspects.* The Free Press.

Gunnar, M. R. (2016) How secure attachment relationships reduce the effect of stress in children. College of Education and Human Development. University of Minnesota. *Improving lives*, Friday 19th August. [Online] Available from: https://cehdvision2020.umn.edu/blog/secure-attachment-relationships/

Hare, R. D. (1985) Comparison of procedures for the assessment of psychopathy. *Journal of Consulting and Clinical Psychology*, **53**, pp. 7-16.

Hart, H. and Rubia, K. (2012) Neuroimaging of child abuse: a critical review. *Frontiers in Human Neuroscience*, **6**(52).

Hawkley, L. C., Thisted, R. A., Masi, C. M. and Cacioppo, J. T. (2010) Loneliness predicts increased blood pressure: 5-year cross-lagged analyses in middle-aged and older adults. *Psychology and Aging*, **25**(1), pp.132-41

Hemingway, H. and Marmot, M. (1999) Evidence-based cardiology: psychosocial factors in the aetiology and prognosis of coronary heart disease. Systematic review of prospective cohort studies. *The British Medical Journal*, **318**(7196), pp. 1460-1467.

Herrera, B. M. and Lindgren, C. M. (2010) The genetics of obesity. *Current Diabetes Report*, **10**(6), pp. 498-505.

Holt-Lunstad, J., Smith, T. B., Baker, M., Harris, T. and Stephenson, D. (2015) Loneliness and social isolation as risk factors for mortality: a meta-analytic review. *Perspectives on Psychological Science*, **10**(2), pp. 227-237.

Holt-Lunstad, J., Smith, T. B. and Layton, J. B. (2010) Social relationships and mortality risk: a meta-analytic review. *PLoS medicine*, **7**(7), e1000316.

House of Commons Health Committee (2004) *Obesity: Third report of session 2003-04*, volume 1. [Online] Available from: https://publications.parliament.uk/pa/cm200304/cmselect/cmhealth/23/23.pdf

Indregard, A-M. R., Knardahl, S. and Nielson, M. B. (2018) Emotional dissonance, mental health complaints, and sickness absence among health- and social workers. The moderating role of self-efficacy. *Frontiers in Psychology*, **9**(592).

Jackowska, M., Hammer, M., Carvalho, L. A., Erusalimsky, J. D., Butcher, L. and Steptoe, A. (2012) Short sleep duration is associated with shorter telomere length in healthy men: Findings from the Whitehall II cohort study. PLOS ONE [Online] Available from: https://journals.plos.org/plosone/article?id=10.1371/journal.pone.0047292.

Jonason, P. K., Li, N. P., Webster, G. D. and Schmitt, D.P. (2009) The dark triad: facilitating a short-term mating strategy in men. *European Journal of Personality*, **23**(1), pp.5-18.

Jonason, P. K. and O'Conner, P. J. (2017) Cutting corners at work: an individual difference perspective. Personality and Individual Differences, 107, pp. 146-153).

Kane, M. J. and Engle, R. W. (2003) Working memory capacity and the control of attention: The contributions of goal neglect, response competition, and task set to Stroop interference. *Journal of Experimental Psychology: General*, **132**(1, pp. 47-70.

Kaufman, S. B. (2015) The emotions that make us creative. *Creativity*. [Online] Available from: https://hbr.org/2015/08/the-emotions-that-make-us-more-creative.

Krohne, H.W. (2002) *Stress and Coping Theories*. Johannes Gutenberg-Universitat Mainz Germany.

Levenson, M., Kiehl, K. A. and Cory, M. F. (1995) Assessing psychopathic attributes in non-institutionalised population. *Journal of Personality and Social Psychology*, **68**(1), pp. 151-158.

Levy, B. R., Slade, M. D., Kunkel, S. R. and Kasl, S. V. (2002) Longevity increased by positive self-perceptions of aging. *Journal of Personality and Social Psychology*, **83**(2): pp. 261-270.

Levy, B. R., Slade, M. D., Murphy, T. E. and Gill, T. M. (2012) Association between Positive age stereotypes and recovery from disability in older persons. *The Journal of the American Medical Association*, 308(19), pp.1972-1973.

Liao, Y., Shonkoff, E. T. and Dunton, G. F. (2015) The acute relationship between affect, physical feeling states, and physical activity in daily life: A review of current evidence. *Frontiers in Psychology*, 23rd December. [Online] Available from: https://www.frontiersin.org/articles/10.3389/fpsyg.2015.01975/full

Lindstrom, B. R. and Bohlin, G. (2011) Emotion processing facilitates working memory performance. *Cognition and Emotion*, **25**(7), pp. 1196-1204.

Maes, H. H., Neale, M. C. and Eaves, L. J. (1997) Genetic and environmental factors in relative body weight and human adiposity. *Behaviour Genetics*, **27**(4), pp. 325-351.

Mackay, D. G. and Ahmetzanov, M. V. (2005) Emotion, memory and attention in the taboo Stroop paradigm. *Psychological Science*, **16**(1), pp. 25-32.

Marmot, M. (2015) *The health gap.* Bloomsbury.

Marcus Aurelius (2006). *Meditations.* Translated by M. Hammond. Penguin Classics.

Marcus, D. K., Zeigler-Hill, V., Mercer, S. H. and Norris, A. L. (2014) The psychology of spite and the measurement of spitefulness. *Psychological Assessment*, **26**(2), pp. 563-574.

Markus, H. R. and Kitayama, S. (1998) The culture of Psychology of personality. *Journal of Cross-Cultural Psychology*, **29**(1), pp 63-87.

Mayer, B. and Sullivan, J. (2018) Consumption and income inequality in the US since the 1960s. *VOX: CEPR Policy portal.* [Online] Available from: https://voxeu.org/article/consumption-and-income-inequality-us-1960s

(The) Mental Health Foundation (2013) *Let's get physical: The impact of physical activity on well-being.* [Online] Available from: https://www.mentalhealth.org.uk/sites/default/files/lets-get-physical-report.pdf

(The) Mental Health Foundation (2016) *Relationships in the 21st century: The forgotten foundation of mental health and well-being.* [Online] Available from: https://www.mentalhealth.org.uk/sites/default/files/Relationships-in-21st-century-forgotten-foundation-mental-health-well-being-full-may-2016.pdf

Malkin, C. (2015) *The Narcissist Test: How to spot outsized egos...and the surprising things we can learn from them.* Thorsons/ Element-GB.

Miller, G. E. and Chen, E. (2010) Harsh family climate in early life presages the emergence of a proinflammatory phenotype in adolescence. *Psychological Science*, **21**(6), pp. 848-856.

(The) National Health Service (UK) (2019) *Overview: Obesity.* [Online] Available from: https://www.nhs.uk/conditions/obesity/

Nolen-Hoeksema, S. (2000) The role of rumination in depressive disorders and mixed anxiety/ depressive symptoms. *The Journal of Abnormal Psychology*, **109**(3), pp. 504-511.

Novakova, S., Blahutkova, M., Muchova, M. and Lepkova, H. (2016) Influence of Physical Activities on Stress Reduction among Third Age University Students. dLibra Digital Library, *Wydawnictwo im. Stanisława Podobińskiego Akademii im.* [Online] Available from: http://dlibra.bg.ajd.czest.pl:8080/dlibra/docmetadata?id=4061&from=publication.

O'Boyle, E., Forsyth, D. R., Banks, G. and McDaniel, M. A. (2011) A metaanalysis of the dark triad and work behaviour: A social exchange perspective. *Journal of Applied Psychology*, **97**(3), pp. 557-579.

O'Donovan, A., Tillie, J., Dhabhar, F. S., Wolkowitz, O. M., Blackburn, E. H. and Epel, E. S. (2009) Pessimism correlates with leukocyte telomere shortness and elevated interleukein-6 in post-menopausal women. *Brain, Behaviour and Immunity*, **23**(4), pp. 446-449.

(The) Office for National Statistics (ONS) (2018) *Overview of the UK population: November 2018.* [Online] Available from: https://www.ons.gov.uk/peoplepopulationandcommunity/populationandmigration/populationestimates/articles/overviewoftheukpopulation/november2018.

Oomen, C. A., Soeters, H., Audureau, N., Vermunt, L., van Hasselt, F. N., Manders, E. M., Joels, M., Lucassen, P. J. and Krugers, H. (2010) Severe early life stress hampers spatial learning and neurogenesis but improves hippocampal synaptic plasticity and emotional learning under high stress conditions in adulthood. *Journal of Neuroscience*, **30**(19), pp. 6635-6645.

The Organisation for Economic Cooperation and Development (OECD, 2015) *In it together: why less inequality benefits all.* [Online] Available from: https://www.oecd.org/social/in-it-together-why-less-inequality-benefits-all-9789264235120-en.htm

The Organisation for Economic Cooperation and Development (OECD, 2018) *Inequalities in household wealth across OECD countries: evidence from the OECD wealth distribution database.* [Online] Available from: https://www.oecd.org/officialdocuments/publicdisplaydocumentpdf/?cote=SDD/DOC(2018)1&docLanguage=En

(The) Organisation for Economic Development (OECD) (2019a) *Inequality: Inequality and income.* [Online] Available from: http://www.oecd.org/social/inequality.htm

(The) Organisation for Economic Development (OECD) (2019b) *Income inequality.* [Online] Available from: https://data.oecd.org/inequality/income-inequality.htm

Paskov, M. and Dewilde, C. (2012) Income inequality and solidarity in Europe. *Research in Social Stratification and Mobility*, **20**(4), pp. 415-432.

Paulhus, D. L. and Williams, K. M. (2002) The dark triad of personality: narcissism, Machiavellianism and psychopathy. *Journal of Research in Personality*, **36**(6), pp. 556-563.

Pearlin, L. I. and Schooler, C. (1978) The structure of coping. *Journal of Health and Social Behaviour*, **19**(1), pp. 2-21.

Pickett, K. E. and Wilkinson, R. G. (2010) Inequality: an underacknowledged source of mental illness and distress. *British Journal of Psychiatry*, **197**(6), pp. 426-428.

Pickett, K E. and Wilkinson, R. G. (2015) Income, inequality and health: a causal review. *Social Science and Medicine*, **128**, pp. 316-326.

Raskin, R. and Hall, C. S. (1979) A narcissistic personality inventory. Psychological Reports, inventory. *Psychological Reports*, **45**, pp.590.

Repetti, R. L., Taylor, S. E. and Seeman, T. E. (2002) Risky families: family social environments and the mental health and physical health of offspring. *Psychological Bulletin*, **128**(2), pp. 330-366.

Ribeiro, S., Bauer, W., Andrade, A., York-Smith, M., Pan, P. M., Pingani, L., Knapp, M., Coutinho, E. S. F. and Evans-Lacko, S. (2017) Income inequality and mental illness related morbidity and resilience: a systematic review and meta-analysis. *The Lancet Psychiatry*, **4**(7), pp. 554-562.

Robertson, T., Batty, G. D., Der, G., Fenton, C., Shiels, P. G. and Benzeval, M. (2013) Is socioeconomic status associated with biological aging as measured by telomere length? *Epidemiologic Reviews*, **35**(1), pp. 98-111.

Semenyna, S. W. and Honey, P. L. (2015) Dominance styles mediate sex differences in dark triad traits. *Personality and Individual Differences*, **83**, pp.37-43.

Seneca (2004) Penguin great ideas: on the shortness of life. (UK ed) Translated by C. D. N. Costa. Penguin.

Sigman, M. (2018) *The secret life of the mind*. Williams Collins.

(The) Social Metrics Commission (2018) A new measure of poverty for the UK. [Online] Available from: https://socialmetricscommission.org.uk/

Smith, J. C. (2002) *Stress Management: A comprehensive handbook of techniques and strategies*. Springer Publishing Company.

(The) *state of obesity: better policies for a healthier America. Adult obesity in the United States* (2018). Available from: https://www.stateofobesity.org/adult-obesity/

Stults-Kolehmainen, M. A. and Sinha, R. (2015) The effects of stress on physical activity and exercise. *Sports Medicine*, **44**(1), pp. 81-121.

Sue, D. W. and Sue, D. (1990) *Counselling the culturally different: Theory and practice (2nd Ed)*. New York: Wiley.

Surtees, P. G., Wainwright, N. W., Luben, R. N., Wareham, N. J., Bingham, S. A. and Khaw, K. T. (2008) Psychological distress, major depressive disorder, and risk of stroke. *Neurology*, **70**(10), pp.788-794.

Taleb, N. N. (2007) *The Black Swan: The impact of the highly improbable*. New York: Random House.

Teicher, M. H. and Samsung, J. A. (2016) Annual research review: Enduring neurobiological effects of childhood abuse and neglect. *Journal of Child Psychology and Psychiatry*, **57**(3), pp. 241-266.

Teicher, M. H., Samsung, J. A., Polcari, A. and Mcgreenery, C. E. (2006) Sticks and stones and hurtful words: relative effects of various forms of childhood maltreatment. *American Journal of Psychiatry*, **163**, pp. 993-1000.

Theal, K. P., Brett, Z. H., Shirtcliff, E. A., Dunn, E. C. and Drury, S. S. (2013) Neighborhood disorder and telomeres: Connecting children's exposure to community level stress and cellular response. *Social Science and Medicine*, **85**, pp. 50-58.

Travis, J. W. and Ryan, R. S. (2004) *Wellness workbook: How to achieve enduring health and vitality (1943)* (3rd ed). Celestial Arts, Berkeley.

Triandis, H.C. (1996) The psychological measurement of cultural syndromes. *American Psychologist*, **51**(4), pp. 407-415.

Uslaner, E. M. (2012) *Segregation and mistrust: diversity, isolation and social cohesion*. Cambridge University Press.

Vernon, P. A., Villani, V. C., Schermer, J. A. and Petrides, K. V. (2008) Phenotypic and genetic associations between the big five and trait emotional intelligence. *Twin Research and Human Genetics*, **11**, pp. 524-530.

Vernon, P. A., Villani, V. C., Vickers, L. C. and Harris, J. A. (2008) A behavioural genetic investigation of the dark triad and the big 5. *Personality and Individual Differences*, **44**, pp. 445-452.

Wassertheil-Smoller, S., Shumaker, S., Ockene, J., Talavera, G. A., Greenland, P., Cochrane, B., Robbins, J., Aragaki, A. and Dunbar-Jacob, J. (2004) Depression and cardiovascular sequelae in post-menopausal women. The Women's Health Initiative (WHI) *Archives of Internal Medicine*, **164**(3), pp. 289-298.

Wilkinson, R. G. and Pickett, K. E. (2006) Income inequality and population health: a review and explanation of the evidence. *Social Science and Medicine*, **62**(7), pp. 1768-1784.

Wilkinson, R. G. and Pickett, K. (2010) *The spirit level: why equality is better for everyone*. London: Penguin.

Wilkinson, R. and Pickett, K. (2019) *The inner level: how more equal societies reduce stress, restore sanity and improve everyone's well-being*. Penguin.

Wilson, T. D. and Schooler, J. W. (1991) Thinking too much: introspection can reduce the quality of preferences and decisions. Journal of *Personality and Social Psychology*, **60**, pp.181-192.

Wilton, N. (2013) *Human Resource Management: An introduction*. London. Sage Publications Limited.

Winston, R. and Chicot, R. (2016) The importance of early bonding on the long-term mental health and resilience of children. *London Journal of Primary Care*, 8(1), pp. 12-14.

(The) World Health Organisation (WHO) (2017) *Mental Health. Depression: Let's talk*. Online. Available at: http://www.who.int/mental_health/management/depression/en/.

(The) World Health Organisation (2018a) *Prevalence of insufficient physical activity among adults*. [Online] Available from: https://www.who.int/gho/ncd/risk_factors/physical_activity/en/.

(The) World Health Organisation (2018b) *Obesity and overweight.* [Online] Available from: https://www.who.int/news-room/fact-sheets/detail/obe0sity-and-overweight.

Zeidner, M. and Endler, N. S. (1996) *Handbook of Coping: Theory, research applications.* New York: Wiley.

Zucman, G. (2019) Global wealth inequality. *The National Bureau of Economic Research.* (Working paper: 25462) [Online] Available from: https://www.nber.org/papers/w25462.

Chapter 8: Training and development

Allstate (2011) New Allstate survey shows Americans think they are great drivers- habits tell a different story. [Online] Available from: https://www.prnewswire.com/news-releases/new-allstate-survey-shows-americans-think-they-are-great-drivers---habits-tell-a-different-story-126563103.html.

Brinol, P., Gasco, M., Petty, R. E. and Horcajo, R. E. (2013) Treating thoughts as material objects can increase or decrease their impact on evaluation. *Psychological Science*, 24(1), pp. 41-47.

Cherniss, C. (2000) Social and emotional competence in the workplace. In R. Bar-On and J. D. A. Parker (Eds.), *The handbook of emotional intelligence: Theory, development, assessment, and application at home, school, and in the workplace*, pp. 433-458.

Clarke, N. (2006) Developing emotional intelligence through workplace learning: Findings from a case study in healthcare. *Human Resource Development International*, **9**(4), pp. 447-465.

Cohen, J. (2006) Social, emotional, ethical, and academic education: creating a climate for learning, participation in democracy, and well-being. *Harvard Educational Review*, 76(2), pp. 201-237.

Cooper, R. K. (1997) Applying emotional intelligence in the workplace. *Training and Development*, **51**(12).

Creswell, J. D. (2017) Mindfulness interventions. *Annual Review of Psychology*, 68, pp. 491-516).

Davidson, R. J., Kabat Zinn, J., Schumacher, J., Rosenkranz, M. A., Muller, D., Santorelli, S. F., Urbanowski, F., Harrington, A., Bonus, K. and Sheridan, J. F. (2003) Alterations in brain and immune function produced by mindfulness meditation. *Psychosomatic Medicine*, **65**(4), pp. 564-570.

Davis, D. M. and Hayes, J. A. (2011) What are the benefits of mindfulness? A practice review of psychotherapy related research. *Psychotherapy*, 48(2), pp. 198-208.

Dierdorff, E. C. and Rubin, R. S. (2015) Research: we're not very self-aware, especially at work. *Harvard Business Review.* [Online] Available from https://hbr.org/2015/03/research-were-not-very-self-aware-especially-at-work.

Doidge, N. (2007) *The brain that changes itself: stories of personal triumph from the frontiers of brain science.* Penguin Books.

Duranso, C. (2018) Walk for well-being: The main effects of walking on approach motivation. *Motivation and Emotion*, pp. 1-10.

Duval, S. and Wicklund, R. A. (1973) Effects of objective self-awareness on attribution of causality. *Journal of Experimental Psychology*, 9(1), pp. 17-31.

Fulton, P. R. (2005) Mindfulness as clinical training. In C. K. Germer, R. D. Siegel and P. R. Fulton (Eds.), *Mindfulness and psychotherapy*. New York: Guilford Press, pp. 55–72

Germer, C. K., Siegel, R. D. and Fulton, P. R. (2005) *Mindfulness and psychotherapy*. New York: Guilford Press

Goleman, D. (1998) *Working with emotional intelligence*. Bantam Books: New York.

Goleman, D. (2012) Self-awareness (question and answer). [Online] Available from: http://www.danielgoleman.info/on-self-awareness.

Grant, A. M. (2007) Enhancing coaching skills and emotional intelligence through training. *Industrial & Commercial Training*, 39(5), pp. 257-266.

Haley, B., Heo, S., Wright, P., Barone, C., Rettiganti, M.R. and Anders, M. (2017) Relationships among active listening, self-awareness, empathy, and patient-centred care in associate and baccalaureate degree nursing students. *NursingPlus Open*, 3, pp. 11-16.

Hebb, D. (1949) *The Organisation of Behaviour. A Neuropsychological Theory*. Wiley, New York, NY.

Hicks, A. L., Adams, M. M., Martin Ginis, K., Giangregorio, L., Latimer, A., Phillips, S. M. and McCartney, N. (2005) Long term body weight supported treadmill training and subsequent follow up in persons with chronic SCI: effects on functional walking ability and measures of subjective well-being. *Spinal Cord*, 43, pp. 291-298.

Holiday, R. (nd) Daily stoic: what is stoicism? A definition and 9 stoic exercises to get you started. [Online] Available from: https://dailystoic.com/what-is-stoicism-a-definition-3-stoic-exercises-to-get-you-started/

Kabat-Zinn, J. (1990) *Full catastrophe living: Using the wisdom of your body and mind to face stress, pain, and illness*. Piatkus.

Kabat-Zin, J., Massion, A. O., Kristeller, J., Peterson, L. G., Fletcher, K. E., Pbert, L., Lenderking, W. R. and Santorelli, S. F. (1992) Effectiveness of a meditation-based stress reduction program in the treatment of anxiety disorders. *The American Journal of Psychiatry*, 149(7), pp. 936-943.

Kahneman, D. and Krueger, A. B. (2006) Developments in the measurement of subjective well-being. *Journal of Economic Perspectives*, 20(1), pp. 3-24.

Kerrigan, D., Chau, V., King, M., Holman, E., Joffe, A. and Sibinga (2017) There is no performance, there is just this moment: The role of mindfulness instruction in promoting health and well-being among students at a highly ranked university in the United States. Journal of Evidence-Based Integrative Medicine. [Online] Available from: https://journals.sagepub.com/doi/abs/10.1177/2156587217719787

Killingsworth, M. A. and Gilbert, D. T. (2010) A wandering mind is an unhappy mind. *Science*, 330(6006), pp. 932

Kruger, J. and Dunning, D. (1999). Unskilled and unaware of it: how difficulties in recognizing one's own incompetence lead to inflated self-assessments. *Journal of Personality and Social Psychology.* **77** (6), pp. 1121–34

Luttrell, A., Brinol, P. and Petty, R. E. (2014) Mindful verses mindless thinking and persuasion. In: A. Ie, C.T. Ngnoumen, and E. J. Langer. *The Wiley Blackwell Handbook of Mindfulness (Volume 1).* Wiley Blackwell. pp. 258-278.

McConville, J., McAleer, R. and Hahne, A. (2016) Mindfulness training for health profession students- The effect of mindfulness training on psychological well-being, learning and clinical performance of health professional students: A systematic review of randomised and non-randomised controlled trials. *Explore,* **13**(1), pp. 26-45.

Nader, K. and Einarsson, E. O. (2010) Memory reconsolidation: an update. *Annals of the New York Academy of Sciences,* **1191**, pp. 27-41.

Nelis, D., Kotsou, I., Quoidbach, J., Hansenne, M., Weytens, F., Dupuis, P. and Mikolajczak, M. (2011) Increasing emotional competence improves psychological and physical well-being, social relationships, and employability. *Emotion,* **11**(2), pp. 354-366.

Palmer, B., Walls, M., Burgess, Z. and Stough, C. (2001) Emotional intelligence and effective leadership. *Leadership and Organisational Development Journal,* 22(1), pp. 5-10.

Penedo, F. J. and Dahn, R. J. (2005) Exercise and well-being: a review of mental and physical health benefits associated with physical activity. *Current Opinion in Psychiatry,* **18**(2), pp. 189-193.

Sapolsky, R. (1996) Why stress is bad for your brain. *Science,* **9**(273), pp. 749-750.

Sapolsky, R. (2018) *Behave: The biology of humans at our best and worst.* Vintage.

Segal, Z. V., Williams, J. M. G. and Kabat-Zinn, J. D. (2012) *Mindfulness-based cognitive therapy for depression (2nd).* Guilford Press.

Simmons, E. (2018) The dark side of mindfulness: It's supposed to be calming. But there's growing evidence the fashionable therapy can be harmful. The Daily Mail 1st December 2018, [Online] Available from: https://www.dailymail.co.uk/home/you/article-5661321/Can-mindfulness-bad-you.html.

Slaski, M. and Cartwright, S. (2003) Emotional intelligence training and its implications for stress, health and performance. *Stress and Health: Journal of the International Society for the Investigation of Stress,* **19**(4), pp.233-239.

Stanford-News Service (1996) *New studies of human brains show stress may shrink neurons.* [Online] Available from: https://news.stanford.edu/pr/96/960814shrnkgbrain.html.

Stevenson, B. and Wolfers, J. (2008) Economic growth and subjective well-being: reassessing the Easterlin paradox. Brookings Papers on Economic Activity. *The Brookings Institution,* **39**(1), pp. 1-102. [Online] Available from: https://www.nber.org/papers/w14282.

Williams, J. M. G., Teasdale, J. D., Segal, Z. V. and Kabat-Zinn, J. (2007) *The mindful way through depression: freeing yourself from chronic unhappiness.* Guilford Press.

Williams, M. and Penman, D. (2013) *Mindfulness: a practical guide to finding peace in a frantic world.* Piatkus.

Wilson, B. M., Mickes, L., Stolarz-Fantino, S., Evrard, M. and Fantino, E. (2015) Increased false-memory susceptibility after mindfulness meditation. *Psychological Science,* **26**(10) pp. 1567-1573.

Zell, E. and Krizan, Z. (2014) Do people have insight into their abilities? A metasynthesis. *Perspectives on Psychological Science,* **9**(2), pp. 111-125.

Zijlmans, L., Embregts, P., Gerits, L., Bosman, A. and Derksen, J. (2014) The effectiveness of staff training focused on increasing emotional intelligence and improving interaction between support staff and clients. *Journal of Intellectual Disability Research,* **59**(7), pp. 599-612.

Chapter 9: Emotional intelligence: does it really matter?

Bar-On, R. (1997) *The Emotional Inventory (EQ-i): Technical manual.* Toronto: Multi-Health Systems.

Burnett, D. (2016). *The Idiot Brain.* Guardian Books, London

Craig, A. D. (2002) How do you feel? Introception: The sense of the physiological condition of the body. *Nature Reviews Neuroscience,* **3**(8), pp. 655-666.

Craig, A. D. (2004) Human feelings: why are some more aware than others? *Trends in Cognitive Sciences,* **8**(6), pp. 239-241.

Davidson, R. J. and Begley, S. (2012) *The emotional life of the brain: How to change the way you think, feel and live.* Hodder and Stoughton.

Dweck, C. (2017) *Mindset: changing the way you think to fulfil your potential.* Robinson.

Eysenck, M. W. (2004) *Psychology: an international perspective.* Psychology Press Ltd.

Foer, J. (2012) *Moonwalking with Einstein: the art and science of remembering everything.* Penguin.

Gardner, H. (1983) *Frames of mind: The theory of multiple intelligences.* New York: Basic Books.

Gardner, H. (1999) *Intelligence reframed. Multiple intelligences for the 21st century.* New York. Basic Books.

Goleman, D. (1995) *Emotional Intelligence: Why It Can Matter More than IQ.* Bantam Books, New York. NY.

Goleman, D. (1998) *Working with emotional intelligence.* Bantam Books: New York.

Ghosh, S. and Collier, A. (2012) *Churchill's pocketbook of diabetes.* Elsevier Ltd.

Helm, K. M. (2016) Hooking up: *The psychology of sex and dating.* ABC-CLIO, LLC.

International Labour Organisation (2011) *A skilled workforce for strong, sustainable and balanced growth: a G20 training strategy.* International Labour Office, Geneva. [Online] Available from: https://www.oecd.org/g20/summits/toronto/G20-Skills-Strategy.pdf

Irvine, W. B. (2015) *Putting the Greek back into stoicism.* BBC News [Online] Available from https://www.bbc.co.uk/news/magazine-33346743.

Kazim, E. (2011) *Scientific commentary of Suratul Faatehah* (3rd ed). Nice Printing Press, Delhi.

Kim, M. J. and Whalen, P. J. (2009) The structural integrity of an amygdala-prefrontal pathway predicts trait anxiety. *Journal of Neuroscience,* **29**(37), pp. 11614-11618.

Kirsch, P., Esslinger, C., Chen, Q., Mier, D., Lis, S., Siddhanti, S., Gruppe, H., Mattay, V. S., Gallhofer, B. and Meyer-Lindenberg, A. (2005) Oxytocin modulates neural circuitry for social cognition and fear in humans. *The Journal of Neuroscience,* **25**(49), pp. 11489-11493.

LeDoux, J. (1999) *The emotional brain: The mysterious underpinnings of emotional life.* W. and N.

LeDoux, J. (2003) *Synaptic self: How our brains become who we are.* Penguin Books.

LeDoux, J. (2019) *The deep history of ourselves: How ancient microbes became conscious brains.* Viking.

Lubuschagne, I., Phan, K. L., Wood, A., Angstadt, M., Chua, P., Heinrichs, M., Stout, J. C. and Nathan, P. J. (2010) Oxytocin attenuates amygdala to fear in generalised social anxiety disorder. *Neuropsychopharmacology.* **35**(12): pp. 2403-2413.

Marcus Aurelius (2006). *Meditations.* Translated by M. Hammond. Penguin Classics.

Mayer, J. D. and Salovey, P. (1997) What is emotional intelligence? In: P. Salovey, and D. Sluyter, (Eds). *Emotional Development and Emotional Intelligence: Educational Implications,* (2nd ed). Basic: New York, pp. 3-31.

Neurath, O. (1935/1983) Pseudo rationalism of falsification. In R. S. Cohen and M. Neurath (Eds and Trans) *Philosophical Papers (1913-1946).* Dordrecht/ Boston: D. Reidel Publishing Company, pp.121-131.

Peterson, R. L. (2007) *Inside the investor's brain: the power of mind over money.* John Wiley and Sons.

Petrides, K. V. (2009a) Psychometric properties of the Trait Emotional Intelligence Questionnaire. In: C. Stough, D. H. Saklofske, and J. D. Parker, *Advances in the assessment of emotional intelligence.* New York: Springer.

Petrides, K. V. (2009b) *Technical manual for the trait emotional intelligence questionnaire (TEIQue).* London, England: London Psychometric Laboratory.

Petrides, K. V. and Furnham, A. (2001) Trait emotional intelligence: Psychometric investigation with reference to established trait taxonomies. *European Journal of Personality,* **15**, pp. 425-448.

Petrides, K. V. and Furnham, A. (2003). Trait emotional intelligence: Behavioural validation in two studies of emotion recognition and reactivity to mood induction. *European Journal of Personality,* **17**(6), pp. 39–57.

Pinker, S. (2019) *Enlightenment now: the case for reason, science, humanism and progress.* Penguin.

Popper, K. (1962) *Open Society and its enemies (4th ed).* Routledge.

Sabihi, S. (2017) *Role of oxytocin and GABA in the prefrontal cortex in mediating anxiety behaviour.* Ohio state University.

Salovey, P. and Mayer, J. D. (1990) Emotional Intelligence. Imagination. *Cognition and Personality,* **9**, pp. 185-211.

Sapolsky, R. (1996) Why stress is bad for your brain. *Science,* **9**(273), pp. 749-750.

Sapolsky, R. (2018) *Behave: The biology of humans at our best and worst.* Vintage.

Sigman, M. (2018) *The secret life of the mind.* Williams Collins.

Simon, H. A. (1997) Models of bounded rationality. *Empirically grounded economic reason.* The MIT Press, **3**.

Sloman, S. and Fernbach, P. (2017) *The knowledge illusion: The myth of individual thought and the power of collective wisdom.* Pan.

Stanford-News Service (1996) *New studies of human brains show stress may shrink neurons.* [Online] Available from: https://news.stanford.edu/pr/96/960814shrnkgbrain.html.

Taleb, N. N. (2012) *Antifragile: Things that gain from disorder.* Penguin Books.

Taleb, N. N. (2019) *Skin in the game: hidden asymmetries in daily life.* Penguin Books.

Thomson, H. (2018) *Unthinkable: an extraordinary journey through the world's strangest brains.* John Murray.

Wilkinson, R. and Pickett, K. (2019) *The inner level: how more equal societies reduce stress, restore sanity and improve everyone's well-being.* Penguin.

(The) World Economic Forum (2018) *The future of jobs report 2018. Centre for the new economy and society.* World Economic Forum. [Online] Available from: http://www3.weforum.org/docs/WEF_Future_of_Jobs_2018.pdf

Other good sources

Abe, J. A. A. (2011) Positive emotions, emotional intelligence, and successful experiential learning. *Personality and Individual Differences,* **51**(7), pp.817-822.

Asberg, A. (2018) Burnout: The exhaustion funnel. Mindfulnext. [Online] Available from: http://mindfulnext.org/burnout-the-exhaustion-funnel/

Ashkanasy, N. M. and Dasborough, M. T. (2003) Emotional Awareness and Emotional Intelligence in Leadership Teaching. *Journal of Education for Business,* **79**(1), pp. 18-22.

Bakker, A. B. and Demerouti, E. (2007) The job demands-resources model: state of the art. *Journal of Managerial Psychology,* **22**(3).

Bennion, K. A., Ford, J. H., Murray, B. D. and Kensinger, E. A. (2013) Oversimplification in the study of emotional memory. *Journal of the International Neuropsychological Society,* **19**(9), pp. 953-961.

Bouchard, T. J. (1994) Genes, environment and personality. *Science,* **264**, pp. 1700-1701.

Cacioppo, J. T., Hughes, M. E., Waite, L. J., Hawkley, L. C. and Thisted, R. A. (2006) Loneliness as a specific risk factor for depressive symptoms: cross-sectional and longitudinal analyses. *Psychology and Aging,* **21**(1), pp. 140-15.

Carlson, L. E., Beattie, T. L., Giese-Davis, J., Faris, P., Tamagawa, R., Fick, L. J., Degelman, E. S. and Spec, M. (2014) Mindful based cancer recovery: The development of an evidence-based psychological oncology intervention. *Cancer Cytopathology,* **121**(3).

The Centre for Disease Control and Prevention (USA) *Adult obesity facts.* [Online] Available from: https://www.cdc.gov/obesity/data/adult.html.

Chang, M. L. (2009) An appraisal perspective of teacher burnout: Examining the emotional work of teachers. *Educational Psychology Review,* **21**(3), pp. 193–218.

Cherniss, C., Goleman, D., Emmerling, R. J., Cowan, K. and Adler, M. (1998) Bringing Emotional Intelligence to the Workplace: a technical report. *Consortium for Research on Emotional Intelligence in Organizations: Rutgers University.* [Online] Available from: http://www.eiconsortium.org/reports/technical_report.html.

Cole, N. N., Nonterah, C. W., Utsey, S. O., Hook, J. N., Hubbard, R. R., Opare-Henaku, A. and Fischer, N. L. (2014) Predictor and moderator effects of ego resilience and mindfulness on the relationship between academic stress and psychological well-being. *Journal of Black Psychology,* May. [Online] Available from: https://journals.sagepub.com/doi/abs/10.1177/0095798414537939.

Damasio, A. R., Everitt, B. J. and Bishop, D. (1996) The somatic marker hypothesis and possible functions of the prefrontal cortex (and discussion). *Philosophical Transactions: Biological Sciences* **351**(1346), pp. 1413-1420.

Davidson, R. J., Goleman, D. J. and Schwartz, G. E. (1976) Attentional and affective concomitants of meditation: A cross-sectional study. *Journal of Abnormal Psychology,* **85**(2), pp. 235-238.

Davidson, R. J., Schwartz, G. F. and Rothman, L. P. (1976) Attentional style and self-regulation of mode-specific attention: An electroencephalographic study. *Journal of Abnormal Stability,* **85**(6), pp. 611-621.

De Jesus, M., Puleo, E., Shelton, R. C. and Emmons, K. M. (2010) Associations between perceived social environment and neighbourhood safety: Health implications. *Health and Place,* **16**, pp. 1007-1013.

Diener, E. (1984) Subjective well-being, *Psychological Bulletin,* **95**(3), pp. 542-575.

Diener, E., Diener, M. and Diener, C. (1995) Factors predicting the subjective well-being of nations. *Journal of Personality and Social Psychology,* **69**(5), pp. 851-864.

Dougal, S. and Rotello, C.M. (2007) Remembering emotional words is based on response bias, not recollection. *Psychonomic Bulletin and Review,* **14**(3), pp. 423–429.

Emmons, R. A. (1984) Factor analysis and construct validity of narcissistic Personality Inventory. *Journal of Personality Assessment,* **48**, pp. 291-300.

Fang, X., Sauter, D. A. and Van Kleef, G. A. (2018) Seeing mixed emotions: The specificity of emotion perception from static and dynamic facial expressions across culture. *Journal of Cross-cultural Psychology*, **49**(1), pp.130-148.

Fredrickson, B. L., Cohn, M. A., Coffey, K. A., Pek, J. and Finkel, S. M. (2008) Open hearts build lives: Positive emotions, induced through loving-kindness meditation, build consequential personal resources. *Journal of Personality and Social Psychology*, **95**, pp. 1045-1062.

Frijda, N. H., Ridderinkhof, K. R. and Rietveld, E. (2014) Impulsive action: emotional impulses and their control. *Frontiers in Psychology*, **5**(518).

Gadzella, B., Carvalho, C. and Masten, G. (2008) Differences among Gender-Role Identity Groups on Stress. *American Journal of Psychological Research*, **4**(1), pp. 40–52.

Gottlieb, G (1998) Normally occurring environmental and behavioural influences on gene activity: from central dogma to probabilistic epigenesis. *Psychological Review*, **105**(4), pp. 792-802.

Gross, J. J. (2001) Emotion regulation in adulthood: timing is everything. *Current Directions in Psychological Science*, **10**(6), PP. 214–219.

Guilford, J. P. (1967) *The nature of human intelligence*. New York: McCraw Hill.

Hamann, S. (2001) Cognitive and neural mechanisms of emotional memory. *Trends in Cognitive Sciences*, **5**(9), pp. 394-400.

Halbesleben, J. R. B. and Buckley, M. R. (2004) Burnout in work organisational life. *Journal of Management*, **30**(6), pp. 859-879.

Hargreaves, A. (1998) The emotional practice of teaching. *Teaching and Teacher Education*, **14**(8), pp. 835–854.

Healthprep (2018) *Types of workplace bullies to look out for*. [Online] Available from: https://healthprep.com/mental-health/types-workplace-bullies/?utm_source=google&utm_medium=search&utm_campaign=1584963333&utm_content=59619819757&utm_term=harasser.

Horner, K. L. (1996) Locus of control, neuroticism, and stressors: Combined influences on reported physical illness. *Personality and Individual Differences*, **21**, pp. 195-204.

ICD-10 (2016) International Statistical Classification of Disease and Related Health Problems (10th Revision) *World Health Organisation* (WHO) version. [Online] Available from: http://apps.who.int/classifications/icd10/browse/2016/en#/V

Ickes, W. J., Wicklund, R. A. and Ferris, C. B. (1973) Objective self-awareness and self-esteem. *Journal of Experimental Social Psychology*, **9**(3), pp. 202-219.

Impett, E. A., Daubenmier, J. J. and Hirschman, A. L. (2006) Minding the body: Yoga, embodiment, and well-being. *Sexuality Research and Social Policy*, **3**(4), pp. 39-48.

Johnson, R., Robertson, W., Towey, M., Stewart-Brown, S. and Clark, A. (2017) Changes over time in mental well-being, fruit and vegetable consumption and physical activity in a community-based lifestyle intervention: a before and after study. *Public Health*, **146** (May), pp. 118-125.

Johnson, R. B., and Onwuegbuzie, A. J. and Turner, L. A. (2007) Toward a definition of mixed methods research. *Journal of Mixed Methods Research*, **1**(2), pp. 112-133.

Kaszniak, A. W. (2011) Meditation, mindfulness, cognition and emotion: Implications for community-based older adult programs. *Enhancing cognitive Fitness in Adults*, pp. 85-104.

Kerr, C. E., Jones, S. R., Wan, Q., Pritchett, D. L., Wasserman, R. H., Wexler, A., Villanueva, J. J., Shaw, J. R., Lazar, S. W., Kaptchuk, T. J., Littenberg, R., Hamalainen, M. S. and Moore, C. I. (2011) Effects of mindfulness meditation training on anticipatory alpha modulation in primary somatosensory cortex. *Brain Research Bulletin*, **85**(3-4), pp. 96-103.

Kotsou, I., Nelis, D., Gregoire, J. and Mikolajczak, M. (2011) Emotional plasticity: Conditions and effects of improving emotional competence in adulthood. *Journal of Applied Psychology*, **96**(4), pp. 827-839.

Laine, M. K., Eriksson, J. G., Kujala, U. M., Raj, R., Kaprio, J., Backmand, H. M., Peltonen, M. and Sarna, S. (2015) Effect of intensive exercise in early adult life on telomere length in later life in men. *Journal of Sports, Science and Medicine*, **14**(2), pp.239-245.

Leung, D. Y. M., Nelson, H. S., Szefler, S. J. and Busse, W. W. (2004) Stress and atopy: The mind-body connection. *The Journal of Allergy and Clinical Immunology*, **113**(6), pp.1012.

Lindquist, K. A. and Feldman Barrett, L. (2012) A functional architecture of the human brain: emerging insights from the science of emotion. *Trends in Cognitive Sciences*, **16**(11), pp. 533-540.

Ludwig, D. S. and Kabat-Zin, J. (2008) Mindfulness in medicine. *The Journal of the American Medical Association*, **300**(11), pp. 1350-1352.

Maltby, J., Day, L. and Macaskill, A. (2013) *Personality individual differences and intelligence (3rd ed)*. Pearson.

Mayer, J. D., Caruso, D. R. and Salovey, P. (2016) The ability model of emotional intelligence: Principles and updates. *Emotion Review, Special edition*, pp.1-11.

McRaney, D. (2012) *You are not so smart*. Oneworld.

Minocha, S., Banks, D., Holland, C., McNulty, C., Ana-Despina, C. and Ana-Despina, T. (2017) *Investigating the role of wearable activity-tracking technologies in the well-being and quality of life of people aged 55 and over*. Report submitted to Sir Halley Stewart Trust, The Open University, Milton Keynes, UK. [Online] Available from: http://oro.open.ac.uk/43718/

Miyazaki, T., Takase, K., Nakase, K., Nakajima, W., Tada, H., Ohya, D., Sano, A., Goto, T., Hirase, H., Malinow, R. & Takahashi, T. (2012) Disrupted cortical function underlies behaviour dysfunction due to social isolation. *The Journal of Clinical Investigation*, **122**, pp. 2690–2701.

Mushtaq, R., Shoib, S., Shah, T. and Mushtaq, S. (2014) Relationship between loneliness, psychiatric disorders and physical health. A review of the psychological aspects of loneliness, *Journal of Clinical and Diagnostic Research*, **8**(9).

Nathanson, C. Paulhus, D. and Williams, K. M. (2006) Personality and misconduct correlates of body modification and other cultural deviance markers. *Journal of Research in Personality*, **40**(5), pp.779-802.

Palfrey, J. and Gasser, U. (2010). *Born Digital: Understanding the First Generation of Digital Natives.* Basic Books.

Patrick C. J. and Lang, A. R. (1999) Psychopathic traits and intoxicated states: Affective concomitants and conceptual links. In M. E. Dawson, A. M. Schell, and A. H. Boehmelt (Eds). *Startle modification: Implications for neuroscience, cognitive science, and clinical science.* New York: Cambridge University Press.

Pessoa, L. (2008) On the relationship between emotion and cognition. *Nature Reviews Neuroscience*, **9**(2), pp. 148-158.

Petrides, K. V., Vernon, P. A., Schermer, J. A. and Veselka, L. (2011) Trait emotional intelligence and the dark triad of personality. *Twin Research and Human Genetics*, **14**(1), pp.35-41.

Pinquart, M. and Sorensen, S. (2001) Influences on loneliness in older adults: A meta-analysis. *Basic and Applied Social Psychology*, **23**, pp. 245–66.

Plomin, R. and Daniels, D. C. (1987) Why are children in the same family so different from one another? *Behavioural Brain Sciences*, **10**, pp. 1-16.

Prior, M., Smart, D., Sanson, A. and Oberklaid, F. (2000). Does shy-inhibited temperament in childhood lead to anxiety problems in adolescence? *Journal of American Academy of Child and Adolescent Psychiatry*, **39**, pp. 461-468

Reisenzein, R. (2007) What is the definition of emotion? And are emotions mental behavioural processes? *Social Science Information*, **46**(3).

Roberts, R. D., MacCann, C., Matthews, G., and Zeidner, M. (2010) Teaching and learning guide for: Emotional intelligence: Towards a consensus of models and measures. *Social and Personality Psychology Compass*, **4**(10), pp. 968-981.

Rubin, K. H., Coplan, R. J. and Bowker, J. C. (2009) Social withdrawal in childhood. *Annual Review of Psychology*, **60**, pp. 141-171.

Ruiz, D. M. and Mills, J. (1997) *The four agreements: A practical guide to personal freedom.* Amber-Allen Publishing.

Simonet, D. V., Tett, R. P., Foster, J. and Bartlett, J. (2017) Dark side Personality Trait interactions: amplifying negative predictions of leadership performance. *Journal of Leadership and Organisational Studies*, **25**(2).

Simon-Thomas, E. R. Role, K. O. and Knight, R.T. (2005) Behavioural and electrophysiological evidence of a right hemisphere bias for the influence of negative emotion on higher cognition. *Journal of Cognitive Neuroscience*, **17**(3), pp. 518-529.

Schmidt, S. R. (2012) Memory for emotional words in sentences: The importance of emotional contrast. *Cognition and Emotion*, **26**, pp.1015–1035.

Sinclair, M. and Seydel, J. (2013) *Mindfulness for busy people: turning frantic and frazzled into calm and composed.* Pearson.

Stemke, C. A. (2013) Distress tolerance and mental health outcomes. *Modern Psychological Studies*, **18**(2).

Stimpson, N. J., Davison, G. and Javadi, A-H. (2018) Joggin' the noggin: Towards a physiological understanding of exercise-induced cognitive benefits. *Neuroscience and Biobehavioural Reviews*, **88,** pp. 177-186.

Tyng, C. M., Amin, H. U. Saad, M. N. M. and Malik, A. S. (2017) The influences of emotion on learning and memory. *Frontiers in Psychology*, **8**(1454).

Tupes, E. C. and Christal, R. C. (1992) Recurrent personality factors based on trait ratings. *Journal of Personality,* **60**(2)**,** pp. 225-251.

Vesely, A. K., Saklofske, D. H. and Nordstokke, D. W. (2014) EI training and pre-service teacher well-being. *Personality and Individual Differences*, **65**, pp. 81-85.

von Haaren, B., Ottenhbacher, J., Muenz, J., Neumann, R., Boes, K. and Ebner-Priemer, U. (2016) Does a 20-week aerobic exercise training programme increase our capabilities to buffer real-life stressors? A randomised controlled trial using ambulatory assessment. *European Journal of Applied Physiology*, **116**(2), pp. 383-394.

Vos, T., Barber, RM., Bell, B., Bertozzi-Villa, A., Biruyukov, S., Bollinger, I. et al (2013). Global, regional, and national incidence, prevalence, and years lived with disability for 301 acute and chronic diseases and injuries in 188 countries, 1990-2013: a systematic analysis for the Global Burden of Disease study 2013. *The Lancet*, **386**(9995), pp.743-800.

Wallace, B. A. (2001) Intersubjectivity in Indo-Tibetan Buddhism. *Journal of Consciousness Studies*, **8**, pp. 209 –230.

Walsh, R. and Shapiro, S. L. (2006) The meeting of meditative disciplines and western psychology: A mutually enriching dialogue. *American Psychologist*, **61**, pp. 227–239.

Weinberger, L. A. (2002) Emotional Intelligence: Its Connection to HRD Theory and Practice. *Human Resource Development Review,* **1**(2), pp. 215-243.

Weiss, R. (1975) Loneliness: the experience of emotional and social isolation. MIT Press.

West, D. A., Kellner, R. and Moore-West, M. (1986) The Effects of Loneliness: A Review of the Literature. *Comprehensive Psychiatry*, **27**(4), pp. 351–83.

Wright, R. J. (2005) Stress and atopic disorders. *The Journal of Allergy and Clinical Immunology*, **116**(6), pp. 1301-1306.

Wright, R. J., Cohen, R.T. and Cohen, S. (2005) The impact of stress on the development and expression of atopy. *Current Opinion in Allergy and Clinical Immunology*, **5**(1), pp. 23-29.

Index

A

ability model, xvii, 2, 4, 5, 6, 18
Advisory, Conciliation and Arbitration Service (UK), 61
Allport, 99
Aristotle, xxii, xxiv
Arthritis Research UK, 140
Avoidance coping, 70

B

Babiak and Hare, 152
Bar-On, xvii, 1, 4, 8, 9, 10, 16, 102, 187
beehive, xix, 109, 131, 133
big 5, xviii, 12, 13, 101, 102, 103, 104, 105, 106
Binet, 110
Binet-Simon intelligence test, 110
bounded rationality, xxv, 191
breaking point, 187
British Association for Behavioural and Cognitive Psychotherapies, 66
Bullying, xviii, 48, 61, 62
burnout, xviii, xxviii, 19, 30, 38, 39, 40, 41, 44, 55, 154, 217, 244

C

Cattell, 99
Chartered Institute of Personnel and Development, 20, 137, 231
chronic stress, xviii, 19, 38, 39, 43, 58, 103, 155, 156, 159
Cicero, xxiii
Cognitive behavioural therapy (CBT), 65
cognitive bias, 171
cognitive control, 155
collective wisdom, 122
conforming, xix, 116, 163, 188
coping strategies, xviii, 33, 63, 69, 71, 74, 75, 76, 84, 91, 95, 97, 135, 142
Cortisol, 25, 26, 189
creativity, 149
crystallised intelligence, 113

D

Damasio, xxi, 14, 148, 232
dark triad, xix, 136, 152, 154, 159, 185, 186, 193, 247
Deep acting, 30
Descartes, xxiv
distress, xviii, 19, 23, 24, 25, 26, 27, 33, 38, 43, 63, 64, 69, 71, 102, 187, 189
Distress toleration, 63
DSM-5 (Diagnostic and statistical Manual), 56
Dunning-Kruger effect, 171

E

Emotion focused coping, 70
Emotion focused therapy, 64
Emotion processing, 64, 65
emotional contagion, 50
emotional dissonance, xviii, 29, 30, 55, 56, 147
emotional labour, 30, 44, 55
emotional style, 50, 51

Emotional support, 76
enlightenment of the modern age, 191
eudaimonic, 15, 94, 186
Eustress, xviii, 23, 43

F

flashbulb memory, 148
fluid intelligence, 113
Freud, 99
fuzzy generalisations, 74

G

Galen, xxiii, xxiv
general intelligence, 111
glucocorticoids, 165, 189
Goleman, xv, xvii, 1, 3, 4, 6, 7, 8, 10, 16, 18, 54, 102, 122, 123, 124, 170, 187
Group coping, 130
group emotional intelligence, 123
Groupthink, xix, 118

H

harassment, xviii, 48, 61, 62, 67, 215
Health and Safety Executive, 19, 20, 31
high demand and low control, 24
Higher Education Statistics Agency, 34, 36
Hippocrates, xxiv
hyperactive stress syndrome, 156

I

I can take it, xix, 146, 147, 158, 162, 174, 178, 186, 190
illusion of explanatory depth, 121
Inequality, 143

instrumental support, 76
introspection, 156
introspection illusion, 171

J

James, xxv, 49, 50, 99

K

Kabat-Zinn, 166, 167, 175

L

learned helplessness, xviii, 48, 56, 59
learned optimism, xviii, 10, 48
Loneliness, 122

M

Marcus Aurelius, 156, 191, 193
meditation, 42, 44, 60, 91, 157, 166, 178, 190, 192, 245, 246
Memes, 121
memory, 179
Mental Health Foundation, 20, 42, 44, 58, 138, 141
mindfulness, xix, 54, 60, 65, 91, 157, 162, 165, 166, 167, 175, 178, 190, 192, 246
mindset, xix, 23, 82, 156, 160, 162, 169, 170, 175, 178, 181, 183
mind-set, 23
mixed model, 2, 4, 6, 7, 8, 9, 10, 18, 102
modes of appraisal, 47
multiple intelligences, xvii, 1, 187

N

National Health Service (England), 20

noradrenaline, 25
nudge theory, 118

O

obesity, 155
oxytocin, 25, 26, 155, 189

P

passions, xxi, xxii, xxv, 47
perfectionist, 39
Personality traits, 99
Petrides and Furnham, xvii, 1, 4, 11, 12, 13, 14, 16, 17, 18, 102, 187
physical exercise, 138
Plato, xxi, xxii
positive emotions, xviii, 19, 29, 51, 59, 101, 148, 174, 232
positive self-image, 156
Primary appraisal, 47
Problem focused coping, 70
psychological strain, 24, 105, 109, 127, 128, 131, 133
Psychological stress, 20, 70, 221
psychopathy, 153

R

reference values, 69

S

Salovey and Mayer, xvii, 1, 3, 4, 5, 16, 18, 102, 187
say it like it is, 25
saying it like it is, 56
Secondary appraisal, 47
self-awareness, xix, xxvii, 3, 6, 7, 8, 9, 48, 51, 54, 123, 124, 162, 170, 171, 172
Seneca, xxiii, 160

senescence, 151
serotonin, 25, 26
seven deadly sins, xxiv
Simonides of Ceos, 179
smiling, 168
Social connectedness, 142
Social Metrics Commission, 146
social networking, xix, 120, 121
Socrates, xxi, xxii, 118
Spearman, 111
Stoics, xxiii
stress is debilitating, 23
stress-is enhancing, 23
Stroop test, 147
subjective well-being, 15, 224
substance misuse, 38, 186
surface acting, 30
sympathy, xxii, 52
Systematic stress, 70

T

teaching, xviii, xxvii, 20, 22, 24, 28, 30, 31, 32, 39, 48, 52, 53, 54, 55, 66, 74, 82, 84, 87, 93, 95, 104, 106, 245
team cohesiveness, 124
telomeres, 150
The knowledge Illusion, 121
The white room, xix, 172
therapies, xviii, 63, 66
Thomas Aquinas, xxiv
Thurstone, 112
tipping point, 120
trait model, xvii, 2, 16, 18
two back test, 147
two-factor theory, 50

W

walking, 168

Wechsler adult intelligence scale, 112
Wechsler scale for children, 112
white room, 162, 172, 173, 174, 175
wired to connect, 109, 122, 132
work/life balance, xviii, 19, 27, 32, 33, 42, 43, 84, 97
World Economic Forum, 21, 181
wrong food, 26
Wundt, xxv

Y

Yerkes, 111

Z

Zeno of Citium, xxiii

www.ingramcontent.com/pod-product-compliance
Lightning Source LLC
Chambersburg PA
CBHW071812300426
44116CB00009B/1287